Buddhist Warfare

Buddhist Warfare

Edited by

MICHAEL JERRYSON AND

MARK JUERGENSMEYER

OXFORD
UNIVERSITY PRESS

2010

OXFORD
UNIVERSITY PRESS

Oxford University Press, Inc., publishes works that further
Oxford University's objective of excellence
in research, scholarship, and education.

Oxford New York
Auckland Cape Town Dar es Salaam Hong Kong Karachi
Kuala Lumpur Madrid Melbourne Mexico City Nairobi
New Delhi Shanghai Taipei Toronto

With offices in
Argentina Austria Brazil Chile Czech Republic France Greece
Guatemala Hungary Italy Japan Poland Portugal Singapore
South Korea Switzerland Thailand Turkey Ukraine Vietnam

Published by Oxford University Press, Inc.
198 Madison Avenue, New York, New York 10016

www.oup.com

Library of Congress Cataloging-in-Publication Data
Buddhist warfare / Michael Jerryson and Mark Juergensmeyer (editors).
p. cm.
Includes bibliographical references.
ISBN 978-0-19-539483-2 ISBN 978-0-19-539484-9 (pbk.)
1. War–Religious aspects–Buddhism.
2. Violence–Religious aspects–Buddhism.
I. Jerryson, Michael K. II. Juergensmeyer, Mark.
BQ4570.W3B83 2009
294.3'37273–dc22 2009012194

Printed in the United States of America
on acid-free paper

Acknowledgments

Without the permission and assistance of many people, this book could have never come together. We would like to express our gratitude to the Instituts d'Extrême-Orient du Collège de France for granting us permission to translate and include Paul Demiéville's article in this volume. We would also like to thank the *Journal of Southeast Asian Studies* for its permission to include Michael Jerryson's article. Brenda Turnnidge was kind enough to share her photograph of a Burmese novice monk overlooking the Irrawaddy River (cover picture), which was taken in August 1988. Throughout its various drafts, we were fortunate to have the assistance of Rhella Kessler and Fawn Jerryson, who have helped to bring cohesion and coherence to the diverse chapters. We would also be remiss if we did not thank Oxford University Press's anonymous reviewers, whose extremely insightful and generous suggestions molded the book in its final stages.

Finally, a word about the role played by each of the co-editors of this book. Michael Jerryson organized the original panel at the American Academy of Religion that produced the first draft of many of these essays, communicated with the authors, and wrote the introductory chapter. Mark Juergensmeyer was the commentator on the original panel and provided insight about the comparative study of religion and violence, which was useful for the introduction and for the project as a whole; he also helped to edit the introduction and to shepherd the manuscript through the publication process.

Contents

Contributors

Paul Demiéville (1894–1979) is considered one of the eminent architects of the Franco-Belgian school of Buddhology that drew upon Sanskrit texts and their corresponding commentaries in Mandarin and Tibetan. He was appointed as Chair of Chinese Language and Literature at the College de France in 1946, where he supervised the development of important Buddhist Studies scholars such as Wapola Rahula and Bernard Faure. He co-edited the *T'oung Pao* until 1976 and published numerous books in French, among them *Anthologie de la Poésie Chinoise Classique* (1962), the French translation of the *Dunhuang manuscripts* (1971) and *Choix d'études Bouddhiques, 1929–1970* (1973).

Bernard Faure is the Kao Professor of Japanese Religion at Columbia University. He received his Ph.D. (Doctorat d'Etat) from Paris University in 1984. His work has focused on topics such as the construction of orthodoxy and heterodoxy, the Buddhist cult of relics, iconography, and sexuality and gender. His current research deals with the mythico-ritual system of esoteric Buddhism and its relationships with medieval Japanese religion. He has published a number of books in French and English. His most recent English publications include *The Red Thread: Buddhist Approaches to Sexuality*; *The Power of Denial: Buddhism, Purity, and Gender*; and *Double Exposure*. He is presently working on a book on Japanese gods and demons.

Stephen Jenkins was trained at Harvard University and is currently the chair of Religious Studies at Humboldt State University.

His doctoral work and publications focus on problems in the interpretation of compassion in the Indian Buddhist literature.

Michael Jerryson is Assistant Professor of Religious Studies at Eckerd College. His publications have surveyed religious traditions from across Asia, including Singapore and, most recently, Thailand. One of his more recent publications, *Mongolian Buddhism: The Rise and Fall of the Sangha*, explores the development of Mongolia's state religion until its demise in the twentieth century under the Soviet Union.

Mark Juergensmeyer is a professor of sociology and global studies and the director of the Orfalea Center for Global and International Studies at the University of California, Santa Barbara. He is the author or editor of twenty books on global religion and politics, including *Global Rebellion: Religious Challenges to the Secular State* and *Terror in the Mind of God: The Global Rise of Religious Violence.*

Michelle Kendall is the translator of *The Cradle of Humanity* and *The Unfinished System of Non-Knowledge* by Georges Bataille and *Sade and Lautreamont* by Maurice Blanchot. Currently, she is pursuing her doctorate in French literature at the University of California, Santa Barbara.

Daniel W. Kent received his Ph.D. in religious studies from the University of Virginia with a dissertation entitled "Shelter for You, Nirvana for Our Sons: Buddhist Belief and Practice in the Sri Lankan Army," which was based on extensive ethnographic research on two different military bases in Sri Lanka. Kent is currently revising his dissertation for publication, beginning work on a new project on Buddhist-Muslim tensions in contemporary Sri Lanka, and teaching courses on Theravāda Buddhism at the University of Virginia and at Mary Baldwin College.

Derek F. Maher received his Ph.D. in history of religions and Tibetan studies from the University of Virginia. He now teaches at East Carolina University, where he is the co-director of the Religious Studies Program. He writes about religious biographical writings, the intersection of religion and politics, and religious history. His most recent publications are an annotated translation of Tsepőn Shakabpa's *One Hundred Thousand Moons: An Advanced Political History of Tibet* and a co-edited volume with Calvin Mercer, *Religion and the Implications of Radical Life Extension.*

Brian Daizen Victoria is a native of Omaha, Nebraska, and a 1961 graduate of Nebraska Wesleyan University in Lincoln. He holds an M.A. in Buddhist studies from the Soto Zen sect–affiliated Komazawa University in Tokyo and a Ph.D. from the Department of Religious Studies at Temple University. In addition to his most recent book, *Zen War Stories*, Victoria's major writings include *Zen at War* and an autobiographical work in Japanese entitled *Gaijin de ari,*

Zen bozu de ari (As a Foreigner, as a Zen Priest). Currently, he is a professor of Japanese studies at Antioch University and the director of the Antioch Education Abroad Buddhist Studies in Japan Program.

Vesna A. Wallace is the holder of the Numata Chair in Buddhist Studies at the University of Oxford. She has published several books and a series of articles on Indian esoteric Buddhism and on different aspects of Mongolian Buddhism.

Xue Yu has undertaken Buddhist studies for more than twenty-five years. He has studied Mahāyāna Buddhism, Theravāda Buddhism, Japanese Buddhism, and Chinese Buddhism in China, Sri Lanka, Japan, and the United States. Having received a Ph.D. from the University of Iowa in 2003, he began research on Buddhism and modern society, particularly humanistic Buddhism. Xue Yu is now an assistant professor in the Department of Cultural and Religious Studies at the Chinese University of Hong Kong and also serves as the director for the Study of Humanistic Buddhism jointly sponsored by the Chinese University of Hong Kong and Foguan Shan. His recent book *Buddhism, War, and Nationalism* investigates the activities of Chinese monks and nuns against Japanese aggressions during the Republic era (1912–1949).

Buddhist Warfare

Introduction

Michael Jerryson

> It is a well-known fact that the first of all the commandments of the Buddhist creed is "Thou shalt not kill" [but] Chinese books contain various passages relating to Buddhist monks who freely indulged in carnage and butchery and took an active part in military expeditions of every description, thus leaving no room for doubt that warfare was an integrate part of their religious profession for centuries.
>
> —J. J. M. de Groot, 1891

Violence is found in all religious traditions, and Buddhism is no exception. This may surprise those who think of Buddhism as a religion based solely on peace. Indeed, one of the principal reasons for producing this book was to address such a misconception. Within the various Buddhist traditions (which Trevor Ling describes as "Buddhisms"), there is a long history of violence.[1] Since the inception of Buddhist traditions 2,500 years ago, there have been numerous individual and structural cases of prolonged Buddhist violence. This book explores instances in which Buddhist ideas and religious leaders have been related to structural violence in one of its most destructive and public form: warfare. The motivations for this volume are many, but chief among them is the goal of disrupting the social imaginary that holds Buddhist traditions to be exclusively pacifistic and exotic. Most religious traditions, whether Judaic, Christian, Buddhist, Islamic, or Hindu, is quintessentially social in nature; and because religious traditions are social, they suffer from the negative elements inherent in the human condition. The chapters in this volume investigate this dark underbelly of Buddhisms, with particular attention to the monastic interplay with warfare.

This investigation is conducted by means of both textual and ethnographic approaches. The first of these chapters is Paul Demiéville's article "Buddhism and War," which was initially published in French in 1957 as a postscript to G. Renondeau's "The History of the Warrior Monks of Japan." Demiéville surveys East Asia's history of soldier-monks and the Buddhist principles applied in times of war. As a Buddhist studies scholar, Demiéville's training was similar to the training of the other contributors to this volume who were educated in and/or teach religious studies. The second chapter is by Stephen Jenkins, who bases his analysis on South Asian texts; Jenkins's focus is more on Buddhist philosophical stances toward violence. The subsequent five chapters rely on textual analyses, refer to specific regional and historical events, and thematically follow in chronological order. Derek Maher reviews the development of just-war ideology during the Tibetan-Mongol war in 1642. Vesna Wallace examines the historical development of corporal punishment in theocratic Mongolia from the early sixteenth century to the late twentieth century. Brian Victoria offers a critique of Japan's wartime soldier-Zen during the first half of the twentieth century. The role of Buddhist monks during the Korean War of the 1950s is related by Xue Yu. Then, two chapters use ethnography to examine contemporary conflict zones in South and Southeast Asia. Daniel Kent investigates the Buddhist sermons given to Sri Lankan soldiers between 2004 and 2006. Michael Jerryson traces the Thai state's militarization of Thai Buddhism in an area under martial law between 2004 and 2008. The concluding chapter is by Bernard Faure, who reviews the arguments in this volume and then paves the way for larger subsequent discussions on the topic of Buddhisms and violence.

While most of the contributors locate violence within Buddhist traditions, Brian Victoria's chapter disavows a relationship between Buddhisms and violence. For Victoria, Buddhists who perform acts of violence are not acting as Buddhists; Buddhisms, in this scenario, remain unsoiled by the trappings of human frailty. Victoria's stance is shared by other Buddhologists and Buddhist studies scholars, many of whom (like Brian Victoria) are current or former monks. An example of this comes from the Sri Lankan Buddhist monk and religious studies scholar Mahinda Deegalle, who raises a similar argument in his article "Is Violence Justified in Theravada Buddhism?" Deegalle confronts a difficult passage in the *Mahāvaṃsa*, one in which a Buddhist monk consoles the Sinhalese king Duttagamani (Pāli: Duṭṭagāmaṇī, Sinhala: Duṭugämuṇu) for killing "evil unbelievers"; the monk explains that the acts carry no more weight than killing animals. Deegalle argues that this passage is not a Buddhist justification for violence—rather, that it is heretical to the teachings of the Buddha.[2]

Indeed, there are scholars of other religious traditions that take a similar position when facing violent acts in the name of their religion. In other religious traditions, some adherents have also been adamant that violence has no legitimate place in their faiths. Christian pacificists have often argued that the injunction of Jesus to "turn the other cheek" rather than to fight is a mandate for absolute nonviolence. In the Hindu tradition, Mohandas Gandhi thought that Hindu scriptures gave no room for religiously sanctioned violence, even going so far as to reinterpret the traditional battle scenes in the *Mahābhārata* and Rāmāyaṇa epics as allegories for the struggle between truth and falsehood.

Can people, as Buddhists, commit acts of violence? It is ultimately up to the reader to decide which of these perspectives to adopt. Beyond these differing perspectives on authenticity lie two questions that demand attention: (1) how can Buddhist scripture be interpreted for warfare? and (2) how *is* it interpreted for warfare?

Before exploring the relationship between Buddhisms and warfare, it is critical to define these two terms. For the purposes of this volume, "Buddhisms" is a web of interconnected cultural entities predicated on the teachings of the Buddha, whether he is conceived as historical and/or cosmological. This definition is deliberately broad in order to encompass the fluid and polythetic characteristics found in self-ascribed Buddhist traditions, specific beliefs, texts, and leaders related to Buddhist organizations. There is an enormous diversity in Buddhist principles and followers, which raises the question of whether we should use value-laden terms that are all-encompassing, such as "Buddhism." This is similar to the concern that religious studies scholar Jonathan Z. Smith poses in regard to Judaisms. Smith calls on scholars to dismantle old theological and imperialistic impulses toward totalization and integration, explaining that the "labor at achieving the goal of a polythetic classification of Judaisms, rather than a monothetic definition of early Judaism, is but a preliminary step toward this end."[3] It is this totalizing impulse found in the term Buddhism that demands change, if not critical reflection.[4]

Although virtually every Buddhist tradition holds the Four Noble Truths (Pāli: *cattāri ariyasaccāni*)[5] as its core principles, there is no unifying canonical scripture that interprets and explains them in detail.[6] One can easily find variegated descriptions of the Noble Truths when comparing the Sinhalese, Thai, Burmese, Sanskrit, Pāli, and Khmer canonical scriptures (and there are geographical variations within each linguistic category). In addition, each Buddhist tradition contains unique practices and doctrines (which constitute the very nature of a tradition): for example, Mongolian Buddhists circumambulate cairns made of rock and wood; Thai Buddhists believe that people have two different spirits, the *winyan* and *kwan*;[7] and monks from the Jogye school initiate their followers to Korean Buddhism by placing five incense sticks on the initiate's arm. Although each tradition contains unique practices and beliefs, Buddhists associate these variegated beliefs and practices with the teachings of the Buddha.

Warfare is another term that encompasses a plethora of actions and meanings. For the purposes of this volume, warfare refers to the processes and activities affiliated with war, and specifically for the purpose of defeating an enemy or gaining property. Wars are not simply physical conflicts in our cosmos, they can manifest in the spiritual dimension as well.[8] One example of this dual nature of warfare is found in Vesna Wallace's chapter "Legalized Violence: Punitive Measures of Buddhist Khans in Mongolia." Mongolian khans subjugated shamans and believers in different schools in their attempts to convert the populace. When Wallace examines Buddhist state-sanctioned violence, she finds that it is motivated by both physical wants (i.e., the confiscation of property) and the spiritual desire to create a religiously and politically harmonious nation. Indeed, throughout this volume, nationalism is found embedded within different forms of warfare. *Nationalism* is also a contested term. For the purposes of this book, we will use Mark Juergensmeyer's definition of nationalism, by which he means "not only the xenophobic extremes of patriotism but also the more subdued expressions of identity based on shared assumptions regarding why a community constitutes a nation and why the state that rules it is legitimate."[9]

The topic of warfare introduces the larger category of violence. *Violence* is a slippery term to define, as many astute scholars such as Walter Benjamin, Emmanuel Levinas, and Jacques Derrida have shown. The act of "violating" another person can take many subtle forms. Bruce Lawrence, for instance, regards violencc as a "process" of domination that is endemic in the human condition.[10] A similar breadth is found in the Sanskrit term for violence, *hiṃsa*. *Hiṃsa*is the root of *ahiṃsa*, the word for nonviolence made popular by Mohandas Gandhi. The literal definition of *hiṃsa* means "to desire to harm." In this volume, however, the authors will confine themselves to the simplest definition of violence—inflicting physical injury or death on another person—whether portrayed symbolically or as part of a social act, such as punishment or warfare.

Buddhist violence is by no means limited to the scope of warfare. For instance, the ethical justification for killing animals for food is much debated throughout Buddhist traditions; there have been and continue to be differing opinions on this issue. Whereas most Chinese Buddhist traditions have prescribed a vegetarian lifestyle, Tibetan and Mongolian Buddhist traditions wholeheartedly have embraced the practice of slaughtering animals for sustenance. Aside from splinter groups such as Santi Asoke that prohibit their monks from eating meat, Theravādin Buddhist monks in countries such as Sri Lanka, Burma, and Thailand are required to accept any food offered to them, meat or otherwise.

Other instances of Buddhisms' relationship with violence relate to recent technological and medical developments. The issue of abortion is a case in point. In Tibetan Buddhism, the Fourteenth Dalai Lama has tacitly condoned abortion in specific circumstances, rationalizing the need for this form of violence.[11] In Japan after an abortion, Buddhist women participate in the ceremony *Mizuko Kuyo* in order to appease possibly wrathful spirits. Medical advances also have introduced the topic of euthanasia. The ethics of euthanasia is debated among Buddhist scholars, many of whom equate it with suicide. According to the *Vinaya* (monastic guidelines), people commit a sin if they encourage another person to commit suicide; however, the action of the person who commits suicide is much more ambiguous and doctrinally debated.

Suicide as a form of martyrdom for political purposes is particularly controversial within Buddhist circles. Some of the most well-publicized examples of this type of Buddhist suicide occurred during the U.S. war in Vietnam, when Vietnamese monks immolated themselves, sacrificing what they regarded as their impermanent bodies to trigger a change in social consciousness. While their intentions were nuanced by a unique context, monastic suicides are not uncommon in the Buddhist traditions. One infamous example of monastic suicide occurred following the Buddha's lecture on detachment and meditating on the loathsomeness of the body. Shortly after the lecture, the Buddha went into seclusion for fifteen days and then returned to find that over a hundred monks were dead, either by suicide or by asking a local recluse, Migalandika, to kill them. In this instance, only those who deprived *others* of life were condemned to excommunication.[12] Suicides abound in the Buddha's birth stories (Skt. *jātaka*), when the Buddha sacrifices himself for the greater good; they also exist in the biography of the historical Buddha, Siddhārtha Gautama (Pāli: Siddhattha Gotama). It is said that Siddhartha was fully aware of his eventual demise when he accepted ill-prepared pork.

Thus, issues of violence have been part of the ethical choices of Buddhists as individuals throughout history. These issues have also been part of the structural and systemic patterns of political organizations and institutions for many centuries. The present-day proponents of these forms of organized Buddhist violence often refer to Buddhist mythohistories that justify violence, histories that are rife with tales of warfare.

In Buddhisms, as in every religious tradition, warfare is related to religion in several different ways. Some wars are conducted to defend a Buddhist community against enemies from a different faith. In other instances, it is two different schools of Buddhists that clash with each other over which version of the faith is valid and which community is stronger. In yet other instances, Buddhist ideas and monastic leaders have lent their legitimacy to wars that otherwise might have been characterized simply as wars of defense, conquest, or vengeance. In Sri Lanka, for instance, members of the Buddhist political party Janatha Vimukthi Peramuna (JVP) were alleged to have blurred the lines between sacred duty and murder; they traced their justifications back to the Sinhalese mythohistorical chronicle called the *Mahāvaṃsa*. In this work, the Buddhist king Dutthagamani wages a sacred war against foreign invaders led by Tamil king Eḷāra in the second century BCE. In the contemporary Buddhists' view, the killing of Tamil heathens did not constitute murder because Tamil warriors were neither meritorious nor, more important, Buddhist.[13]

Chinese Buddhist revolts during the sixth century framed the fight as between the Buddha and his legendary nemesis Māra, the god of desire and illusion. Under the leadership of Faqing, Chinese Buddhist monks murdered barbarians as part of the larger cosmic battle against Māra. In some accounts, Faqing is labeled as the messianic figure Maitreya.[14] There are also military activities relating to the millenarian accounts of Buddhism, which often revolve around the buddha-to-be, Maitreya (Pāli: *Metteya*). Between 1699 and 1959, in eight revolts against Siamese and Thai governments, Buddhist revolutionaries held to a belief in imminent catastrophes that were to be followed by material bliss. Half of these revolts centered on the coming of Maitreya (Thai: *Si Ariya*).[15]

Buddhist messianic violence persists in contemporary times, with the latest violent outbreak occurring in Japan. In 1995, Asahara Shōkō's Aum Shinrikyō unleashed Sarin nerve gas into the Tokyo subway, killing a dozen people and injuring many more. Part of Aum Shinrikyō's ideology is based on the *Lotus Sūtra*, one of the most popular and influential *sūtras* (scriptures) in Mahāyāna Buddhism.

Buddhist battles also have occurred due to ideological differences between Buddhist traditions. This is especially evident in the Tibetan Buddhist tradition, whose history includes battles between different schools of Buddhist thought over issues of political and ideological supremacy. Derek Maher's chapter in this book, "Sacralized Warfare: The Fifth Dalai Lama and the Discourse of Religious Violence," explores one of these moments. Examples may also be found in other Buddhist traditions of wars that were fought in order to spread Buddhist beliefs. The Indian *Kālacakratantra* describes an eschatological war in which the army of the bodhisattva king of Shambhala conquers and annihilates Muslim forces and reestablishes Buddhism.[16] And in Japan, Zen became a mechanism of the state and a motive to fight—to convert the heathens. Japanese Buddhist military objectives in the early 1900s were to kill unbelievers and to convert their state to Buddhism. In accordance with Mahāyāna principles, people who were not enlightened would be reborn; therefore, there was no true destruction of life. Once the state became Buddhist, unbelievers would be reborn in a Buddhist country. Brian Victoria writes that, in this context of Buddhist war, murder becomes a form of *upāya* (skillful means), since sentient beings are ultimately saved.[17] When Buddhist states have attempted to preserve Buddhist principles and values, popular forms of Buddhist nationalism and fundamentalism have been simultaneously elicited.[18]

Thus, the chapters in this book contain examples that span both centuries and countries. All of these cases of bloodshed counter the popular (and also exoticized) notion that Buddhism is an entirely pacifist—and, in this sense, mystical—religion. In fact, these chapters reveal that, in regions where Buddhism is part of the ideology of statecraft, there is a pervasive tendency for Buddhists to sanction state violence. For instance, in this volume, Michael Jerryson's and Daniel Kent's ethnographic works on Buddhist monastic practices highlight the important distinction between how Buddhism is *lived* as opposed to how it is *taught* or *perceived*. This distinction reveals that, in some cases, the practices of Buddhist monks have become inextricably intertwined with military exercises and charged with violent rhetoric.

This insight into the violent side of Buddhist monastic practices has been confirmed by some of the most distinguished scholarly observers of Buddhist culture. For instance, the violence was noted by the Chinese Buddhist scholar J. M. M. de Groot in his article "Militant Spirit of the Buddhist Clergy in China," written in 1891 (an excerpt of which appears in the epigraph of this introduction). While Demiéville rightly critiques de Groot's textual evidence, the value of de Groot's insight into the militancy within the Chinese Buddhist traditions remains. This insight and those of other scholars tend to have been neglected in the general discourses on Buddhist studies. The historical examples of monks participating in violence force the question that Brian Victoria addresses in his chapter: does the foundation of Buddhisms forbid violence, or does it provide a space for it? This question is prompted especially in Paul Demiéville's "Buddhism and War" and in Bernard Faure's "Afterthoughts."

The early period of South Asian Buddhism provides an understanding of the politicized nature of Buddhisms and, more important, of Buddhisms' ambiguous platform concerning violence. As Stephen Jenkins, Derek Maher, and Xue Yu discuss in this volume, early ambiguity toward violence could explain how Buddhist practices reached the point of advocating compassionate killings. Buddhist doctrine and practice, from their nascency, grew within a state-supported politicized environment. This political climate deeply affected monastic decisions and ultimately affected the Buddha's discussions and judgments on state (kingdom) violence.

Some scholars speculate that the militant side of Buddhism can be traced to its founder, Siddhārtha Gautama, purportedly born between 500 and 400 BCE in what is now Nepal. A common epithet for Siddhartha Gautama is Śākyamuni—Sage of the Śākyas. According to Romila Thapar, the Śākya clan—although having a ruler—was part of a greater governmental network called *gaṇa-sanghas*.[19] Siddhārtha, prior to the spiritual enlightenment that transformed him into the Buddha—the Awakened One—was a member of the warrior caste. He was raised to be the ruler of his clan and had an intimate knowledge of statecraft, particularly of the *gaṇa-sanghas*. It was this governmental structure that deeply affected the construction of Buddhist monasticism, later called the *sangha*. As a prince growing up, the future founder of Buddhism was inculcated in an environment imbued with practices of diplomacy and warfare. He was well aware of the regional *gaṇa-sanghas*, oligarchies that lacked a monarch. These regional oligarchies had a joint council of princes or local dignitaries who made decisions for the collective states. These governmental systems were usually wrought through financial successes, i.e., merchants-cum-rulers, and were adverse to the Brahmanical system of support. Uma Chakravarti and Thapar note that, by the time Siddhartha founded Buddhism, the powers of the *gaṇa-sanghas* were waning in North India.[20] Eventually, they would fall before the might of two expanding monarchies: Magadha and Kosala.

While early political structures informed and helped to construct Buddhist monasticism, the first Buddhist *sangha* affected the early polities around it. One example of this is in the relationship between state and *sangha* laws within the kingdoms of Magadha and Kosala. Bridging the notion that the Buddhist *sangha* was adapted from the political structure of *gaṇa-sanghas*, Buddhist *sangha* monks (Pāli: *bhikkhu*; Skt. *bhikṣu*) acted like foreign diplomats and were thus accorded immunity to state laws. There are documented cases in the *Vinaya* of state officials appealing to either the Magadhan or Kosalan ruler to intervene and punish monks for various incidents; yet, in all accounts, the ultimate decisions were deferred to the Buddha. In one instance, a king's guard was suspected of thievery by Buddhist monks, and the Buddha tried the case. His verdict was then accepted by the king.[21]

This political influence was not one-sided, however. State laws and state pressure made an enormous impact on Buddhist interdictions. The resulting tension between advocating morality and maintaining positive state relations became a constant presence in Buddhist societies. In Kent's chapter in this volume, "Onward Buddhist Soldiers: Preaching to the Sri Lankan Army," he carefully assesses the actions of Buddhist monks as they preach to Sinhalese soldiers. The situation he describes exemplifies the resulting tensions between advocating morality and maintaining positive state relations—and how they are still evident in the twenty-first century. While many of the monastic codes of conduct (Pāli: *Vinaya*) pertain to internal issues of purity, many were the result of tensions generated through the Buddha's diplomacy with Magadha and Kosala. In another chapter in this volume, "Militarizing Buddhism," Michael Jerryson discusses contradictions between the Buddhist interdiction against ordaining soldiers and the reinterpretations that are necessary to support state needs. During the time of the Buddha, a high rate of soldiers abandoned their posts. In order for the *sangha* to continue to enjoy the critical financial support of the Magadha and Kosala kingdoms, it was crucial that it prevent derelict soldiers and criminals from finding refuge in the *sangha*.

Thus, the interdictions placed upon the *sangha* during the time of the Buddha can be seen as the result of compromises necessary in order to maintain the monks' immunity to state rules. Subsequent conflicts did arise in Theravāda history between the *sangha* and state. In circumstances such as in Ceylon, where kings had the power to banish monks from the island, this immunity has been redrawn. During the time of the Buddha, there had been a shift in the strengths of political systems. Previously, *gaṇa-sanghas* had been the more powerful system in northern India (as in the *Licchavis*), but by the time of Buddhisms's institutional growth, they were being replaced by centralized monarchies. The expanding kingdoms of Magadha and Kosala turned to the Buddhist *sangha* for support and guidance, particularly with respect to issues of morality. For instance, the Magadhan ruler Ajātasatta asked the Buddha's advice before invading the neighboring kingdom of Kosala.[22] This instance demonstrates not only the important influence of the Buddha and the *sangha* upon state decisions, but also the high regard in which they were held by the state. The ruler of Kosala (Pasenadi) was an avid supporter of the Buddha; in seeking the Buddha's advice, Ajātasatta might have wanted to reduce or avoid angering the Buddhist *sangha*. The implication is that the *sangha* had political leverage and power similar to that of a kingdom.

From Buddhisms's inchoation, we find that kingdoms were important stakeholders in supporting the sustenance and growth of Buddhist monasticism, and Buddhist doctrine reflected the importance of state relations. One political influence that brought together the *sangha* and the state was the Buddhists' promulgation of a social contract. In the *Dīgha Nikāya*, the *Mahāsammata* goes into a great deal of detail over the rights of citizens and their rulers. Similar to Hobbes's *Leviathan* or even the political ideas of John Locke, the *Dīgha Nikāya* stresses the intertwined obligations of citizens and their ruler. The ruler was morally bound to protect his citizens and to maintain a civilized society. If the ruler failed to uphold these responsibilities, the citizens were justified in disregarding the ruler's legitimacy. This is explicitly detailed in a dialogue between the Buddha and King Pasenadi. As if to illustrate the ruler's motivations for following this social contract, the Buddha explains the systematic degradation of society, starting with the ruler. A celestial society that upholds the *dhamma* (in this case, the "rule") begins to break down when the ruler disregards the teachings of the Buddha and fails to protect the civility of his kingdom. When poverty arises, it in turns brings about criminality, and finally there is absolute chaos throughout the kingdom.[23] As described in Brian Victoria's "A Buddhological Critique of 'Soldier-Zen,'" the Japanese used and extended this rationale for preserving the kingdom in order to justify their empire building.

Though the social contract bound Buddhist rulers to a civic obligation, it also conceded to them certain rights to violence. There are detailed references to this in "Legalized Violence," Vesna Wallace's account of Mongolian state-sanctioned torture. Anthropologist Stanley Tambiah has written extensively on Buddhist traditions in Thailand and Sri Lanka; he indicates that texts on Buddhist civic obligations predominantly emphasize their application *when* the king is ruling, rather than in *how* the king reaches the throne and assumes power.[24] The most famous of these cases is the Mauryan emperor Aśoka who, after massacring thousands of people and conquering most of South Asia, converted to Buddhism and then enjoyed a peaceful, stable reign. Buddhist monks and texts often herald Aśoka for his peaceful rule, yet few focus on the bloody prequel to his rise to power. Balkrishna Gokhale points out that Aśoka never disbanded his army after his Buddhist epiphany. Gokhale notes that "history knows of Buddhist kings who have waged wars, often very devastating, against other Buddhist kings." This leads one to conclude that, while Buddhist ideology was adopted by states, the ideology did not preclude the states from perpetrating violence. Gokhale hypothesizes, "Buddhists recognized that they had little influence in the matter of war and territorial acquisition and felt that the most they could do in these matters was to influence the minds of kings to keep the horrors of wars within reasonable limits."[25] This hypothesis became actualized in the thoughts of twenty-first-century Sri Lankan monks who, according to Daniel Kent's account, rationalized their sermons to the Sinhalese military in similar terms.

There is no consistent platform from which the Buddha propounds on state violence. Even in situations in which a king is ruling, violence has been ambiguously noted within the texts. As Stephen Jenkins states as the main theme of his chapter in this volume, "Making Merit through Warfare According to the *Ārya-Bodhisattva-gocara-upāyaviśaya-vikurvāṇa-nirdeśa Sūtra*," *dhamma* (in this context, "order") becomes an issue requiring compromise: it permits the ruler the right to rule—*and* to enforce his rule through violence. At the same time, any transgression of Buddhist *dhamma* (in this case, the "social contract") would result in a fall from grace and would lead the ruler as well as his kingdom into unfolding chaos and political delegitimation.

Scholars may debate the interpretation of the official Buddhist doctrinal stance on violence, but history confirms a widespread propensity among states to adopt Buddhisms as the official religion and for Buddhisms to provide the rationalization for the state's sanctioned use of violence. State applications of Buddhisms were so pervasive in ancient India that they became an assumed practice. One of the leading scholars of early Buddhisms, Balkrishna Gokhale, has argued that early Buddhist thinkers always took for granted the power of the state, and that this "organization of force or violence" was "largely restricted to the king."[26] The implicit Buddhist understanding of state and violence is such that, as it says in the *Vinaya*, "those who administer torture and maiming are called kings."[27] Uma Chakravarti argues that Buddhist ideas on power are invariably expressed through the medium of the king. Buddhists, she writes, "do not seem to envisage a political and social system without the institution of kingship."[28] Numerous Buddhist canonical texts stress the intrinsic relationship between Buddhism and the state. One of these is "The Lion's Roar on the Turning of the Wheel" (Pāli: *Cakkavatti-Sīhanāda sutta*) in the largest collection of discourses, the *Dīgha Nikāya*. In discourse, the Buddha explains to his retinue of monks the importance of a just rule. He tells the story of a monarch named Dalhanemi, who is unable to preserve order in his realm because he fails to correctly administer the *dhamma* in his state policies—in this particular instance, by not giving property to the needy. Thus, one incorrect policy by the king catalyzes a concatenation of events that result in depravity and disorder.[29]

The inability to conceive of a state without Buddhism alludes to a kind of religious nationalism. Religious nationalism thus becomes a way of conceptualizing the state and its society as *necessarily* Buddhist. This concept was actualized in such Buddhist societies as sixteenth-century Tibet. After examining the relationship between the Fifth Dalai Lama and Gushri Khan, the Mongol ruler, Derek Maher in this volume offers a cogent example of how the interests of the state and of religion coalesce. Buddhist nationalism becomes a way of thinking and a rationale for justifying warfare, either to defend the nation or to extend the power of the nation. The phenomenon of soldier-Zen and the just-war ideology in support of the Japanese in World War II is addressed in Victoria's chapter. Another chapter in this volume, Xue Yu's "Buddhist Monks in China during the Korean War (1951–1953)," provides a more recent example of Buddhist nationalism. He reveals Chinese Buddhist justifications for engaging in the Korean War. In Paul Demiéville's chapter, we find reoccurring Buddhist justifications for warfare in Chinese, Korean, and Japanese societies.

The final chapters herein relate Buddhist warfare to other aspects of violence. Michael Jerryson's chapter notes that violence is often associated with the role of a Buddhist monk as a political symbol in Buddhist countries. He theorizes that one catalyst for Buddhist violence might be an attack upon a Buddhist monk, which would then lead to violent acts of retaliation. Jerryson's observations are based on the Buddhist-Muslim conflict in Thailand, but the pattern may hold true throughout Buddhist societies. In "Afterthoughts," Bernard Faure urges us to look beyond the popular associations of violence with war and to consider more nuanced aspects of violence. This intellectual nudge puts into context the self-immolation of Vietnamese monks during the U.S. war in Vietnam, the Spivakian category of epistemic violence, and even Buddhist perspectives on anorexia and bulimia. Hence, this volume on Buddhist warfare in such countries as Tibet, India, China, Mongolia, and Sri Lanka counters the pervasive illusion that Buddhism is a pacifistic religion and raises the issue of the relationship of violence to spirituality in Buddhisms. Hopefully, in a wider sense, this volume will help to bring Buddhist examples to the discourse about sacred violence in general. The problematic idea of religious war is an intellectual challenge not only for historical reflection, but also for understanding the social tensions of the contemporary age.

NOTES

1. Trevor Ling uses the term "Buddhisms" to underline the importance that history, politics, and society have on a transnational religion such as Buddhism. For more information on this, see the introduction in *Buddhist Trends in Southeast Asia*, ed. Trevor Ling (Singapore: Institute of Southeast Asian Studies, 1993), 1–5.

2. Mahinda Deegalle, "Is Violence Justified in Theravada Buddhism?" *Ecumenical Review* 55.2 (April 2003): 125.

3. Jonathan Z. Smith, *Imagining Religion: From Babylon to Jonestown* (Chicago: University of Chicago Press, 1982), 80.

4. Buddhist studies scholars have critically reexamined the parameters and implications of Buddhism since the mid-1990s. For examples of such work, see Donald Lopez, ed., *Critical Terms for the Study of Buddhism* (Chicago: University of Chicago Press, 2005); Hilda Gutiérrez Baldoquín, ed., *Dharma, Color, and Culture: New Voices in Western Buddhism* (Berkeley, Calif.: Parallax, 2004); and Steven Collins, *Nirvana and Other Buddhist Felicities* (Cambridge: Cambridge University Press, 1998).

5. The first truth addresses the nature of suffering (Pāli: *dukkha*), the second truth locates the origin of suffering, the third is that there is a cessation from suffering, and the fourth is the path to this cessation.

6. For examples of variations, see the description in the *Saṃyutta Nikāya* of the Pāli canon, the *Mahāparinirvana Sūtra*, and the *Angulimaliya Sūtra*.

7. The amalgam of *kwan* and *winyan* are specific to Thailand; however, each has a different origin. The practice of venerating the *kwan* can be traced back to tenth-century China, whereas the propitiation of the *winyan* comes from early Sanskrit India.

8. The New Testament offers an excellent example of mythic warfare in 2 Corinthians 10:4–5, "For the weapons of our warfare are not carnal, but mighty through God to the pulling down of strong holds; casting down imaginations, and every high thing that exalteth itself against the knowledge of God, and bringing into captivity every thought to the obedience of Christ."

9. Mark Juergensmeyer, *Global Rebellion: Religious Challenges to the Secular State, from Christian Militias to Al Qaeda* (Berkeley: University of California Press, 2008), 6.

10. Bruce Lawrence and Aisha Karim, eds., *On Violence: A Reader* (Durham, N.C.: Duke University Press, 2007).

11. Claudia Dreifus, "The Dalai Lama," *New York Times*, November 28, 1993.

12. "Whatever monk should intentionally deprive a human being of life, or should look about so as to be his knife-bringer, he is also one who is defeated, he is not in communion." I. B. Horner, trans., *The Book of the Discipline* (Oxford: Pali Text Society, 1992), 1:123. See also a slightly abridged account in Bhikkhu Bodhi, trans., "Ānāpānasaṃyutta," in *Saṃyutta Nikāya, Mahāvagga* (Boston: Wisdom, 2000), 1773 and 1774.

13. Michael Jerryson, "Militarizing Buddhism: Violence in Southern Thailand," in this volume.

14. Paul Demiéville, "Buddhism and War," in this volume.

15. Chatthip Nartsupha, "The Ideology of 'Holy Men' Revolts in North East Thailand," in *History and Peasant Consciousness in Southeast Asia*, ed. Andrew Turton and Shigeru Tanabe (Osaka: National Museum of Ethnology, 1984), 123.

16. Lambert Schmithausen, "Aspects of the Buddhist Attitude towards War," in *Violence Denied: Violence, Non-Violence and the Rationalization of Violence in South Asian Cultural History*, ed. E. M. Houben and K. R. Van Kooij (Leiden: Brill, 1999), 58.

17. Brian Victoria, *Zen at War*, 2nd ed. (Boulder, Colo.: Rowman & Littlefield, 2006), 88, 119.

18. For a survey of fundamentalism in Theravāda Buddhism, see Donald Swearer, "Fundamentalist Movements in Theravada Buddhism," in *Fundamentalisms Observed*, ed. Martin E. Marty and R. Scott Appleby (Chicago: University of Chicago Press, 1992), 628–690.

19. Romila Thapar, *Early India: From the Origins to AD 1300* (Berkeley: University of California Press, 2002), 152–155.

20. Uma Chakravarti, *The Social Dimensions of Early Buddhism* (Delhi: Munshiram Manoharlal, 1996), 8. Thapar, *Early India*, 175.

21. Durga N. Bhagavat, *Early Buddhist Jurisprudence* (Poona, India: Oriental Book Agency, 1939), 60.

22. A strong analysis of this is in Elizabeth J. Harris, "Violence and Disruption in Society: A Study of the Early Buddhist Texts," *Dialogue* 17.1–3 (Jan.–Dec. 1990): 35.

23. Balkrishna Gokhale addresses this in "The Early Buddhist View of the State," *Journal of the American Oriental Society* 89.4 (Oct. 1969): 731.

24. Tambiah takes a distinct stance on early Buddhism's perspective on violence, explaining, "Kings must be good killers before they can turn to piety and good works." Stanley J. Tambiah, *World Conqueror and World Renouncer: A Study of Buddhism and Polity in Thailand against a Historical Background* (Cambridge: Cambridge University Press, 1976), 522.

25. Gokhale, "The Early Buddhist View of the State," 734.

26. Balkrishna Gokhale, "Dhamma as a Political Concept," *Journal of Indian History* 44 (Aug. 1968): 251.

27. I. B. Horner, trans., The Book of the Discipline (Suttavibhanga) (Oxford: Pali Text Society, 1992), 1:74.

28. Chakravarti, Social Dimensions of Early Buddhism, 150.

29.

> Thus, from the not giving of property to the needy, poverty became rife, from the growth of poverty, the taking of what was not given increased, from the increase of theft, the use of weapons increased, from the increased use of weapons, the taking of life increased—and from the increase in taking of life, people's life-span decreased.

"Cakkavatti-Sīhanāda Sutta: The Lion's Roar on the Turning of the Wheel," in *The Long Discourses of the Buddha: A Translation of the Dīgha Nikāya*, trans. Maurice Walshe (Boston: Wisdom, 1995), 399, 400.

I

Buddhism and War

Paul Demiéville
Translated by Michelle Kendall

General Renondeau's superb text on Japan's warrior-monks (*sōhei*) precedes this. In it, the thrice-endowed expert of Japanology, Buddhism, and military history presents a few observations and musings that go further than usual; these I would now like to summarize.[1] Is Buddhism's militarization just a phenomenon found in Japan, or do we see other examples in the general history of Buddhism? How is this explained, how was it explained, this departure from a doctrine whose main cardinal precept is to refrain absolutely from killing any living being? What might the social, economic, and political motives of this phenomenon have been? What logic do the guilty parties use to ideologically justify their deviation from the prescribed doctrine? Such are the questions I am given the opportunity to consider, thanks to Renondeau, in this Chinese-style postscript.

When the Hieizan monks took up arms to go off to war their faces were veiled. Their heads were wrapped in a cloth that left only their eyes uncovered. It can surely be said that they were in bad faith, and for good reason. Murder, harming living creatures, as is said in Sanskrit (*prāṇātipāta*), the act of killing (*cha-cheng*) or cutting short life (*touan cheng-ming*) as the Chinese say, are all in fact the subject of the first of the five precepts (*pañca-śīla*), which every practitioner in the Buddhist community must observe, laypersons as well as monks. Within this not inherently Buddhist pentalogy,[2] the precept of not-killing comes before stealing, sexual misconduct, lying, and the taking of intoxicants, all of which war also exploits, in addition to murder. Yet, there is nothing more worthy than not-killing. The canonical tradition is unanimous on this: "Murder is the most serious of all sins."[3] It is also ranked number one in the ten major sins that we call "negative paths of karma" (*akuśala-karma-patha*) and which are forbidden to the clerics, beginners, catechumen, monks, and nuns. No other precept is followed so strictly by all Buddhists, even now. Not-killing is a characteristic so anchored in Buddhism that it is practically considered a custom.[4]

It has its distinctive quality. My reverend friend Bhikkhu Walpola Rahula has often told me that, until her death, his mother (a simple peasant from Ceylon) had never killed a living creature, not even an insect. In the *Vinaya*, the set of rules regulating the monastic community, the killing of any being (animal or plant) is considered a sin requiring purification. Hence, the clergy were required to take precautions such as using filters, abstaining from nightly walks or walks soon after rainfall, etc., as a measure to protect the lives of even the tiniest sentient beings. For monks and nuns, killing a human being is one of the four transgressions that are grounds for excommunication and definitive expulsion from the monastic community (*pārājika*). On the canonical list of transgressions that qualify for excommunication, murder is ranked third, after sexual misconduct and stealing, but before lying. Yet, the Chinese interpreters of the Great Vehicle insist that this classification must be rectified and that murder must be placed first.[5]

Buddhist pedagogy was observed when it came to the sin of killing. This sin is defined as more than the act of killing itself, it includes simply provoking or even approving of a murder committed by someone else, or likewise contributing in any way to one. Hence, it follows that with war, responsibility is collective in nature:

> When soldiers join together toward the same goal, they are all equally as guilty as the one who does the actual killing. In fact... communally they egg each other on, if not with words, then in the mere fact that they are all there together to kill.... Even [if] it is out of duty that they have joined the army, they are guilty, except if they have made this pledge: I will not kill a living being, even to save my own life.[6]

On this point, the Buddhist logicians concur with every antimilitarist logician, from Mö-tseu to Tchouang-tseu, from Pascal to La Bruyère:[7] "If a man steals a buckle, he's put to death; yet if a man steals a principality, he becomes a prince"[8]; or like the French proverb states, "If a man steals money, he's condemned. If he steals a nation, he's crowned."

They go even further, and not without pushing the logic of their own dogma to its near limits, it seems: better to die than to kill, they teach; better to observe the taboo on someone else's life than to preserve one's own life.[9] With this, we are touching on one of the fundamental paradoxes in Buddhist doctrine (the other one concerning us is the antinomy of karma and the negation of all personality, *nairātmya*), paradoxes stemming no doubt from the conflict between the Buddhist reformation's innovations and old, immemorial principles that were anchored in the collective unconscious.[10] The Buddhist axiom is that everything is suffering, but that there is a way to end this suffering: this path leads to nirvana, which principally consists in the end of rebirth. The condemnation of life is evident, and naïve logic would favor these eleventh-century Chinese sectarians who massacred their contemporaries while declaring that, since life is suffering, killing one's neighbor is doing him a favor.[11] This is a simple-minded heresy for there is karma which cannot be extinguished by death.[12] The most misleading of all temptations therefore would be using suicide as an option. Dually noted in various texts of the *Vinaya* is the condemnation of suicide as preceding that of murder or which serves as the preliminary opportunity for it.[13] Certainly suicide is not as serious as murder:[14] it is only a wrong action (*duskṛta*) or a serious misdeed (*sthūlātyaya*) and is not, like murder, cause for excommunication (*pārājika*) or for purification (*pāyantika*).[15] The common monk is no less formally counseled against suicide, for it prevents him from continuing the cultivation of pure conduct (*brahmacaryā*), in other words good karma (*kuśala-karman*), and therefore from his salvation.[16] Certainly, we notice on many occasions in Buddhist texts where suicides have not been condemned;[17] but it usually concerns the saints of the Lesser Vehicle who were ready for nirvana and, "having done what there was to do" (*kṛta-kṛtya*), no longer have to accumulate redemptive karma. Or it concerns the bodhisattva[s] sacrificing their lives for the good of others. As La Vallée Poussin notes, the example of a saint like Vakkali—who attains nirvana while slicing his own throat (with the Buddha's approval)—is completely different from the example of the average suicide victim who covets non-existence, and for whom suicide is an act of passion and not the result of a supreme peace of mind.[18] Vakkali was "beyond reproach, without remorse"; he was ready for deliverance (*vimukti*); Vakkali was mature.[19] As for the Great Vehicle, we read in the *Treatise on the Great Perfection of Wisdom* attributed to Nāgārjuna that suicide is not a sin of killing, because it does not destroy the life of another.[20] Further, is not the other's life more precious than my own life? Certainly, according to the Great Vehicle, whose moral is essentially altruistic. So why do the Lesser Vehicle texts like those referenced earlier, teach that in war it is better to let oneself be killed than to kill? Admittedly, Buddhist altruism is not an innovation of the Great Vehicle; it only develops it.

The saint of the Great Vehicle, the bodhisattva, must "contribute to the life of everything that exists."[21] But, what is this thing called "me"? What is the "me" of another living being? Why compassion, why altruism, why would I sacrifice myself out of respect for another living being if it does not exist in itself, if it is only an aggregate of continually changing aggregates, as Buddhism asserts? "Why combat suffering if the suffering being does not exist?"[22] And as for killing, what is it really, since the aggregates (*skandha*) are short-lived (*kṣaṇika*)?[23] "The destruction of things is spontaneous," states a well-known treatise from the Lesser Vehicle. "[T]hings perish on their own, because it is in their nature to perish. As they perish with no help from the other, they perish in being born; perishing in birth, they are short-lived."[24] What then is the role of the murderer? We are told that he puts an end to the vital breath (*prāṇa*) by inhibiting it to continue to recur. What is more, he annihilates the very organ that houses the life force (*jīvitendriya*), by obstructing the birth of a new "moment." However, if there is no person, no entity endowed with breath (*prāṇin*) who is killed: what dies, as what lives, [is] simply a material body complete with sense organs.[25] Therefore, killing is allowed to be defined as "cutting short the series, of a predetermined duration, of a sentient being."[26] Mahāyāna doctors do not hesitate to jump to the conclusion:

> [S]ince the living being [*sattva*] does not exist, neither does the sin of murder. And since the sin of murder does not exist, there is no longer any reason to forbid it. . . . In killing then, given that the five aggregates are characteristically empty, similar to the visions of dreams or reflections in a mirror, one commits no wrongdoing.[27]

Not surprisingly with such definitions, the Buddhism of the Great Vehicle was able to engender a reasoning which the clergy only had to draw upon to justify its warrior aberrations. The Lesser Vehicle, which tends to condemn life, remains firm in its interdiction of killing; the Great Vehicle lauds life, and it is the Great Vehicle that will in the end find excuses for murder, and will even glorify it.

We will discuss these ideas in even more detail than the Buddhists from the Far East have done, though they have had numerous opportunities to bring them to the fore. Among the treatises on discipline in which the Great Vehicle devises to thwart the *Vinaya* of the Lesser Vehicle, none has had more success, in China, as well as in Japan, and in neighboring countries, than the work entitled the *Brahma Net Sūtra* (*Brahmajāla Sūtra*). This was purportedly translated from the Sanskrit at the beginning of the fifth century, but its authenticity is, to say the least, dubious. For instance, we have found no evidence of it outside China. Nevertheless, this text strongly insists upon the responsibility that befalls the children of the Buddha; in other words, the follower who has taken his bodhisattva vows in line with the Great Vehicle is to take no part whatsoever in war. It forbids them to possess arms, to "stockpile" any object destined for the killing of other living beings, such as knives, sticks, bows or arrows, spears, axes, fishing nets, or hunting lassos.[28] When armies come into contact with one another, they are to refrain from getting involved with each other, from going back and forth between camps, and especially from participating in any armed combat against the state, all while following their missions.[29] They will not attend battles wishing ill on the other.[30] They will not kill. They will not make the other kill. They will not attain the means for killing. They will refrain from praising killing and from approving of it when they find themselves witnessing it. They will abstain from being accomplices of murder through the use of black magic, etc.[31] For all intents and purposes, their mind must always be filled with charitable and submissive thoughts, thoughts of the other's salvation; for them, killing will lead to their excommunication (*pārājika*).[32]

This was a long insistence on warlike temptations that most assuredly were assailing the Buddhists at the time this text was written, a time in China's history when peasant uprisings were rife with Buddhist inspiration.[33] Perhaps in other parts of its vast and expanding domain Buddhism contributed to softening, if not eliminating war. I recollect having read that a king from Indianized Indochina had the tips of soldiers' arrows rounded. Even in India, I don't believe Buddhist monks ever took up arms; they left that to the *yogin* and *sannyāsin* ascetic orders which were still overrunning the countryside in the eighteenth century and which the British administration had to suppress.[34] The emperor Aśoka seems to have been converted to Buddhism through his experience of the horrors of war:

> Eight years after his coronation, the King Piyadasi, the Beloved-of-the-Gods, conquered Kalinga. One hundred thousand people were deported; one hundred thousand were killed; this number many times over perished. Then, once Kalinga was taken, his fervent supporters were for the Beloved-of-the-Gods the enforcement of the Law, the love of the Law, the teaching of the Law. Regret took hold of the Beloved-of-the-Gods after he conquered Kalinga. Seeing that conquering an independent country is murder, it means death or captivity for its people.[35]

Also, Buddhist nonviolence (*avihiṃsā*) most certainly contributed to the weakening of the lamaist, Tibetan, and Mongol military. As early as the eighth century a Turkish khan was advised to be wary of Buddhism (and of Taoism), for it was said that these doctrines "make one good and weak, and are usually against using war or forceful conflict as an option."[36] Likewise, in the thirteenth century, Khubilai [Qubilai] had to use Buddhism to politically neutralize Tibet.[37]

Yet we do not see Buddhism making the people it came in contact with (be it in China, nor Japan, or even in countries of Chinese development) more pacifistic. In these countries, it was contending with "closed-minded," well-established nations, built mostly on Confucianism. Here, the relationship between church and state was posing problems the likes of which history has scarcely seen except in Europe.[38]

So many different solutions! It is significant that in the history of China the question of Buddhist monks serving in the military was never discussed in ideological terms, only in economical ones. Buddhist clergy maintained a privileged status with regard to the state that exempted them from paying taxes and exempted them from any state-required civic duty, such as military service.[39] In exchange for these privileges, the state expected religious benefits for its welfare, the welfare of the dynasty, and all its citizens. Rites were performed against natural calamities, such as droughts, as well as against human calamities, such as war or enemies. Subsequently, most notably in Tantric liturgy, we see Buddhist rituals used toward military ends continuously throughout the Far East. For this, they used such apocryphal manuscripts as the well-known text from the *Perfection of Wisdom*, the *Diamond Sūtra*.[40] As the first Christian rulers in Europe relied on Christianity to win wars, so it was with the barbarians in northern China, and later in Japan: one of the principal reasons for adopting Buddhism was the hope of gaining some military advantages.[41]

Nevertheless, the exemption from civic duties, principally military service, attracted among the clergy ranks a group of retractors who were escaping their military service. In the beginning of the Tang dynasty, approximately 621–626, this burgeoning dynasty was in mid-military expansion. The famous Fou Yi, in his anti-Buddhist memoirs, scolded Buddhist clergy not only for being sworn to celibacy (which diminished future available manpower), but especially for dodging military service in favor of its special status.[42] In addition, he proposed the marrying of monks and nuns and the massive enlistment of the empire's entire clergy, which he said would have generated no less than six armies.[43] Again a century later, circa 706, another critic of Buddhism, Li Xiao, expressed criticism in these terms:

> The national defense depends on those required to fulfill civic duties. If all of these citizens became monks, and if all the soldiers went into religion as a profession, how will military campaigns be assured success? And who will pay the taxes?[44]

During the Tang dynasty, the same antiphon returns chronically under the pen[s] of statesmen. However neither in their diatribes nor in the retorts of either the Buddhists or their supporters, was the moral or religious argument condemning war (found in Buddhist doctrine) invoked.[45] Much to the contrary, and it is biting to state this, at the end of the Tang dynasty militarism had broken down internally; with the weakened central power, the soldiers recruited by the statesmen of the provinces threatened the dynasty.

In the Confucian bureaucrats' missives, the Buddhist parasites are seen associated with the factious military. A writer from the period, Yuan Tchen (779–831), a friend of the poet Po Kiu-yi, did not hesitate to put the two in the same category:

> Far from cultivating purity which eliminates luxury and renounces the world, Buddhists take advantage of their preferential treatment thanks to which they balk at civic duties and shirk pain and suffering. On the other hand, soldiers, far from demonstrating bravery, jumping on their tank, deploying their military force, exhibit an arrogance that makes them commit acts of violence indiscriminately and to mistreat civic administrative personnel. And so, nine out of ten men in the empire are parasites with neither hearth nor home.[46]

Then, in the first half of the ninth century, the Emperor Wen-tsong declared to his cabinet:

> Not long ago there were three consumers for the production of one farmer; now we must add to that a Buddhist monk and a soldier. But it is especially the monks who bring nothing but unhappiness to my people.[47]

At the end of the eighth century, there was collusion among the eunuchs of the imperial guard (sworn enemies of the Confucian hierarchy) and the Buddhists under their control. This collusion ranged within the scope of imperial metropolis and possibly further. It contributed gravely to compromising the church and to preparing for the great proscription of 845. This proscription marked the triumph of the state over the church, a triumph from which Buddhism in China has never been able to recover; collectively this assured the state's upper hand on the central military power and on the Buddhist church.[48]

If Buddhism had played a role in the deterioration of the Chinese empire at the end of the Tang dynasty, a deterioration that would have opened the door to new barbarian invasions, it seems to have had only an economic and social impact. Its pacifistic doctrines had no bearing on historical texts and were of no influence in the empire's demise. It goes without saying that these historical texts emanated from civil servants who saw the church only from the state's and from the Confucian perspective; they were keen on attaching only self-interested, sordid motives to Buddhist draft dodgers. Even in Buddhist texts, rarely to my knowledge, are there references to ideological conflicts. One such case was that of an officer from the Leang dynasty, who was descended from a long lineage of civil servants. In 536, at the age of twenty, as he was about to leave for war in the northwest, he deserted the army to enter religion, invoking the Lao-tzu quote on "arms, these instruments of destruction," which prevent us from ever attaining enlightenment.[49]

In his piece against Buddhism, Fou Yi mentioned more than ten Buddhist monk uprisings against the secular authority "since antiquity";[50] the details of these events unfortunately have been lost.[51] Although in China they never became noted (as they did in Japan), essential historical facts, the seditions, insurrections, or uprisings directed, fomented, or inspired by the Buddhists were never lacking throughout history. As was also the case in Japan, these periods seem to coincide with the breakdown of a centralized government. Whether or not religion has been incorporated within a societal feudal system, whenever the centralized power relaxes its control the same actions occur. We see monks from the community either forming armed gangs or leading a peasant uprising, often while partly connected to factious nobility, or to local government officials lacking autonomy.

One of these periods occurred during the reign of the Turkish Mongol Wei Tabgatch, whose dynasty was in control in northern China from 386 to 534. Tabgatch was the third emperor from this dynasty under which Buddhism was to know various fortunes. In 445, the Emperor T'ai-wou infiltrated Tch'ang-ngan to suppress an uprising that for appearance's sake had nothing to do with Buddhism. However, in a convent he discovered a large quantity of bows and arrows, and spears and shields, that local government officials and statesmen of the region had stored there.[52] Concluding that these objects had nothing to do with Buddhism, he suspected the monks were collaborating with the rebels. In any case, he had the Tch'ang-ngan clergy put to death and had all Buddhist icons destroyed. This was a tactical stance he maintained for the duration of his empire.[53] This marked the first of the four Buddhist persecutions that are traditionally enumerated in the history of Chinese Buddhism. Without a doubt the Emperor T'ai-wou erred in mistrusting the Tch'ang-ngan monks.

During the Tabgatch Empire throughout the fifth and sixth centuries, Buddhist-inspired revolts increased in number. In his work on Buddhism in this period, M. Tsukamoto Zenryū counts no less than six between the years 402 and 517.[54] In 515, the monk Faqing commanded the last and most typical uprising. This occurred in what is now the province of Ho-pei, where the population number at that time was very dense. It was a characteristic uprising; according to M. Tsukamoto it was due principally to the continual warfare that had ravaged the region, to the Tabgatch dynasty's recruits against the Leang Chinese dynasty, to the barbaric acts that the central administration ordered the Tabgatch prefects to commit, and to the sumptuary ventures involving the court and the Buddhism-obsessed Tabgatch nobility.

The court and the Tabgatch nobility raised taxes and increased the amount of civic duties owed them by the people. We can undoubtedly add to this, without risking anachronism, the Chinese reaction to the barbarians. Faqing took the title of "Great Vehicle," and declared the arrival of the new Buddha. His lieutenant was a Chinese aristocrat and a friend of the people, to whom he granted the titles "King Who Pacifies the Land of the Han, Commander of the Demon-Vanquishing Army, Tenth-Stage Bodhisattva" (there are ten successive "stages," in Sanskrit *vihāra*, in the spiritual hierarchy of the bodhisattva). Faqing had under his command more than fifty thousand men who do not seem to have been monks. When a soldier killed a man, he earned the title of first-stage bodhisattva. The more he killed, the more he went up the echelon toward sainthood; with the tenth killing he advanced to the tenth stage. Murder was a charitable act in the crusade against Māra; the insurgents were given an alcoholic drug that made them crazy to such an extent that fathers and sons, older and younger brothers no longer recognized one another and didn't think twice before killing each other; "the only thing that mattered was killing."[55] The recruits had to have been illiterate peasants who became crazed by such ideas. They were convinced that they were killing for a "new Buddha," which they seemingly identified as the messiah Maitreya, the cult of which was booming in China. The texts do not specify precisely if Faqing referred to himself as the Buddhist bodhisattva Maitreya, one of his precursors, or one of those universal sovereigns who accompanied his arrival.[56] Faqing married a nun named Houei-houei. We know that at this time, most notably in Serindia, monastic celibacy was not observed. This shift did not spare conventional Buddhism, now completely under the control of the government of the Wei [and] ensconced in the hierarchy. The monasteries had been ravaged. The ecclesiastic authorities were sponsored by the government. The regular clergy, which was placed under its control and its protection, was decimated and sacred texts and icons were burned: "A new Buddha has come to the world, to conquer the old Māra(s)!" The Wei needed to assemble an army of a hundred thousand foot-soldiers and cavalrymen against those crazed armed men. The army was placed under the command of a Tabgatch prince who also devastated the region. Faqing and his nun were decapitated. Their lay lieutenant was publicly executed on the capital steps. The carnage was only finally suppressed in 517.[57]

Most of the other Buddhist revolts at this time were quite similar. They involved peasant insurgences not only against the authority of the state but also against the authority of the officiating church. The Maitreyan messianism, the belief connected to the advent of a "Son of God" or to a utopian *cakravartin*, fueled the rebels.[58] They do not seem to have been recruited directly from the clergy or even from an unorthodox clergy, but rather from the peasantry at the instigation of an inspired monk who claimed to be the incarnation or the precursor of the bodhisattva Maitreya, or that he's the originator of a dynasty destined to establish the Great Peace on Earth and the reign of the Real Law.

These are aspects found in many of the armed revolts that Buddhism must have been provoking in China for centuries. Here are a few random examples, taken from various texts.[59] At the beginning of the Tang dynasty, in one of his memorials from 621–626, Fou Yi let it be known that in his time there were monks so inclined to rebel. He added that, if the barbarians were threatening China and debasing themselves with the two hundred thousand monks and nuns of the empire in order to "conquer the hearts of men," this would result in a crisis which should be guarded against.[60] Was he possibly alluding to a military threat presented by the clergy?

These were troubled times, as was each change of dynasty; the Tang had just recently taken power and their regime was already under threat. The fall of the Sui (581–617), in which the Buddhists had assuredly played a role, had been marked by chaos even though this dynasty had ardently protected them. The officiating clergy seem to have supported the Sui dynasty against the Tang dynasty. In 613 two uprisings are noted. One took place in Tang-hien (present-day Ho-pei), where every five years a certain layperson named Song Zixian, who "excelled in black magic and knew how to metamorphose into the Buddha," took advantage to recruit troops at these large Buddhist gatherings celebrating the advent of the bodhisattva Maitreya.[61] The other uprising was in Fufeng prefecture, near Tch'ang-ngan, where a monk named Xiang Haiming, who also claimed to be an incarnation of the bodhisattva Maitreya, took the title of emperor and the name "The White Raven." He acquired followers in the tens of thousands up to the highest classes from the capital. They even had to send an entire expedition out against him.[62]

At the beginning of 619, shortly after the ascension of the Tang dynasty, a banquet was organized in Houai-jong (present-day Chahar), not far from Peking in the northwest. It was during this Buddhist banquet, organized by the local magistrate and with many in attendance that five thousand monks under the command of the monk Kao T'an-cheng, revolted.[63] They massacred the local magistrate and his military colleague[s]. The monk prepared to repeat the heroic deeds of the rebel monk Faqing of the Wei dynasty. Similarly, he declared himself emperor with the same title of "Great Vehicle," bestowed on a nun the title of "Empress Yashodhara" (this was the name of the Buddha's wife, who became a nun after *bodhi* or enlightenment), and decreed the inauguration of an era named "The Wheel of Dharma." He then formed an alliance with Kao K'ai-tao, a general in the region who turned to crime and took the title of the prince of Yen. Soon this henchman turned against the Buddhist "emperor" and assassinated him ignominiously.[64]

At this time, the founder of the Tang dynasty, Li Che-min (then the prince of Ts'in), was dealing with more serious insurgencies, one of which was in Ho-nan, commanded by the veritable general Wang Che-tch'ong, who had taken the title of prince of Tcheng, and who aspired to the empire. Wang Che-tch'ong surrendered on June 4, 621. The following day Li Che-min invaded Lo-yang, the capital of the Sui. He had the palace destroyed, the capital's principal edifice as well as the main door to the palace confines and the one to the imperial city.[65] Additionally, and in our opinion of much more significance, he decreed the elimination of every Buddhist monastery and the secularization of every monk and nun in Lo-yang. The only exception was the thirty monks and thirty nuns particularly renowned for their virtues.[66] This tactical measure can clearly be understood, not as hostility against Buddhism in principle, but as a fundamental distrust that the Lo-yang clergy must have inspired. They were most likely aligned with the Sui in the dynastic conflict. Even outside Lo-yang, there were other instances of the Buddhist clergy opposing the Tang dynasty's endeavors. When, in 619 the "rebel" general Lieou Wou-tcheou infiltrated the Kiai prefecture in the Chan-si, he scaled the surrounding wall with the use of Buddhist prayer flags that the monk Tao-teng hung out for him.[67] In 621, a character from the Sui prefecture in the Chen-si and a "maleficent monk" named Tche-kiue together wove a plot against the Tang dynasty.[68]

No doubt Fou Yi was alluding to these sorts of factions in his memoir. They no longer had anything to do with peasant insurrections. They were more likely the result of Buddhists' involvement in the political battles of the times.

Epigraphy fills us in on another of Buddhism's involvements which, as far as I know, is not documented in any historical text. The monastery of the woods near the Shaoshi peak, on the Song-chan or central peak in the province of Ho-nan, not far from Lo-yang, is known among all the Buddhist monasteries in China as one of the original locales of the Dhyāna school. This is where, in the fifth and sixth centuries, Bodhidharma stayed and practiced "mural contemplation" for nine years; it subsequently became a center for the art of boxing. We know that the Boxers who rose up against foreigners at the end of the nineteenth century, and besieged the Peking delegation in 1900, were part of a secret society with more or less Buddhist origins. And yet, Chao-lin sseu, the monastery in the woods near the Shaoshi peak, houses an inscription from the Tang dynasty with a reproduction of Li Shemin's signature, believed to be actually by the engraver.[69] It was a message left by the prince of Ts'in, the future Taizong (627–649). He left it for the community of Chao-lin, its eldest member, its superior, and also its military and civic leaders who, along with the monks, were obviously found to be involved in the affair, the subject of Li Shemin's message. This message is dated the thirtieth day of the fourth moon, which can only be May 26, 621. In it, Li Shemin disparages the unrest afflicting the world; anarchy and disharmony are compromising even the existence of Buddhism. This message glorifies the huge undertaking of the pacification of the Tang dynasty and faults Wang Che-tch'ong, the rebel general who the message urges its addressees to catch. The message also praises the addressees for all they already know how to do for the good cause, and promises them abundant rewards in exchange for their services.

On June 4, 621, as noted above, Wang Che-tch'ong surrendered to Li Shimin, who was invading Lo-yang. Li Shimin did not wait long to extensively reward the Chao-lin sseu monks. They were truly gifted in knowing exactly when to side with the Tang dynasty and, seemingly before his victory, had regained control over a strategic point known as the Cypress Valley Estate, located fifty *li* northwest of Chao-lin sseu. This is where Wang Che-tch'ong's troops must have set up camp. Immediately after his victory, Li Shimin gave them 1,000 pieces of silk fabric. Then, in 624, he exempted them from the general method of Buddhist clergy secularization and from [the payment on] taxable goods that he decreed in 621 or in 622.[70] In the end, in 625, he granted them forty *k'ing* (some five hundred acres) of land located in the Cypress Valley Estate. It was designed to be a private prefecture with a water-mill for the Chao-lin sseu (exempt from taxes). Further, in order to acknowledge their good conduct in Cypress Valley and also the land they had taken during the Lo-yang invasion in 621,[71] the monks were awarded official titles. This leaves us with no doubt as to their abilities as soldiers. T'an-tsong, who stormed the Cypress Valley Estate, was named great general, as was the elder of Chao-lin sseu, Chan-hou, his superior, Tche-ts'ao, and his acting-general, Houei-tch'ang.[72] What's more, they seem to have refused these titles, which hardly went with religious status. Without them, they were not any less illustrious in history; they were examples of military merit which Chao-lin sseu acquired in the centuries that followed, as we will see below.[73]

Around the end of the Tang dynasty, when the dynasty was beginning to falter, government officials were inciting unrest on all sides to arrogate regional power. Another monk from the Song-chan monastery (we are not told if this is an offshoot of the Chao-lin sseu or not), Yuan-tsing, played a key role in overthrowing the imperial palace of Lo-yang in 815.[74] His accomplice was Li Che-tao, who was of Korean descent; his grandfather Li Tcheng-ki had enlisted in China's army as a general and become a naturalized citizen in 778. As a military commander in Chan-tong, he carved out a vast territory which he controlled nearly autonomously and which afterward his son Li Na took over, followed by his grandson Li Che-kou. These last two finished by openly rebelling against the central government. Meanwhile, Li Che-kou's younger brother, Li Che-tao, had inherited just as much power. In most of their activities and official titles, the imperial court of the Tang dynasty continuously affirmed Li Che-tao's power. Nevertheless, he kept close guard over his independent sovereignty, especially on his subordinates whose wives and children he kept hostage, and whom he put to death at the slightest sign of defection or conspiring with the central authority.

In 815, Li Che-tao took advantage of the government's vulnerability resulting from simultaneous insurgences of other military leaders. He, too, decided to revolt. He kept himself informed by spies who worked under cover, alongside hired hands in his Lo-yang residence. He terminated the project by setting fire to the imperial palace and raining fire and brimstone upon the capital. The plot was exposed in time. As Li Che-tao's armed participants were retreating from Song-chan, the imperial army crushed them. When they were taken prisoner, it was discovered that they had been under the command of the monk Yuan-tsing, a seasoned veteran, according to the *Tang chou*, since he had already served as general in Che Sseu-ming (703–761). He was Ngan Louchan's lieutenant in the great insurrection that had placed the Tang dynasty about a hair from its ruin, just after the middle of the seventh century. Yuan-tsing is described as a man of unmatched courage and savagery.

In 815, when he was captured, Yuan-tsing had already passed his eightieth birthday. He observed that, when his executioners tried to torture him with a hammer, they found his bones to be so hard that they were unable to break his legs. Yuan-tsing then began to curse them: "These vermin!" he said, "they are *brave men*, and they do not even know how to break a leg!"[75] So, he positioned his legs and showed them how to break them himself. At the moment of his death, he exclaimed, "I missed my shot! I wasn't able to make blood flow in the city of Lo-yang!" It is reported that Li Che-tao had been paid through donations apparently destined for the restoration of the Song-chan convent, Fo-Kouang sseu.[76] Nevertheless, it most assuredly was not for the protection of the *sangha*'s residence that this soldier-monk loved to take up arms. More likely, he was one of those dynamic, wild leaders who rebel against all authority, like his contemporary, Yi-hiuan († 867). Yi-hiuan, the founder of the Lin-tsi sect, was called the "general of Lin-tsi." It was said about him, "If he had not been a monk, he would have most assuredly been a great ringleader."[77] He ardently preached spiritual murder and the "reversal of all values." "Kill everything you encounter, internally as well as externally! Kill the Buddha! Kill the patriarchs! Kill the saints! Kill your father and mother! Kill your closest friends! This is the path of deliverance, the way to escape the bondage of things; this is freedom!"[78]

Buddhist monks in China do not seem to have often taken up arms to protect their belongings and land, as they most likely did in Japan. The authority of the state remained strong, and the church remained very much a vassal of the state. In the case of the Yuantong monks, on the Lou-chan, north of Kiangsi, they had received a thousand *k'ing* of land and all sorts of favors from the poet-emperor Li Yu, the last one from the Southern Tang dynasty. When the Song dynasty troops marched on Nankin in 975 to oust Li Yu, the monks formed an advance guard numbering in the several hundreds to retain them on the banks of the Yangtze River.[79] Here we see monks entering into war to defend a dynasty that had supported them. This is a rather common motive for the militarization of the clergy in the history of China.

As early as the sixth century, the last emperor from the Northern Wei dynasty, Hiao-wou-ti, had to flee his capital, Lo-yang, only to go to Tch'ang-ngan where death and disaster awaited him and where his courtesans abandoned him like vermin leaving a boat in distress. A Buddhist church dignitary, Houei-tchen, acting general of the *sangha*, was charged afterward with carrying the imperial shield and sword and protecting the monarch.[80] In 755, at the time of the Ngan Lou-chan insurrection, one of the loyalist generals who intervened on the side of the Tang dynasty was a temporarily defrocked monk, Tao-p'ing. He commandeered one of the armies of the guard,[81] and fought several times against rebel troops. After regaining Tch'ang-ngan in 756, he refused the official titles bestowed on him and reentered the clergy.[82]

During the twelfth and thirteenth centuries, during the Jurchen and Mongol invasions, numerous monks were seen fending off the invaders. When Pien-leang (Kaifeng) was taken by the Jurchens, in 1126, the monk Tsong-yin (a descendant of the Song dynasty's imperial clan, and known for his interest in the art of war) was recruited into General Fan Tche-hui's army staff with the provisionary titles of advisor to the commanding general and cavalry inspector. General Fan Tche-hui was attempting to regain control over the Song capital. Accordingly, he organized an army of monks who were given the name August Victory Squadron. He also organized one of young volunteers calling them the Pure Victory Squadron. The first of these squadron names is a Chinese translation of Vijaya, "the Victorious," or Vikirṇa, "the Destroyer," deities from the Tantric pantheon.[83]

At this time (1126), in the Chan-si province, a monk from Wutai shan mountain range, Tchen-pao, sided similarly with the Song dynasty. He did so with so much heroism that his biography had to be included in the *History of the Song Dynasty*, listed alongside those imperial statesmen worthy of commemoration for their loyalty and sense of duty.[84] Once he had learned of the arrival of the Jurchens in the Wutai shan region, Tchen-pao began to dispatch his disciples on the mountain. The Emperor Kintsong, the last of the Northern Song dynasty, ordered him to Pien-leang and lavished him with encouragement. When the Jurchens showed up in front of the Tai prefecture at the foot of the Wutai shan mountain range, he protected it himself, since the prefect had defected. He was overwhelmed by the vast numbers arrayed against him. Consequently, the monasteries were consumed by flames. The Jurchen general had Tchen-pao brought back to him alive. So taken aback was the general by Tchen-pao's superb moral makeup, he was unable to decide to have him executed. He attempted to get around it, but in vain: "In my law," the monk told him, "it is a sin not to keep your word. I promised the Song emperor I'd die for him: how could I take it back?"

Thirty years later, the monk Yi-touan was also passionate about military things. He was involved in a Chinese insurrection against the Jurchen in the Shandong region. He organized a military outfit of a thousand men and placed them under the command of Keng-King, the head of the insurrection. One evening, however, the monk ran off, taking with him the insurgents' seal. He was recaptured and put to death before he succeeded in gaining control of the Jurchen camp.[85] In the thirteenth century, Mo Kien-tche from Yi-hing was another Buddhist monk whose conduct was even more commendable. In 1275, in the Kiang sou province, west of Tai-hou Lake, when the Khubilai troops were invading, Mo Kien-tche gathered a group of volunteers to defend the region. The last emperor of the Southern Song dynasty, Kong-ti, named Mo Kien-tche police chief of the subprefecture of Li-yang. He died in battle and was given posthumously the title of superior officer, for his military merits.[86] It was reported that at the time, in the southern part of the Kaingsi province, the Wan-ngan monks put their own troops up against the Mongols. They carried flags with inscriptions on them like: "Down with the Māra(s)!" or even: "In times of danger, we become generals; once the matter is resolved, we become monks once more!" These monks were killed in combat.[87]

Nevertheless, in China, Buddhist monks from the Dhyāna sect were the most famous for going to war to serve the homeland. They went to war against Japanese pirates at the time of the Ming dynasty (a dynasty whose very founder was a monk-turned-ringleader-turned-general). In the fifteenth and sixteenth centuries, China's coasts were infested with Japanese pirates who scavenged the seas, more or less under the official blessing of the Ashikaga lords. The Ming government had to then rely on masses of relief troops to halt the progress of the incursions of these pirates, even on their internal coastal territories. Among these ad hoc recruited troops there were bandits, salt merchants, coolies of the salt tax, salt furnace operators, fishermen, hunters, miners, brigands. They were a completely haphazard soldiery that, with the guidance of ordinary troops, in the end, was right about the islander looters. Nevertheless, all the source material recognizes that when it came to courage, the Chao-lin sseu monks were superior. The names of about twenty of them are known. Documents from the period describe them in combat, in the Shanghai region, under the command of regular army officers, with their hair dyed vermillion and their faces smeared with indigo like actors. They chased the terrified Japanese while flailing their arms about with clubs in hand. Next they cleaved them with iron picks.[88] Their exploits were the premise of a play in the modern repertory theater.[89] In addition, I have read in a Chinese newspaper from December 29, 1936, that a conference on the same subject was presented by a Tsiang Kiai-che army officer to the Nankin Buddhist monks to encourage them to obey the national government—without balking at the order for clergy to enlist.[90] The monks and nuns were, in fact, formally recruited into the Chinese National Army during the Sino-Japanese War, which preceded, announced, and accompanied the last world war. These monks and nuns were usually under the sign of the Red Cross, which they wore on their sleeves. Nonetheless, they were given military uniforms and taught how to use and handle their weapons. In Nankin, 1937, because the clergy had the financial means, they used their own money to pay their military instructors to enforce two hours of training a day.[91]

There remains still a lot to discuss about the sects, such as the White Lotus sect, the White Cloud sect, Maitreya, and others, which were more or less Buddhist. In addition, there are the secret societies that were somewhat connected to these sects and played an integral role in this still misunderstood story. A part of history still intensely investigated today is the insurrectional trends and revolts which plagued China for two millennia.[92] These sects and secret societies were always tainted with heresy or marked by a syncretism with Taoism, or even by the old shamanist roots of the reigning religion of the day. The regular Buddhist clergy preferred to keep their distance from these sects and secret societies. The official church turned a blind eye to this tumultuous unrest. The influence of the government, however, was much stronger in China than in Japan. The Chinese government considered this turmoil an illegal and clandestine activity (except when said government might benefit from using these sects and societies to further its own interests). We can conclude from the documentation collected above, although very incomplete and still very anecdotal, that militarization of the Buddhist clergy as such seems to have been only an episodic and sporadic phenomenon in China.

It was not the same in the neighboring countries, most notably in Korea, and especially in Japan. One reason for this is that Buddhism was introduced in these countries from China at the same time as civilization itself. Also, this was a time when, even though the Chinese civilization was saturated with Buddhism, Buddhism had to contend with national traditions. Buddhism ultimately absorbed them. As a result, it was changed in a very decisive and enduring way. As for the populace in China (often referred to as barbarians), Chinese culture was usually exported in the form of Buddhism, whereas even in China this religion was continuously given a thrashing as barbaric. It follows that in these countries, Buddhists participate more effectively and openly in state-run life than in China. This very Chinese phenomenon of secret societies has scarcely ever existed there. Military history, however, does not escape such an inclination.

I cannot keep from discussing Korea more in depth; there is such an abundance of material. On many occasions Korean kings enlisted in their own armies to fight against foreign invaders; the Korean peninsula was always seriously vulnerable. Monks were enlisted in the thousands. In the twelfth century they were recruited against the Jurchens; in the fourteenth, against the Mongols; in the sixteenth, against the Japanese from Hideyoshi; in the seventeenth, against the Manchu people. In return, this armed force often allowed the great Buddhist abbots to address the royal authority and to incite turmoil.[93]

In Japan, we can say that Buddhist military groups truly became an institution. For six or seven centuries (roughly speaking from the tenth to the sixteenth century), they represented an essential fact in the nation's history and in particular, its military history. We note in passing that before the modern era, Japan's military history was hardly more than a history of its own civil wars. Yet, this is a country wherein the virtues of the warrior have always been revered. Japan's insularity protected it against foreign aggressors who were then too weak. Until modern times this continued to be the case; as a result, it could support extensive initiatives for external expansion. So it was among themselves that the Japanese let loose their combative impulses. Furthermore, this trait is even found in the history of Japanese Buddhism; Japan has never really experienced religious unity. The Buddhist church was divided into multiple sects and then even subdivided in an entire hierarchy of branches and ramifications. A spirit of competition has continued for centuries between all these factions. The effects of this rivalry can still be felt and have contributed to the militarization of the clergy. However this was nothing like the syncretism that had led to total integration in China.[94]

What is remarkable about the history of the *sōhei*, which General Renondeau so meticulously recounted, is that it takes place between the two periods when Japan was governed by centralized and unified regimes. During this period the state had established itself as the authority. Warrior monks appeared at the beginning of the Heian era, after the disintegration of the Nara Empire. This empire was very similar to the Chinese empires wherein Buddhism had been firmly supervised, regulated, bureaucratized. It was an administration modeled on the Tang dynasty and aimed at assimilating both the *sangha* and the state, as is now the case in present-day Thailand.[95] After the tenth century, the royal court instituted a monopolizing and oppressive aristocracy in Heian (present-day Kyoto). The people were crushed by over taxing; as a consequence, the royal court pushed the peasants to seek refuge in Buddhist convents that were exempt from taxes and from civic duties, as they were in China.[96]

The large monasteries benefited from this influx of manpower, for one reason because they were then able to exploit or clear their rather extensive property. This donated land had rendered them quite well off, even in China. These estates were incorporated into the "villas" (*shō, shōen*) or the nobility's private domain. They were given by the imperial administration and received tax-exempt status.[97] Moreover, this influx of manpower soon served as the monasteries' armed defense (which in China rarely ever transpired) against the intrusion of government administration and also against the nobility, who did not look highly upon the monasteries unjustifiably assuming rights of true manorial authority. Soon groups of monks could be found armed and beginning to rebel against their own abbots, who were often of noble birth and in collusion with the royal court.[98] At the same time, military barons from the provinces instigated insurrection against the royal court. This must have resulted in the formation of what we have every right to call a feudal regime. Such formations have not been seen in China since pre-imperial antiquity, or perhaps to some extent under the Six Dynasties, or at the end of the Tang dynasty—periods in which we actually see Chinese Buddhists becoming agitated and taking up arms.[99]

In Japan, religion was feudalized at the same time society was. Armed conflicts between the sects and the imperial court, between the sects and the nobles, and then even among the sects themselves, are commonplace within feudalism. Occasionally the sects were in league with the provincial barons. Since they were established in the provinces of large communities, they were like pockets of decentralization. They escaped the control of imperial power with the help of local nobles who sometimes commended them to the court, all while appropriating tax revenue. Sometimes the local nobles protected them. Sometimes the local nobility was protected by the sects.[100] According to

General Renondeau, in the middle of the twelfth century the imperial domain had nearly all but disappeared, with no more than a hundredth of the land left among the provincial statesmen. The remaining land formed *shō*, private property. Accordingly, Buddhism became involved in the formation of medieval feudalism in Japan. As indicated by some authorities on the subject, feudalism might even have originated in Buddhist convents.[101]

Another point I found particularly fascinating in General Renondeau's work was the diverse composition of the personnel in the monasteries. We are beginning to distinguish the complex elements that compose what we call essentially Buddhist clergy.[102] Regular monks who were given support by the state had to be recorded on the state's register; others were supported by a good family, and even others by popular associations. In contrast, atypical monks were vagabonds, hermits, deserter soldiers, farmers cheating on their taxes, ecclesiastical employees, and the entire population of what's called "peasant monks." Peasant monks depended on the monasteries, but we cannot say too much about how they were actually connected to them or if they were, strictly speaking, truly monks or just laypersons. There was great diversity under the imprecise designation of the word *sangha*. In Japan, besides the monks who were there to devote themselves to their studies (*gakuryo, gakushō*) and who formed a purely elite group of ecclesiastics in the monasteries, there was a second tier of monastics (the *shuto*), from whom most of the monastic troops were recruited.[103] These troops, called *kokumin*, were composed of many pure laypeople employed on the grounds and trained with weaponry. They ultimately were combined with the *shuto*. After the fourteenth century, the *shuto* outflanked the *gakuryo*, only to then be outflanked in turn by the *kokumin*.[104] One wonders what proportion of actual monks in fact participated in warlike activity.

As General Renondeau indicates, there was an evolution in policy in Japan toward the valorization of all these social trends. This policy evolution was, of course, nothing more than a reflection of these social trends, as the Marxists assert. At this time, around 1200, the *sōhei* were booming; sects of the common people began to appear in reaction to the aristocratic Buddhists from the Heian monastery, where esoteric, extravagant ritualism (Shingon sect) was blended with verbose scholasticism (Tendai sect).

The first of these new sects was at Heian, and was of the Pure Land (*Jōdo*), founded by Hōnen (1133–1212). It claimed to follow the Chinese patriarchs (from the Tang dynasty, more than three or four centuries old). In essence, however, it was no less Japanese. None of its principal characters had ever been to China to seek out the sacred doctrine. It taught a very simple method for attaining salvation. "Easy" is what they even called it themselves, and accessible to everyone. It was a fideism that had faith only in the Buddha Amita, to the detriment of texts and practices. These were reduced to devotional orations, even to the simple oral invocation of the name Amita which, if done with the necessary faith entailed, was deemed sufficient to assure rebirth in his Pure Land, in his paradise in the west.

The second sect was the one founded by Nichiren (1228–1282) in the north during the thirteenth century. He was a fisherman's son whose name meant "Sun Lotus" or, with the intended double meaning "Lotus from Japan." This is the only Japanese sect that does not claim to follow any Chinese patriarchy. Its doctrine is an apocalyptic interpretation of the *Lotus of the True Law Sūtra* (*Saddharma-pundarīka Sūtra*) and is characterized by a virulent appeal to popular passions and to nationalism. War didn't take long to rage between the adepts of these two sects. One branch of the Jōdo sect was the so-called true branch (*Shin*)—all dissidents claim to be the only "true" one—[and] must have been particularly combative. Founded in the thirteenth century by Shinran (1173–1262), it soon became much more important than the Jōdo sect itself. The Shin branch had abolished the monastic rule, which it considered to be of no use since the texts themselves were useless. The only thing that counted was grace.

Marriage was allowed, as was the consumption of meat and alcohol. The renunciation of celibacy allowed the leaders of this school to be succeeded by their progeny, no longer by just their spiritual successors but by their own blood descendants, which likens them to hereditary feudal lords, but clothed in the prestige of religion.[105] As complete fanatics, the followers of the Shin sect went into combat. They were convinced that the faith they were defending was true and right and that the paradise of Amita was worth their death. The entire "Warring States period" (*Sengoku-jidai*), in the sixteenth century, was beset with eruptions of violence by "single-minded leagues," *ikko-ikki* as the Shin sect's warrior-monks were designated.[106] Many laypersons and rebel peasants integrated themselves with them as well, stresses General Renondeau.[107] This was also the case in China regarding most of the Buddhist uprisings.

Emerging at the same time as feudalism, the militarization of Buddhist clergy faded along with it. When the Tokugawa regency (the military dictators who were reestablishing unity in Japan) was preparing for war, it had no adversaries more tenacious than the monastic armies who took refuge in fortresses they turned into Buddhist convents. These fortresses bore witness to Oda Nobunaga's unforgettable siege, which lasted from 1570 to 1580. The siege of the Osaka castle was the siege of the Shin sect, the Hongan-ji or the temple of the original vow. These are the incidents upon which the city of Osaka, now the financial center of Japan and one of the largest emporia of the world, has been founded.

Its origins are from a fortified convent around which an urban agglomeration sprang into existence. After the destruction of this convent, Toyotomi Hideyoshi erected a new and formidable castle on the very same site, which he chose to be the seat of government. The center of the Shin sect, or more precisely of the Otani branch, was transferred to Kyoto into two new Hongan-ji, where it still exerts a powerful hold over the popular masses. The filial leaders of the sect, now related by marriage to the imperial family, were granted nobility in 1884. When I was in Japan thirty years ago, they were the "high-and-mighty" which brought to mind the prelates of the Italian Renaissance. In 1938 one of them was minister of foreign affairs. Another was a sergeant in the transportation services. This was not surprising because the clergy enjoyed no statutory privileges and the ecclesiastical personnel had been subject to the draft in Japan from the Meiji restoration. Throughout the Sino-Japanese conflict, Buddhist sects were under the control of the Office of Religious Affairs, which reported to the Ministry of the Interior. The Buddhist sects officially participated in the "spiritual mobilization" declared on September 9, 1937.[108]

Another sect played an important role in Japan's military history, but not as much in the actual fighting of wars (as they did in China). They were integral in the training of the warriors. This was the Dhyāna sect (Zen). Not long after being introduced in Japan from China at the end of the twelfth century, monks from the Zen sect would take arms in an attempted coup d'état of the Hojo government in 1303, and later the Ashikaga government in 1340.[109] In 1339, Soseki Musō encouraged his fellow Zen practitioners to not carry weaponry because, he noted with uncommon good sense, "If one truly observes Buddhist law, one does not amass worldly goods. Therefore, one has no need to defend them with arms in hand."[110] As a result, in 1345 and 1368, during the Tenryūji and Nanzenji sieges, the resident Zen monks did not defend these Zen monasteries against the Tendai monasteries' *sōhei*. It was the troops from the imperial court of Kyoto and from the Kamakura *bakufu* who mounted a defense.[111] During the Muromachi period, between the fourteenth and the sixteenth centuries, the Zen sect was an exceptionally cultured, literate, and artistic elite. In this they were similar to the Tchan masters from the Yuan and Ming dynasties, the recipients of Zen in China who in turn came to teach it in Japan. The Zen sect exerted its influence through diplomacy, commerce, and especially through education, in which it excelled.[112] Yet the Dhyāna school's method of training personnel by encouraging instinctive immediate responses, and by encouraging simple actions to come directly from the depths of the unconscious, lent itself well to military regulation. If *jūdō* or *jūjitsu* is fighting "fluidly" (and take [their] name[s] from Taoism to which Dhyāna is much indebted), in Japan Dhyāna is usually associated with its particular tactical methods of combat in areas such as archery and fencing.[113] Fencing manuals were written by Zen masters and conceived completely in Buddhist terms.[114] During the last world war, when Paris was under the German occupation, a Japanese film was showing in the theaters. It told the story of the formation of a soldier, from the moment he enlisted until the bombing of Pearl Harbor. The methods that were used were glaringly from Zen.

Men are made in such a way that they need reasons to justify bending their principles. Consequently, when they eschew a bad habit, it too often comes back, masked as a virtue. Buddhists have taken many alternative routes trying their utmost to legitimize many habits that run completely counter to the Buddhist precept of no-killing. This precept is the basis of their entire code of ethics. Along these lines, we might add an interesting paragraph to the chapter on "logical derivations." It is interesting to note that Vilfredo Pareto took a perverse pleasure in collecting examples consistent with the Machiavellian or Voltairean traditions.[115] I will only indicate a few of these supporting arguments. Most of them date back all the way to India; however, they have not lost their relevance. Furthermore, at the time of the recent Sino-Japanese conflict I only had to leaf through the news publications of the day from the Far East to find nearly all of these arguments still being used for external and internal propaganda. I also found that journalists lacked anything new to add.[116]

The main, peremptory argument that we extract from the former Buddhist apologists is that the Real Law must be protected from its enemies. This idea is dramatically manifested in its folklore and in its iconography, wherein we find all sorts of divinities taken from the pantheon in India outside Buddhism. These were integrated into Buddhism as protectors of the Buddha, his law, and his community. Indra (Śakra Devendra) for example, the lord of the celestial gods, was one such co-opted lord. Among the celestial gods, the Buddhists are the sworn enemy of Malin. The four god-kings (*devarāja*) who were specifically assigned to guard the four regions of space, were even included along with many others in imagery decorating armor, weaponry, and all the trappings of warriors. In conjunction with this imagery we see such military epithets as "victorious, divine generals," etc. In fact, a mere visit to a Buddhist sanctuary in the Far East, especially if it is affiliated with the Tantric school of Buddhism, belies a religion that is more harsh than sweet in nature. Vaiśravaṇa is one of the four god-kings; he presides over the north. Vaiśravaṇa is shown as the armored warrior holding an umbrella or parasol in one hand and a *stūpa* in the other. For the Buddhists in the north, notably in Serindia, [he] had become a veritable god of war.

Even in China, at the time of the Tang dynasty there were Vaiśravana rituals and Tantric practices to assure victory on the battlefield. It was believed that he "followed the armies to protect the Real Law," like a Homeric god.[117] In Japan, Vaiśravana has become the appointed patron of warriors, who like carrying his image as their amulet. It was reported that, in 587, when Shōtoku Taishi went off to war to establish Buddhism in Japan, he carried a little wooden figurine of Vaiśravana he made with his own hands, stuck in his bun.[118] After returning victorious, he dedicated his first Buddhist establishment in Japan, the Shitennō-ji Temple in Naniwa (Osaka), to the four god-kings, Vaiśravana and the others. Even more recently, while in China the Japanese troops preparing for combat would bow before the icons of the four god-kings in the Chinese temples.[119] Furthermore, Chinese and Japanese Buddhists have no qualms about annexing their native war gods into their pantheon. Also, Kouan-ti, of whom there is often a statue in the Buddhist temples in China and Japan, was bestowed the title of "Buddha Protector of the State" by imperial decree.[120] Finally, in Japan, Hachiman—the Shinto god of war—became a bodhisattva, an avatar of the Buddha Amita.[121]

These warrior figures protect the Real Law. They are usually defending deities. War is justified if it is in defense, is it not? This is a widely held belief in the Far East, where war is generally presented as a form of repression used to reestablish peace. The enemy is perceived as nothing but a troublemaker, and is given labels that mean bandit, rebel, etc. Everyone knows that, according to the etymological play of words of *Tso-tchouan*, war is engaged in order to stop war, to "stop the halberds." Moving from defensive to offensive combat is an easy shift to make when engaging in a preventive war. Heresy must be prevented and evil crushed in utero. General Renondeau cites a speech attributed to Ryōgen more than four centuries before his death.[122] In it, this illustrious superior of the temples on Mount Hiei, near Kyoto, tolerated and even encouraged the arming of his subordinates. Everyone agrees that the arguments, which a writer from the Ashikaga period in 1409 claimed came from Ryōgen's lips, were fabricated. However, at that time, the *sōhei* were in complete full force. It is interesting to see how a contemporary sought to justify these arguments. Here is the author's essential argument.

General Renondeau quotes only one of the two sentences:

> While the great master Jie [Ryōgen's posthumous name] was governing the mountain [Hiei, from 966], he explained things in this way. Without letters, there aren't any rites to make one worship one's superiors. Without weapons, the superiors have no *virtù* to impose on their inferiors. Thus, the world is only well ordered if letters and weapons equally supplement each other. With that accepted, why do we turn to monks [today] who lack intelligence and talent as ranking

> warriors to make up the *shuto* troops?[123] It is because the Real Law is deficient and is no longer the essential Real Law. In high antiquity, in the time of the Counterfeit Law, everyone still respected the Real Law. But, in our time of degeneration [in other words, in our time, the time of the decline of the Law],[124] it is rare for people to have faith. And yet, if, on this high mountain, one lacks oil for the lamp of the Real Law, how could it last very long? Similarly, the troops of the four god-kings protect śakra Devendra, just as our warring troops use force to prevent all sorts of disorder in the land we were given. Through their bravery, they protect us from heretic and depraved sects, thus assuring the preservation of the Real Law and the subsistence of the practitioners of the Dhyāna who safeguard the method.[125]

Moreover, in another of Ryōgen's biographies, also dated in the fifteenth century, we see the following line of thought:

> In 975 . . . , the master [Ryōgen] said: "The time of the Counterfeit Law has come. These reeds who are the listeners [*śrāvaka*, the followers of the Lesser Vehicle], these bamboos who are the lone Buddhas [*pratyeka-buddha*, second of the vehicles and different from the Great Vehicle, which is the one of the *bodhisattvas*], abound like a forest. It is hard to know where to stop this proliferation of undergrowth. Brush does not let itself be eliminated: and still further, the two Vehicles [the lesser ones, the vehicle of *śrāvaka* and the vehicle of the *pratyeka-buddha*, in other words, all the heresies, the adversarial sects, the doctrines, and the practices running counter to those of the Great Vehicle as the Tendai sect on Hieizan understood it]. If we left the bows in their sheaths and neglected the arrows, we would not be ensuring the duration of the Real Law. Didn't the *śāstra* say this? Mañjuśrī has two symbolic attributes (*samaya*): the pointed sword and the Brahmic *pothī* [a Sanskrit book]. . . . This is what our monks study; they are the only Sanskrit books. . . . If we add to this the pointed sword, will we not have hundreds of thousands of living Mañjuśrīs? And henceforth the monks [on Hieisan] began to carry a bow and an arrow.[126]

In the thirteenth century, in his *Treatise on Securing the Peace of the Land through the Establishment of the Correct Buddhist Law* and other writings, Nichiren strongly advocates against adversarial sects.[127] He references numerous passages from the *Mahāparinivāṇa Sūtra*. Interestingly, neither the passages in the aforementioned work on the death of śākyamuni, nor his last teachings (which were in accordance with the tradition of the Lesser Vehicle) interested Nichiren. His interest concerned the treatise on the Great Vehicle, which had to have been composed in India (or in Serindia) at or near the end of the fourth century. It is worth noting that this rather racy doctrine borders on heresy. In it we read in particular what happened to the Buddha in one of his previous existences. It says that he had heretic Brahmans put to death, and then gives two reasons for doing so.

We are told that the first reason was out of pity, to help the Brahmans avoid the punishment they had accrued by committing evil deeds while continuously slandering Buddhism. The Buddha's second reason for putting them to death was to defend Buddhism itself. Regardless, these Brahmans were predestined to infernal damnation (*icchantika*); it was not a sin to put them to death in order to preserve the Real Law, even if it was for their own good [*compelle intrare*].[128] In another passage, this same *sūtra* (scripture) declares that there is no reason to observe the five precepts, or even to practice good behavior, if protecting the Real Law is in question. In other words, one needed to take up the knife and the sword, the bow and the arrow, the spear and the lance. "The one that observes the five precepts is not a follower of the Great Vehicle! Do not observe the five precepts—if it concerns protecting the Real Law, it concerns the Great Vehicle!"[129] Along these lines, the Buddha sings the praises of a king named Yeou-tö, who went to war to defend the *bhikṣu* (monks).[130]

We also find more subtle justifications for killing in Buddhist literature. First, we find statistical justification; killing is permitted if, in killing one man alone, one saves many. For example, this was the case with a particular Brahman who had converted to Buddhism. While he was traveling with a caravan, he approached a canyon where five hundred outlaws were ready to ambush. The one outlaw who seemed to have had some previous relations with the Brahman was sent by his companions on reconnaissance. Taking advantage of this opportunity, the outlaw warned the Brahman of the impending danger to the caravan. The Brahman made the following argument: if I warn my five hundred traveling companions, they will not miss the opportunity to kill the "snitch" outlaw. They would incur considerably painful karmic retributions from this act. If I say nothing, it will be the five hundred outlaws who kill the caravan and reap the terrible fruits of this crime. Consequently, the Brahman decides to kill the outlaw who had warned him. Not seeing him return, the other outlaws decide not to attack the travelers. Thus the Brahman takes upon himself the karmic consequences of the killing, while saving both the outlaws and the travelers. Apprised of the situation after the killing, the outlaws and the travelers convert. It is therefore for the good of nine hundred and ninety-nine people that he killed one. Therefore, his killing was an act of charity.[131]

The following is an even better story. The *Yogācārabhūmi* by Asaṅga, the masterpiece of Buddhist epistemology and psychology, makes it the bodhisattva's duty to commit the sin of killing so as to prevent another from doing so. In other words, it is better to sin than to let the other sin.[132] If a bodhisattva sees an outlaw preparing to kill many men or to commit some other sin, that would be cause for immediate retribution (*ānantarya*). He would say to himself, "If, in killing this man, I go to hell, so be it. This being must not be doomed to hell." And after waiting for the moment when the outlaw has one good thought or at least a neutral thought from a moral point of view, the bodhisattva would kill him. This is both horrific with regard to sin, and yet merciful with regard to the sinner. Once done, not only has the bodhisattva not committed any wrongdoing, instead he has earned a lot of merit.[133]

The same doctrine is found in another treatise by Asaṅga, the *Mahāyāna-saṃgraha*. The commentary relates once again this story of the bodhisattva and the outlaw, using it as an example of "deep-rooted" morality (*gāmbhīriya-śīla*).[134] In 841, while in Tibet, the king Lang Darma, who had been hostile toward Buddhism, was assassinated by a zealot of the Real Law. The historian Bu-ston reports that the assassin set out "with thoughts of commiseration" toward the king.[135] In a note on his translation of Bu-ston, Obermiller refers to Tantra and cites the Tantric text of the *Tanjur*, which reiterates Asaṅga's argument without naming him. It is true that Tantra went far in the "overthrowing of the established values" that characterize late Buddhism.[136] Yet the moral justification of killing precedes the invasion of Buddhism by Tantra. We see this justification as early as the fourth century, in the works of one of the most classic and rational philosophers to which India has ever given birth, Asaṅga, founder of the school of Buddhist philosophy known as the Knowledge Way (*vijñānavāda*).

The School of Emptiness (*śūnyavāda*) raised still other arguments to legitimize killing.[137] In a *sūtra* translated into Chinese as early as the third century, Mañjuśrī attempts to exonerate a repented matricide, claiming that the vacuity of the thoughts that drove the criminal to his crime did not undermine the essential purity of his mind (*citta-mūla-viśuddhi*). His sin did not prevent him from being accepted into the community.[138] In the *Ratnakūta Sūtra*, while five hundred bodhisattvas are repenting their past sins, which prevented them from attaining "profound patience," Mañjuśrī approaches and takes a sword and acts as if he wants to kill the Buddha. The Buddha then praises him for this, saying because everything is an illusion, even emptiness, there isn't any more of me than there is of anyone else. There exists neither human person (*pudgala*), nor living being (*sattva*), nor father or mother, nor saint (*arhat*) or Buddha, nor the Real Law or the Community.... There is therefore no more a crime than there is a criminal, and if Mañjuśrī had killed the Buddha, it would have been a right killing. In fact, what is the Buddha if nothing other than a name, without substance, without reality, misleading and empty like a phantasmagoria [*māya*]? There is no more a sinner than there is a sin. Who could be punished for killing? Between the sword and the Buddha there is no duality.[139]

This line of thought had long been rooted in India.[140] Yet it corresponds to China's long-standing Taoist code of ethics, which was built on the dialectic of opposites. This line of thought is often found in Chinese (and Japanese) texts from the Dhyāna school, and even in such precursors of this school as the great Houei-yuan (334–416). Fortunately, a dialogue that Houei-yuan had with a Chinese layperson, on the question of retribution for one's actions, has been preserved. In it, this layperson asks him the following aporia:

> The Buddhist canonical texts make killing other living beings a sin which has hell as punishment. The infernal judgment responds to it like a shadow or an echo. I have some reservations about this. The body is only made of four elements: solid (the earth), liquid (water), gas (fire), and plasma (wind). They coagulate to form the body which serves as the resting place for the soul. . . . And yet, although the soul depends on the body to exist, in theory it is no less a celestial absolute without it[?]. Between the soul and the body, there is but the difference of subtlety and rudeness. Certainly the soul presents no place wherein it can be wounded. If we destroy the body, this does not annihilate the soul. It is as if we destroyed just the water or the fire elements existing in their natural state in the cosmos.[141]

Here is a fragment of Houei-yuan's response:

> If we admit that the Other and I are identical, and that there is no opposition between our two minds. Then, from the point of view of the transcendent absolute which is one, swords that crisscross are neutralized and there is no conflict between weapons that bang together. Not only does someone who injures others do no harm to the soul, but there is certainly no living being that is killable. It is in this sense that, when Mañjuśrī took up his sword, he was able to have the appearance of going against Buddhist morality, but in reality, he was abiding by it. Although we will have brandished the halberd all day long, there is no place the blade can land.[142]

Above, we saw frantic appeals for (spiritual) killing uttered in the ninth century by the Dhyāna master Yi-hiuan, the founder of the Lin-tsi sect, in the name of freedom.[143] Also, we are familiar with cases concerning the contemporaries Nan-ts'iuan and Kouei-tsong, who did indeed put to death living beings—by cutting them in two, the first a cat, the second a snake—in order to demonstrate *before the very eyes* of their disciples the mortal danger of all duality.[144] In the Zen sect in Japan, they interpreted the argument for taking another's life as "attempting to bring the other's Buddha nature to life" (Buddha nature exists in virtually every living being), "by putting an end to the passions that lead astray and keeping the vision of this nature in mind."[145] Yet once we have "seen," once we have become aware of the essential purity that is the foundation of our being, then what do these precepts matter, and what are moral codes good for? At the point when "every precept is swiftly and completely observed," then the question of killing and not-killing would become inconsequential. There is no more existence than non-existence, no more life than death. No one kills, no one is killed. As the Japanese treatise on morality states, in accordance with Zen:

> [K]eeping track of a difference between killing and not killing violates the arguments. In this sense, what is for the auditors [in other words, for the Lesser Vehicle] the observance of the arguments, is for the bodhisattva a violation of the arguments. This is a complete reversal of values.[146]

Asaṅga classifies the ethics of the Great Vehicle as "deep." They make killing an act of charity. This "deep" quality sometimes leans toward the fantastic. The *Cloud of Jewels Sūtra* (*Ratnamegha Sūtra*) is a dialogue discussing the bodhisattva, in other words, the saint of the Great Vehicle. It was translated into Chinese on four occasions, twice by monks from Bnaṃ (Funan, Cambodia), in the sixth century, a third time in the era of the Empress Wou from the Tang dynasty, at the end of the seventh century, and last, in the time of the Song dynasty, at the beginning of the eleventh century.[147] The original Sanskrit is lost, but some fragments of it have been conserved in an anthology from the seventh century.[148] In it we see exposed most notably different uses of "skillful means" (*upāya-kauśalya*), one of the attributes of a bodhisattva. This is roughly its principle: the ends justify the means.

The fourth kind of skillful means consists in "the removal of remorse" (*kaukṛtya-vinodana*). Herein lies the definition that we read in all the Chinese versions of the *sūtra*. When a saint, a bodhisattva, meets a criminal guilty of the five sins worthy of immediate damnation (patricide, matricide, killing a saint, etc.) or of other serious sins, and finds him so racked with remorse that despair has taken possession of him and any rehabilitation seems impossible for him, the saint, using his miraculous powers (*abhij ā*), will transform himself (before the very eyes of the dejected criminal) into a son, and proceed to commit patricide and matricide. After this, he will resume his previous form. Thus the bodhisattva demonstrates that, after committing two of the sins worthy of immediate damnation, he has lost none of his privileges of sainthood.

Consequently, the dejected criminal concludes that perhaps his crimes were not as unforgivable as he had previously thought. He will begin again to hope, and the saint, taking advantage of this, teaches him how (thanks to Buddhism) he can redeem himself from his most ominous sins. This is what the work of conversion and edification entails, which ultimately will lead the guilty party to salvation.[149]

This dramatic text is famous in China because of the Empress Wou, one of the most spectacular figures in China's national history, who reigned from 690 to 705. She is suspected of citing this text to justify a multitude of assassinations she had perpetrated in order to ensure her continued power.[150] Also famous for her devotion, her Buddhist bigotry is manifest in the various excesses in which she indulged throughout the course of her extraordinarily colorful career. The Empress Wou chose a Herculean ironmonger as her favorite person, a kind of Rasputin who caught her eye in the Lo-yang market. She made him a Buddhist monk to ensure his entrance into the imperial palace, and then bestowed upon him thereafter all kinds of other redundant responsibilities, most notably that of generalissimo of her armies against the Turks. Nonetheless, it was under the command of this strange monk that a committee of translators drafted the Chinese version of the *Cloud of Jewels*. Earlier, I summarized the passage about the magical killings from it.[151]

The Empress Wou did not kill her father or her mother. Still, according to her contemporaries, she had the deaths of two of her sons and numerous relatives of her husband (the Emperor Kao-tsong of the Tang dynasty) on her conscience. We have no positive proof that she made good use of the erroneous Mahāyānist morals of *Cloud of Jewels* to alleviate her conscience. But since she passed herself off as a bodhisattva, and even as an incarnation of Maitreya, some passages (like the one on the magical killings) might have been perfectly applicable. This is how Buddhists from the Ming dynasty understood this matter. A long note inserted into the version from the Buddhist canon, printed during the Ming dynasty, refutes with indignation the authenticity of this passage and denounces it as horrid blasphemy against filial piety, interpolated for the Empress Wou's own use.[152] What else could the prudent editors from the Ming dynasty have gotten wrong? This passage is certainly not apocryphal and indeed must have figured in the original Sanskrit of the *sūtra*.[153] It simply attests to one of these deviations in which all reasoning may get lost from time to time. In the West, we have done much better in this regard.

NOTES

1. Paul Demiéville's article was initially published as "Le bouddhisme et la guerre: Post-scriptum à *l'Histoire des moines guerriers du Japon* de Gaston Renondeau," in *Mélanges publiés par l'Institut des Hautes Etudes chinoises* (Paris: Presses Universitaires de France, 1957), 1:347–385.

2. They are nearly the same as the five *yamas*, or "abstentions," of the *Yoga sūtras* (II, 30–32), the five vows (*vrata*) of the Jain layperson (H. von Glasenapp, *Der Jainismus* [Berlin, 1025], 202), and the Brahmic *dharmaśāstras* (Baudhayana, II, x, 18; Manu, VI, 92)—but not the Hebraic Decalogue.

3. *Mahāprajāpārmitopadeśa: Treatise on the Great Perfection of Wisdom* (Louvain, 1949), 790.

4. How else should one explain the case of a Sui Buddhist colonel who, before becoming a monk, was known as Tche-yen? In 621, he carried suspended from the end of his bow a bag with which to filter water, so as to not kill any insects (*Siu Kao-seng tchouan*, T. 2060, xx, 602b).

5. Mochizuki, *Bukkyo daijiten*, 2931 and what follows; see below, n. 31.

6. *Abhidharmakosa-sostra*, trans. La Vallée Poussin, ch. IV, 152; cf. my *Concile de Lhasa*,I, 224n2. Not everyone shares this opinion; cf. *Abhidharma-mahavibhasa*, T. 1545, CXVIII, 617c:

> If this is required by the king, that we commit murder, is murder then a sin? Some say no, for, they say, we are constrained to do it by the other's strength, not by our own intention. And yet, even in this case, there is the sin of murder; at least we resolve to forgo our own life rather than ever harming that of another: this is the only instance wherein sin is not involved.

7. Mö-tseu, "Against Aggression"; *Tchouang-tseu*, ch. X; Pascal, ed. Brunschvicg, v, 293; La Bruyère, ed. Cayrou, XII, 119.

8. *Tchouang-tseu*, ch. X, ed. Wieger, 278.

9. *Abhidharmakosa*; Mahāprajāpārmitopadeśa, trans. Lamotte, 794.

10. We find interesting remarks on prehistory and the universality of the interdiction of killing in the article by G. Bataille, "What Is Universal History?" *Critique* 111–112 (Aug.–Sept. 1956): 759–761.

11. V. Y. C. Shih, "Some Chinese Rebel Ideologies," *T'oung Pao* 54 (1956), 175. The author makes a huge mistake when he supposes that the explanation of such a doctrine must be sought in Mazdaism or in Manichaeanism and when he adds that "the conception of killing as a way to give another salvation is foreign to every system of thought, and not just to the one of Buddhism."

12. In the *Vinaya*, we see a malevolent divinity (*Marakayika devata*) breathe to Mrgalan dika the idea that killing those who attempt suicide saves them: "You save those who are not saved" (*atinne taresi*). This idea is particularly characterized as heretical (*mithya-dṛṣṭi*). Cf. *Vinaya Pāli*, vol. III, 69, trans. I. B. Horner, 118; T. 1421, II, 7c; T. 1462, x, 744c.

13. The suicide epidemic served as an occasion (*nidana*) to forbid murder by the Buddha. It had also been caused by an excess of meditation on impurity

(*asubha-bhavana*), followed by an excessive disgust with existence for the *bhikṣus*. In most of the *Vinaya* texts, it is not suicide alone that is condemned. It is murder, be it killing with one's own hands those who attempt suicide or having them killed by a third party, or even yet counseling them to kill themselves, encouraging them to do it, and giving them the means to do it, etc. (*Vinaya Pāli*, vol. III, 68, trans. I. B. Horner, 123; Dharmaguptaka, T. 1428, ii, 57b–c; etc.). Moreover, the *Vinaya* of the Mahisasaka (T. 1421, ii, 7b–c) put in the Buddha's mouth, before forbidding murder, defined as *pārājika*, the interdiction of suicide, defined as *sthūlātyaya*. Additionally, in this *Vinaya* text, monks are not only made to kill by their compatriot Mrgalandika (Migalandika), they kill themselves also. This is seen also in other *Vinaya* texts.

14. "In the Vinaya it is said that suicide is not a sin of murder," declares the *Mahāprajñāpārmitopadeśa*, trans. Lamotte, 740–742. I think we need to understand here: "Suicide is not a sin [as serious as the sin] of murder." Mr. Lamotte thinks that "Buddhism never condemned suicide per se." In an essay on suicide in his *Recherches sur l'histoire du boudisme* (Kyoto, 1927), 363, Matsumoto Bunzaburo recalls that upon their arrival in Japan Christian missionaries had caused a sensation by banning suicide. But, suicide was a great honor for the Buddhist *samurais*. Nevertheless, the missionaries sought to convert them (suicide is still seen in Japan, even nowadays, as an expression of either honor, patriotism, or love). This Japanese professor thinks that it is a question of late departure, contrary to the original spirit of Buddhism. This would be to a certain extent my feeling also. However, a deeper examination of the texts would be necessary—particularly the *Vinaya* texts—which is a project I have not undertaken here. In Thailand, suicide is explicitly forbidden to Buddhists in a booklet drawn up by the church's supreme patriarch and published in 1928 with a preface by the king. K. E. Wells, *Thai Buddhism* (Bangkok, 1939), 210.

15. On suicide as *sthūlātyaya*, see n. 12 above. Cf. *Samantapāsādikā*, T. 1462, x, 752c (I do not have the Pāli review in front of me): suicide is a *duskrta*, except in the case of a deathly ill monk who, in order to spare those caring for him unnecessary pain, starves himself and stops taking his medication. He must however be certain that he has reached the end of his long life and that he is in possession of the fruit of the Path, "as if in the palm of his hand."

16. The *Vinaya* of the Mahīśāsakas, T. 1421, n, 8a: A sick monk who has been counseled by his brothers to let himself die in order to avoid further suffering is told that his perfect possession of the *śīla* will not result in a lesser rebirth. He retorts that committing suicide which is anyway condemned by the Buddha as a *sthūlātyaya*, would prevent him from continuing to cultivate *brahmacaryā*; and perhaps he may have a chance to get better, which would allow him to expand his *brahmacaryā*. A bit further on in the same text, some laypeople who had been tortured by outlaws and were suffering terribly are counseled by some *bhikṣu*. They too refuse to commit suicide, for, they say, the suffering one endures in this world teaches how to cultivate the karma of the Buddhist Path.

17. A large number of these have been documented by Lamotte in his *Treatise*, 740n1.

18. *Le dogme et la philosophie du boudisme* (Paris, 1930), 48.

19. *Saṃyutta Nikāya*, vol. III, 119–124; *Samyuktāgama*, T. 99, XLII, 346b–347b; a slightly different version is in *Ekottarāgama*, T. 125, XIX, 642c–643a. Moreover, the *Vinayas* specify that, in the case of an urging toward suicide, or of the murder of a person desiring suicide, there is *pārājika* even if the "suicide" is released from all desire (*vītarāga*; T. 1428, I, 576c), even if he is *śīla-sampanna* or has obtained the fruit of the Path (T. 1421, II, 7c–8a). The only rightful urging that one might make to a person desiring suicide is to think of the Three Jewels without ever stopping until one reaches the natural end of one's life (T. 1462, x, 752b).

20. *Mahāprajñāramitopadeśa*, trans. Lamotte, 741.

21. *Bodhicaryāvatāra*, III, 21 (*bhaveyam upajīvyo 'ham*), VIII, 120, trans. Finot; *La marche à la lumière* (Paris, 1920), 40, 117.

22. Ibid., VIII, 103, trans. Finot, 115. Cf. my article "L'esprit de bienfaisance impartiale dans les civilizations de l'Extrême-Orient," *Revue internationale de la Croix-Rouge* 455 (Aug. 1952): 5.

23. *Abhidharmakośa*, trans. La Vallée Poussin, ch. IV, 153.

24. Ibid., 8.

25. Ibid., 154.

26. Definition by Jiun (Shingon sect, 1718–1804) cited by Sato Kenichi in the journal *Recherches sur le Zen* 10 (June 28, 1929): 76. Cf. *Abhi-dharma-mahāvibhāsā*, T. 1545, CXVIII, 617a[12]–617b:

> How can there be a sin of murder when only things exist [*dharma*: that is to say, the *skandha*, the *dhātu*, and the *āyatana*] and when living beings [*sattva*] do not exist?—There is the sin of murder insofar as we have the notion [*samjñā*] of a living being, although such a being does not exist. In fact, according to the *bhadanta* Vasumitra, the *skandha-dhātv-āyatana* can give rise to the notion of the self [*ātman*], to the notion of a living being [*sattva*], to some notions of life [jīva], of a person who was born [*jantu*], of a person who is fed [*posa*], of the individual [*pudjala*], and it can even give rise to the notion of a permanent person, who is happy and pure [along the lines of a Brahmic *ātman*]; and in this sense, there is the sin of murder in destroying them. According to the *bhadanta* [*dharmatrāta*], the [so-called] living being only exists in a conventional manner [*samvṛti*], but the sin of murder exists in an absolute manner [*paramārtha*]....—What do we call then "killing a living being"? Is it a question of past, future, or present *skandha*? Past *skandha* have already been destroyed [*niruddha*]; future [*skandha*] have not yet come [*anāgata*]; the present *skandha* are limitless [*sthiti*]. We do not see in all this the possibility of murder. Of what, therefore, does murder consist?—It consists of killing future *skandha*, not the past or even the present ones.—But how does one kill future *skandhas*, which have not yet come to be?—Murder consists in preventing, while we are in the present, the gathering of future *skandha*, to obstruct the conditions for the creation of another group of *skandha*....—But present *skandha* are without duration; they self-destruct, without needing to be murdered. In these conditions, what is murder?—Murder consists in cutting short the effectiveness of the *skandhas*, the

effectiveness on the strength of which the present or past *skandhas*, even though they are limitless and self-destruct, have no less the power to be continued one after another in future *skandhas*. And, in this sense, there is the sin of murder even regarding present *skandhas*, insofar as murder prevents them from continuing one after another in future *skandhas*.

27. *Mahāprajñāpāramitopadeśa*, trans. Lamotte, 864.

28. *Fan-wang king*, number ten of forty-eight light precepts, T. 1484, II, 1005c. We might here refer back to J. J. M. de Groot's translation, *Le code du Mahayana en Chine* (Amsterdam, 1893), 46 and passim.

29. Eleventh light precept, ibid., 1005c.

30. Thirty-third light precept, ibid., 1007b. The *Vinaya Pāli*, vol. IV, 103 (trans. Horner, 374), also forbids monks from watching battles.

31. This is a variant on the list of the "ways" to kill (*prayoga*) which we find in the *Vinaya* of the Small Vehicle.

32. The first of ten serious precepts, defined as *pārājika* X, ibid., 1004b. Ranked third of the four *pārājikas* in the *Vinaya* of the Small Vehicle; murder is ranked here number one.

33. Above, 20 and passim.

34. Bibliography in M. Eliade, *Yoga* (Paris, 1936), 304 = *Le Yoga* (Paris, 1954), 405.

35. J. Bloch, trans., *Les inscriptions d'Asoka*, 13th ed. (Paris, 1950), 125.

36. *Lhasa Council*, 1:223.

37. See Paul Demiéville, "La situation religieuse en Chine au temps de Marco Polo," in *Oriente Poliano* (Rome: Instituto Italiano per il Medio ed Estremo Oriente).

38. See, for example, *La guerre et les chrétiens*, 39th book of *La Pierre-qui-Vire*, Yonne (1953).

39. On the organization of military service during the Tang dynasty, see the treatment of E. G. Pulleyblank in his *The Background of the Rebellion of An Lu-shan* (Oxford: Oxford University Press, 1955), ch. 5.

40. T. 245–246. Cf. H. W. de Visser, *Ancient Buddhism in Japan* (Leiden, 1928), 1:116 and passim.

41. Cf. A. F. Wright, "Fo-t'u-têng," *H.J.A.S.* 11 (1948): 325, 339–340.

42. The date of Fou Yi's memorial is not clear; there is contradiction among the sources.

43. *Kouang hong-ming tsi*, T. 2103, VII, 134a–c; Fa-lin, *P'o-sie louen*, T. 2109, I, 482a; *Kieou T'ang chou*, LXXIX, 4b–5a. Cf. Ogasawara Senshū, "Fu I, an Anti-Buddhist in the Tang Dynasty," *Journal of History of Chinese Buddhism* 1.3 (Oct. 1937): 84–93; *Lhasa Council*, 1:223; A. F. Wright, "Fu I and the Rejection of Buddhism," *Journal of the History of Ideas* 12.1 (Jan. 1951): 41; J. Gernet, *Les aspects économiques du boudhisme dans la societé chinoise du Vème au Xème siècle* (Saigon, 1956), 28–29.

44. Biography by Li Kiao, *Sin T'ang chou*, CXXIII, 2b (ed. Po-na).

45. This is only to cajole and weaken the Tibetan "occupants," while we see the Chinese Buddhists maintaining a pacifist discourse (*Lhasa Council*, 1:237 and passim). When it concerns the expulsion of these detested barbarians, the monks are quite

naturally on the side of the supported Chinese military and support them in every way they can (ibid., 249 and passim).

46. *Yuan-che Tch'ang-k'ing tsi*, xxviii, 3b–4a (ed. Sseu-pou ts'ong-k'an).

47. A reference is in *Lhasa Council*, 1:223n2.

48. On the eunuchs as "merit-based stewards," cf. Tsukamoto Zenryū, "The 'Merit-Based Stewards' from the Middle of the Tang Dynasty," *Tōhō gakuhō* 4 (1933): 368–406; E. O. Reischauer, *Ennin's Diary* (New York, 1955), 235–237.

49. *Siu kao-seng tchouan*, T. 2060, vii, 477b, biography by Fa-lang (507–581).

50. *Kouang hong-ming tsi*, T. 2103, vii, 134c.

51. We might find some details if we gathered together a corpus of Fou Yi quotes. Cf. the uprisings mentioned in the Fou Yi quotes to the k. xi of the *Kouang hong-ming tsi*, 160b, 163b.

52. *Wei chou*, CXIV, 12b–13a (*Che-Lao tche*), trans. Ware in *T'oung Pao* (1933): 138–139; O. Franke, *Geschichte des chineischen Reiches*, II, 203; Gernet, *Aspects économiques*, 279.

53. It is explained that the *Net of Brahma* prescribes for the "children of the Buddha" to not possess arms (353).

54. *Shina bukkyōshi kenkyū, Hogu-Gi hen* (Tokyo, 1942), 247–285. See also W. Eberhard, *Das Toba-Reich Nordchinas* (Leiden, 1949), ch. 19, "Die Volkserhebungen," 240–269.

55. In his "Essai d'interprétation du 'Fils du Ciel vêtu de blanc,'" *Yenching Journal* 5 (1948): 234, T'ang Tch'ang-jou points out the analogous practices recommended in the Taoist texts cited in 570 by Tchen Louen in his *Siao-tao louen* (*Kouang hong-ming tsi*, T. 2103, ix, 149c–150a).

56. In the Maitreyan *sūtra* he is called King Thondaman (Śankha-rāja).

57. Tsukamoto, "Merit-Based Stewards," 269–280. Cf. also Eberhard, *Das Toba-Reich Nordchinas*, 252; T'ang, *Siao-tao louen*, 233–234.

58. On the Maitreyan insurgencies in China throughout the centuries, see T'ang, *Siao-tao louen* and also V. Y. C. Shih in *T'oung Pao* 54 (1956). In apocryphal texts noted in the Buddhist bibliographies by the Suis, we find a *sūtra* entitled *The Bodhi of Maitreya and the Submission of Māra*; I'm not sure that the manuscripts were found together in Touen-houang.

59. J. J. M. de Groot, in the anticlerical time of his youth, collected together a certain number of them in an article in the *T'oung Pao*, 1st ser., 2 (1891): 127–139, entitled "Militant Spirit of the Buddhist Clergy in China," an article reprinted two years later in his *Le code du Mahayana en Chine*, 103 and passim. He gathered nearly exclusively his material in the amassed notes entitled "Les moines guerriers du Chao-lin" by Kou Yen-wou and his comments to the k. xxix of the *Je-tche lou* (7a–b of the 1888 lithographic edition). But the Dutch Sinologist neglected to refer back to the original sources, which led him to have many inaccuracies, and the interpretation he gives of this material is just a summary, so that his work does not maintain much interest.

60. *Kouang hong-ming tsi*, T. 2103, vii, 134c, xi, 165b. Cf. Ogasawara, "Fu I, an Anti-Buddhist," 91–93. According to the very low numbers indicated by Fou Yi of the ––– of the various barbarian peoples which he enumerates, it seems that he had

mercenaries serving the nobles. In their response to Fou Yi, as *Kouang hong-ming tsi* notes (vii, 134c), Buddhists recognized that certain monks were guilty of subversive activity, but only on an individual basis.

61. *Tseu-tche t'ong-kien*, CLII, 57a (ed. 1900; Ta-ye IX, 12th moon, day *kia-chen*); see also *Souei chou*, xxiii, 18a–b (*Wou-hing tche*).

62. *Tseu-tche t'ong-kien*, ibid. (days *kia-chen* and *ting-hai*); see also *Souei chou*, iv, 7b (*Penki*), and xxiii, 18b (*Wou-hing tche*).

63. *Wou-to* I, 12th moon, day *keng-tseu*: January 19, 619.

64. *Tse-tche t'ong-kien*, CLI, 36a–b (end of the year *Wou-to* I); also indicated in A. F. Wright and E. Fagan, "Era Names and Zeiteist," *Etudes Asiatiques* 3–4 (1951): 119 (where in note 2, for *Tzu-chih t'ung-chien* 186, 1792, one must read "18b–19a," pagination from the Sseu-pou ts'ong-k'an edition).

65. *Tseu-tche t'ong kien*, CLIX, 58a (*Wou-to* IV, 5th moon, day *ting-mao*).

66. *Tseu-tche t'ong-kien*, ibid. This "expurgation" of the Lo-yang clergy—much lesser known than the one that was ordered by Kao-tsou on March 25, 626 (for all of China), but which scarcely seems to have been followed by any consequences since the abdication of Kao-tsou during this very same year—is confirmed by an inscription by Chao-lin sseu (*infra*, 363n1), and also by a passage from the *Siu kao-seng tchouan* (T. 2060, xxiv, 633c, biography by Houei-tch'eng), wherein we see a monk who compromised himself by siding with the rebel Wou Che-tch'ong against the rebel Li Che-min, receiving from the latter the authorization to preserve his religious status, in Lo-yang, in 621. According to this text, it is not only in Lo-yang, but in each prefecture that, in 621, it would have been authorized for only one Buddhist establishment with thirty monks to remain.

67. *Tseu-tche t'ong-kien*, CLVII, 42b (*Wou-to* II, 6th moon, day *keng-tseu*). In 621, Lieou Wou-tcheou, having been hit by a spear that did not pierce his shield, was compared by an adulator to the Buddha whose "diamond body" (*vajra-kāya*) is invulnerable; he must have been surrounded by Buddhists (*Tseu-tche t'ong-kien*, CLVIII, 54a, *Wou-to* IV, 2nd moon, day *jen-yin*).

68. *Tseu-tche t'ong-kien*, CLVIII, 54a (*Wou-to* IV, 2nd moon, day *jen-yin*).

69. Photographs in *Shodō zenshū* (Tokyo, 1955), 7:fig. 2, 2, and fig. 44, 28; also in Mochizuki, *Bukkyō daijiten*, III, pl. clxiv, fig. 828. Inscription text in *Kin-che ts'ouei-pien tsi-che*, xli, 1a and passim (the 1893 edition has abundant annotations). Also see the beautiful and richly illustrated volume by Washio Junkei, *Bodaidaruma Sūzan shiseki daikan* (Tokyo, 1932), where one will find photographs of the stele (or rather of the two steles, for there is a replica of one in the Cypress Valley; pl. II) and photographs of the inscription (pl. XIII–XXI), with a deciphering of the Chinese text and a commentary in Japanese (22–29 of the section of etchings). Pelliot had the opportunity to say a few words about this inscription in his "Notes sur quelques artistes des Six Dynasties et des T'ang," *T'oung Pao* 22 (1923): 253, n. 1, 262. More recently, the various charters it cites, which are of much interest for the process of imperial annuities, were studied by Niida Noboru, *TōSō hōritsu bunsho no kenkyū* (Tokyo, 1937), 830–838; and by D. C. Twitchett, "Monastic Estates in Tang China," *Asia Major* 5.2 (1956): 131–132.

70. In the 728 inscription from which this information was taken (*Kin-che ts'ouei-pien tsi-che*, LXXIV, 1a and passim), the secularization imposed by Li Che-min,

which the *Teu-tche t'ong-kien* (above, n. 65) dates from 621, is dated from 622 (1b). The monks from Chao-lin sseu protested against this secularization, by citing the services they rendered to Li Che-min, upon which Li Che-min established them, in 624, with personal status privileges and in possession of their own land.

71. This seems to me to pertain to the expresson *fan-tch'eng*, which is repeated several times throughout the 728 inscriptions.

72. *Kin-che ts'ouei-pien tsi-che*, LXXIV, 2a.

73. It is regarding the monks mentioned in these inscriptions that the Chao-lin boxing school is discussed further (s.v. *Ts'eu-hai*); cf. B. Favre, *Les sociétés secrètes en Chine* (Paris, 1933), 120. There is interesting work to be done on Chao-lin sseu's gymnastic and paramilitary traditions: boxing, fencing, stick handling, etc. See the mural paintings reprinted by Chavannes, *Mission archéologique*, figs. 981–982.

74. And not 804 as de Groot says in "Militant Spirit of the Buddhist Clergy in China," 103. On what follows, cf. *Kieou T'ang chou*, CXXLV, 6b–9a; *Sin T'ang chou*, CCXIII, 1a–3a; *Tseu-tche t'ong-kien*, CCIX, 5b–7a (1900). As usual, it is this last source that is the most clear; but we don't really know if it is with Li Che-tao or only with his henchmen that Yuan-tsing was conniving.

75. In the Tang dynasty's military terminology, *kien-eul* meant the regular permanent soldiers in the army (R. des Rotours, *Traité des fonctionnaires*, XLI), or "veterans," as Pulleyblank translates it (*The Background*, 152–153).

76. I have found nothing on this monastery in the contemporary Buddhist literature; one would have to consult the *fang-tche*.

77. E. G. Sargent, "Tchou Hi contre le bouddhisme," in *Mélanges publiés par l'Institut des Hautes Etudes chinoises* (Paris: Presses Universitaires de France, 1957), 1:1–59.

78. *Lin-tsi lou*, T. 1985, 66, of the *Iwanami bunko* edition (Tokyo, 1935).

79. *Tou-sing tsa-tche* by Tseng Min-hing (1118–1175), ed. *Ts'ong-chou tsi-tch'eng*, no. 2775, I, 5–6. The author adds maliciously that "if Li Yu had loved the people like he loved these monks, the people would have known how to show their gratitude toward the dynasty."

80. *Tseu-tche t'ong-kien*, CLV, i, 26b (*Tchoung-ta-t'ong* VI, 7th moon, day *ting-wei*). On the "sword [slicing to the point of cutting apart] a thousand steer," the name is taken from a famous *Tchouang-tseu* anecdote; see Rotours, *Traité des fonctionnaires*, 543n1. The Houei-tchen episode took place the very night of the Hiao-wou-ti escape, when he went to spend the night in a royal villa in Lo-yang's immediate surroundings, on the edge of the Tch'en, flocking from the Lo.

81. The two Kin-wou guards each had a "superior general," a "great general," and two "generals"; see Rotours, *Traité des fonctionnaires*, 530–531.

82. *Fo-tsou t'ong-ki*, T. 2035, IX, 375c; *Seng che liue*, T. 2126, III, 428c.

83. *Song che*, CCCLXII, 14b–15a (ed. Po-na), biography by Fan Tche-hiu.

84. Ibid., CDLV, 24b–25a.

85. Ibid., CDI, 1a–b, biography by Sin K'i-tsi, the famous patriot and poet, friend of Tchou Hi.

86. Ibid., CDLV, 24b–25a.

87. Ibid., 25a.

88. Tch'en Mao-heng, "Ming-tai wo-k'eou k'ao-liue," *Yenching Journal of Chinese Studies* 6 (1934): 152; *Kin-che ts'ouei-pien tsi-che*, XLI, 2a–b. Likewise at the end of the Ming dynasty, during the great Li Tseu-tch'eng and Tchang Hien-tchong insurrections, which ravaged China in the first half of the seventeenth century, an author from the period reports that not only did the rebels not dare to go near Chao-lin sseu, but that the monks from this powerful convent made it their specialty to attack them and to pillage them, and several of these monks waved their military flag like the great generals do; cf. Lin T'ong (1627–1714), *Lai-tchai kin-che-k'o k'ao* (1679), cited in *Kin-che ts'ouei-pien tsi'che*'s commentary, XLI, 1b.

89. *Houo-chao Hong-lien sseu* ("The Red Lotus Monastery Fire") is a piece from the Republican period.

90. *Fo-kiao je-pao* by Chang-hai.

91. *International Buddhist Bulletin* 3.6 (June 1937): 14–15.

92. In his work *The Nien Rebellion* (Seattle, Wash., 1954), Chiang Siang-tseh maintains that the so-called revolt of the Nien-tseu, which erupted between the T'ai-p'ing and the Boxers, was connected through their religious roots to the White Lotus sect.

93. Mochizuki, *Bukkyō daijiten*, 3111; J. A. Haguenauer, 2 (1934): 298 (review of a work by Hatada Takashi).

94. Returning from a study trip in China in 1935, the professor D. T. Suzuki declared that he was particularly surprised by the fusion that had been established between the Pure Land school and the Dhyāna school, which were so clearly separated in Japan on an institutional level and on a doctrinal level. *Eastern Buddhist* 6.4 (Mar. 1935).

95. K. Asakawa, *The Early Institutional Life of Japan* (Tokyo, 1903); "The Place of Religion in the Economic History of Japan," *Annales d'histoires économique et sociale* (1938): 139; Yamada Bunsho, *Nihon bukkyōshi no kenkyū* (Nagoya, 1934), 4, 97.

96. Renondeau, "Histoire des moines guerriers du Japon," in *Mélanges publiés par l'Institut des Hautes Etudes chinoises* (Paris: Presses Universitaires de France, 1957), 1:158–344, 193–195, n. 1. Cf. Tsuh Zennosuke, "Introduction à l'étude des rapports entre le gouvernement et la religion dans l'histoire nationale," *Shūkyō kenkyū* (Religious Studies) 10.1 (Jan.–Feb. 1933): 48.

97. Renondeau, "Histoire des moines guerriers du Japon," 158–344, 182–189.

98. Ibid., 158–344, 196–197 and note, 212–213.

99. On this point, see the opinion of a specialist in European feudalism, Marc Bloch, *La société féodale, les classes et le gouvernement des hommes* (Paris, 1940), 249–252: "Une coupe à travers l'histoire compare." Cf. also *Feudalism in History* (Princeton, N.J., 1956), and the report by J. R. Levenson in *F.E.Q.* 15.4 (Aug. 1956): 569–572.

100. Renondeau, "Histoire des moines guerriers du Japon," 213–216; cf. K. Asakawa, "The Life of a Monastic *Shō* in Medieval Japan," *Annual Reports of the American Historical Association* 1 (1916).

101. Y. Takekoshi, *The Economic Aspects of the History of the Civilization of Japan* (New York, 1930), 1:78.

102. See, for example, Gernet, *Aspects économiques*.

103. Renondeau, "Histoire des moines guerriers du Japon," 190–193.

104. Ibid., 248–249.

105. The proclamation of allegiance to the Buddha Amita and to all his earthly manifestations is typical in this regard. In the fifteenth century, they recited the *Gaike-mon* or the *Ryōge-mon* by Rennyo (1415–1499), who was the eighth leader of the Shin sect (trans. Anesaki, *History of Japanese Religion* [London, 1930], 231).

106. Renondeau, "Histoire des moines guerriers du Japon," 271, 280. *Ikko*, another name for the Shin sect, is an epithet of the exclusive "unilateral" devotion to Amita in the *sūtra* dedicated to him; *ikki* is approximately equivalent to the Chinese *t'ong-tche*, "having the same ideals," from which "comrades" form packs. Cf. Hugh Borton, *Peasant Uprisings in Japan of the Tokugawa Period* (Leiden, 1936), 16n2.

107. Renondeau, "Histoire des moines guerriers du Japon," 248, 273, 280.

108. *International Buddhist Bulletin* 4.1 (January 1938). We might recall that when the Sino-Japanese conflict began, according to the Japanese on January 18, 1932, in Shanghai, acts of violence were being committed against two monks from the Nichiren sect; see *Bukkyō nenkan* (Buddhist Annals) (1933): 350.

109. Renondeau, "Histoire des moines guerriers du Japon," 257–258.

110. Ibid., 258n1.

111. Ibid., 258–265.

112. Ibid., 266 and n. 2.

113. E. Herrigel, *Zen in the Art of Archery*. The author is a German professor who was introduced very intensively to archery by a Zen master during a long stay in Sendai.

114. *Fudōchi shimmyō roku* by Takuan (1573–1645), advisor of the third *shōgun* Tokugawa, Iemitsu; partially translated in Herrigel, *Zen in the Art of Archery*, and by D. T. Suzuki in *Eastern Buddhist* 6.2 (June 1933): 135–136, and *Essays on Zen Buddhism* 3 (1934): 318–319.

115. Vilfredo Pareto, *Traité de sociologie générale* (Paris, 1917–1919).

116. See the 1936 talk to the Nankin Buddhist clergy, above, 34; articles by J. Takausu in *Young East* 8.1 (1938): ex. 13, the "world of the Lotus Embryo," *padma-garbha-dhātu*, which is identified with totalitarianism, with general mobilization; articles from the *International Buddhist Bulletin* 4.1 (Jan. 1938: "the holy war against communism"); etc. I had in my hands a rather big book, *The Buddhist's Idea of War* (*Bukkyō no sensōkan*), published in Tokyo in 1937 by Hayashiya Tomojirō and another Buddhist professor, but I haven't been able to locate it again.

117. *Hobogirin*, art. Bishamon, 81–82.

118. *Nihon shoki*, trans. Aston, II, 114; cf. Coates and Ishizuka, *Hōnen the Buddhist Saint* (Kyoto, 1925), 7.

119. Noted in a Chinese newspaper from Shanghai dated September 15, 1938.

120. T. Watters, *Essays on the Chinese Language* (Shanghai, 1889), 408. This title is not noted in Harada Masami's article "On Some Elements from the Kouan Yu Cult," *Tōhō shūkyō* (Journal of Eastern Religions) 8–9 (Mar. 1955): 29–40, wherein we see mentioned other titles awarded in Kouan-ti under the Ming and the Tsing dynasties; in these titles, the epithet "subjugator of Māra" is usually featured. Kouan-ti is assumed to have received the five precepts, in 591, from the founder of the T'ien-t'ai sect, Tche-yi (*Fo-tsou t'on-ki*, T. 2035, vi, 183c, biography by Tche-yi); this legend was transmitted in Tibet (*Lhasa Council*, 1:357).

121. De Visser, *Ancient Buddhism in Japan*, 1:225.

122. Renondeau, "Histoire des moines guerriers du Japon," 158–344, 172–173.

123. See above, 37–39.

124. On the millenarian doctrine of the three levels of the Real Law, see Renondeau, "Histoire des moines guerriers du Japon," 240–241 and note. In Japan it was believed that the level of the last law had begun in 1051 (or in 1224). The Japanese don't seem to have known that in China the third level traces back much earlier, to the fifth or sixth century.

125. *Yamaga yōki senryaku* by Shunzen (colophon from 1409), text cited in Heki Sōichi, *Nihon sōhei kenkyū* (Tokyo, 1934), 19–20.

126. Keishin, *Jie daishi den* (around 1469), cited in Heki, *Nihon sōhei kenkyū*, 20–21.

127. *Risshō ankoku ron* (1260), trans. Renondeau, *T'oung Pao* 40 (1950): 165–170; *Kaimoku shō* ("For opening eyes," 1272), in *La doctrine de Nichiren*, trans. Renondeau, (Paris, 1953), 199–206; *Épître à Shijō Kingo* (1274), trans. Renondeau, 287–289.

128. *Mahāparinirvāna Sūtra*, T. 374, xvi, 459a–460b.

129. Ibid., iii, 383b–384a.

130. Ibid. Cf. ibid., xii, 434c, the story of King Sien-yu, who had Brahman slanderers of the holy Great Vehicle texts put to death.

131. *Completely Falsified Sūtra on the Salvations Given by the Buddha*, T. 156, vii, 161b–162a.

132. This is very similar to the theme of the William Faulkner novel *Requiem for a Nun* (1951) or the edifying epilogue of *Sanctuary*. In it, we see a black prostitute sanctifying herself by strangling a child so as to spare the child's mother from committing infanticide (and from incurring the death penalty that would follow).

133. *Yogācārabhūmi*, T. 1579, XLI, 517b; Sanskrit text in the *Bodhisattvabhūmi*, ed. Wogihara (Tokyo, 1930), 165–166, and in La Vallée Poussin, "Notes bouddhiques, VII: Le Vinaya et la pureté d'intention," Académie Royale de Belgique, *Bulletin de la Classe des Lettres*, 5th ser., T. XI (1929), 216, with a translation, 212. On the purity of intention which sanctifies sin, see also La Vallée Poussin, "A propos du *Cittaviśuddhiprakarana* d'Aryadeva," *B.S.O.S.* 6.2 (1931): 411–413.

134. *Mahāyāna-samgraha*, trans. E. Lamotte (Louvain, 1939), 2.2:215–216.

135. Bu-ston, *History of Buddhism*, trans. E. Obermiller (Heidelberg, 1932), 216 and n. 1.

136. This text, the *Ardhyardhaśatikā* (or *Prajñāpāramitā-naya*) from one of the Tantric *Prajñāpāramitās*, is often cited: "O Vajrapāṇi! Anyone who has heard this *naya*, will retain it and will recite it, even if it destroys all the beings of the three *dhātu* [another version: if it kills them], he will not descend into the three *durgati*: for this is in order to tame them." Chinese text edited in Toganoo Shōun, *Rishukyō no kenkyū* (Kōyasan, 1930), 8. Also see J. Filliozat in *L'Inde classique*, §2357.

137. On the argument of the emptiness of the individual, see above, 352–353.

138. *Ajātaśatru-kaukrtya-vinodana* ("The Catharsis of Ajātaśatru's Remorse"), T. 627, iii, 424a–425a, translated in 286c; cf. *Lhasa Council*, 1:160n8; and above, 384n2. The king Ajātaśatru attempted to take his father's, Bimbisāra's, life. This doesn't prevent him, after converting to Buddhism, from becoming an eminent

protector of the Real Law. This episode is sometimes cited in the T'ien-t'ai sect to justify the Emperor Yang-ti (606–617) from the Sui sect's participation in the assassination of his father; the founder of the Tche-yi sect (538–598) had maintained close ties with the future Yang-ti before his accession. Cf. Tch'en Yin-k'iue, *Bull. Ac. Sin.* 5.2 (1935): 141–142.

139. *Ratnakūta Sūtra*, T. 310, CV, 590b–c (*Susthimati-pariprcchā*).

140. *Kausītaki Upanisad*, III, 1, trans. Renou (Paris, 1948), 49: "If you know me you will not lose your estate, even if you know me through flight, or through the abortion (or murder) of a Brahman, or through the murder of your mother, or through the murder of your father." *Bhagavad-gītā*, ii, 18–19, trans. Senart (Paris, 1944), 6: "Bodies end; the soul enveloped by the body is eternal, indestructible, and infinite.... Therefore, fight, O Bhārata! Believing that one does the killing, thinking that the other is killed, is to be dually mistaken; one neither kills, nor is killed"; ibid., xviii, 17 (Senart, 54): "The person who does not is not led astray by his egocentricity [literally: he who does not create a "me," *nāhankrta*], and whose intelligence is not cloudy, might kill every living creature, for he does not kill, he takes responsibility for no chain."

141. Houei-yuan, *Ming pao-ying louen*, in *Kouang hong-ming tsi*, T. 2103, 33b–34b. Cf. W. Liebenthal, *JAOS* 70 (1950): 253.

142. This last sentence was inspired by the *Lao-tseu*, §L.

143. Above, 29.

144. D. T. Suzuki, *Essays on Zen Buddhism* (London, 1927), 1:262 and 270. The saint must make himself as indifferent as the unconscious—innocent—forces of nature, while eliminating all personal and conscious thought within his all "too human" intentionality: through this, he creates a morality "outside good and evil" which allows him to violate the precepts without being responsible for his actions, becoming "pure" in every sense of the word. This is explained in the *Treatise of Absolute Contemplation*, a short text from the Dhyāna school probably from the eighth century, of which several manuscripts have been discovered in Touen-huang in Kuno Hōryū, ed., *Shūkyō kenkyū* 14.1 (Jan.–Feb. 1937): 136–144; and Suzuki Daisetsu in *Bukkyō kenkyū* 1.1 (May–June 1937): 57–68. We read therein, for example (Kuno, 140; Suzuki, 62):

> Can we not, in certain instances, kill a living being?—The brush fire burns the mountain; the hurricane destroys the trees; the cliff that falls asunder kills wild animals; the flood that inundates drowns insects. The man who renders his mind similar [to the forces of nature] is entitled to do equally as much. However, if he feels the slightest hesitation, if he [imagines] he's "seeing" a living being [in the recipient of his act], "seeing" a murder [in his act], if there remains the least bit of thought [not depersonalized], then if he kills only an ant, he is connected to the act [*karma*], and his life is implicated by it.

Or even (Kuno, 143; Suzuki, 67):

> If every living being is just a phantasm or a dream, is it a sin to kill them?—If one "sees" them as living beings, it is a sin to kill them. If one does not

"see" them as living beings, then there are not any living beings that can be killed; as when one kills another man in a dream: upon awakening, there is absolutely no one there.

It is perhaps useless to point out the Taoist inspiration through similar documents wherein the *wou-sin* is a Buddhist adaptation of the *wou-wei*. Nevertheless the unreality of the person, of the "living being" is perfectly in keeping with the most orthodox of Buddhist thought; see above, 352n5. The citation from the *Abhidharma-mahāvibhāsā*, which notes from the Small Vehicle: "The sin of murder exists only insofar as one has the notion of a living being, even though such a thing does not exist."

145. *Enzan wadei-gassui shū*, a collection of works by a Zen author from the fourteenth century, cited in Satō Kenichi, "The Precepts of Zen and the Five Precepts," *Zengaku kenkyū* (June 28, 1929): 86–87.

146. *Zenkai shō* by Dōtan (1668–1773), cited in ibid., 87.

147. T. 659–661; T. 489.

148. Śāntideva, *Śikṣāsamuccaya*, ed. Bendall, notably 168: "It is said in the holy *Ratnamegha* that the murder of a man who intends to commit a sin worthy of immediate damnation is allowed." Cf. La Vallée Poussin, *La morale bouddhique* (Paris, 1927), 244.

149. *Ratnamegha Sūtra*, Tang version, T. 660, iii, 293b–c.

150. Or "theater therapy" as our psychiatrists say today; we are reminded of Moreno's psychodramas. This sort of scenario is found for example in the *Ajātaśatru-kau-kṛtya-vinodana*, cited above, 380, where we also see the theme of the confession coming into play. The following are the particulars of the scenario: to be "cured" of repented matricide, Mañjuśrī begins by transforming himself before the "killer" into a child who begins to argue with his parents and then kills them. In seeing this, the "killer" says to himself that after all he only killed one of his parents, and gradually he calms down. The metamorphosed child leads him before the Buddha, to whom the "child" confesses his crime. After the child's confession, the Buddha teaches him about the emptiness of thoughts and accepts him as a monk. The "killer" then follows the example of the magic criminal. He, in turn, confesses, receives the same teaching from the Buddha, and he too becomes a monk.

151. Manuscript colophons discovered in Touen-houang and elsewhere, edited and studied by Yabuki Yoshiteru in *Sankaikyō no kenkyū* (Research on the Third Level Doctrine) (Tokyo, 1927), pl. XIII and explanatory text, 748–759; and in *Meisha youn* (Echoes of the Singing Sands) (Tokyo, 1933), pl. XCIII and explanatory text, 278–281; see also T. 660, ii, 292a–b.

152. T. 660, 293n4 (note from the Ming edition).

153. The agreement of the four Chinese versions leaves no doubt on the authenticity of the passage; besides, it is confirmed by the citation from the *Siksāsamuccaya* (above, 383, n.).

2

Making Merit through Warfare and Torture According to the *Ārya-Bodhisattva-gocara-upāyaviṣaya-vikurvaṇa-nirdeśa Sūtra*

Stephen Jenkins

The impression of Buddhist pacifism is so strong that it has suggested to historians that it was a significant factor in the downfall of Buddhism in India. Buddhist kings would seem to be implicated in a hopeless moral conflict. No Kṛṣṇa seems to rescue the Buddhist Arjuna from the disempowering moral conflict that arises between a warrior's duty and the values of *ahiṃsā* (nonviolence). However, we can see from the example of the *Ārya-Bodhisattva-gocara-upāyaviṣaya-vikurvaṇa-nirdeśa Sūtra* that Buddhist kings had conceptual resources at their disposal that supported warfare, torture, and harsh punishments. The exploration of its intertextual details opens up an ever-wider view of a sort of Buddhism strongly at odds with the pacifist stereotypes. Here, an armed bodyguard accompanies the Buddha and threatens to destroy those who offend him. Torture can be an expression of compassion. Capital punishment may be encouraged. Body armor and a side arm are among the most important metaphors and symbols of the power of compassion. Celestial bodhisattvas, divinized embodiments of the power of enlightened compassion, support campaigns of conquest to spread the influence of Buddhism, and kings vested with the dharma commit mass violence against Jains and Hindus.

The *Ārya-Bodhisattva-gocara-upāyaviṣaya-vikurvaṇa-nirdeśa Sūtra*, otherwise known as the *Ārya-Satyakaparivarta*, engages a variety of questions in relation to the violence of warfare and punishment. As the two different titles indicate, its name can be a source of confusion. Although it is cataloged under its long title, it is more often cited and better known as the *Satyakaparivarta*.[1] I would translate the long name as "The Noble Teaching through Manifestations on the Subject of Skillful Means in the Bodhisattva's Field of Activity."[2] The doctoral dissertation of Lozang Jamspal contains a translation and study. It is also the subject of a rich research article by Michael Zimmermann, who makes use of the Chinese translations and compares perspectives from the Hindu *Arthaśāstra* and *dharmaśāstras*.[3] Lambert Schmithausen mentions it in passing in a sweeping article with which all students of Buddhism and violence should begin.[4] I will synthesize their contributions and make some observations, corrections, and additions. Dr. Sangye Tandar Naga, the former head of research at the Library of Tibetan Works and Archives in Dharamsala, supported my own study. The merit of this work is largely due to him.

The *sūtra* was translated twice into Chinese less than a hundred years apart. According to Zimmermann, the chapter on royal ethics is missing in the earliest Chinese translation by Guṇabhadra. Zimmermann astutely notes that this type of omission does not necessarily indicate that a chapter is a later interpolation into a *sūtra*. I would add that this is particularly true here, since in China violent or erotic materials were frequently modified or omitted when translating Indian texts.[5] Jamspal notes that the text is frequently cited in Indian Buddhist literature.[6] Its most important citation is in the *Sūtrasamuccaya* attributed to Nāgārjuna.[7] Lindtner takes the attributions of the *Sūtrasamuccaya* to Nāgārjuna by Candrakīrti and Śāntideva quite seriously, and it has been often used as a key source for dating texts.[8] This would seem to give the *Satyakaparivarta* an early date. However, dating texts according to their appearance in compendiums such as the *Sūtrasamuccaya* and *Śikṣāsamuccaya* is highly problematic. This type of text, built around a catalog of *sūtra* citations, is very susceptible to interpolation and *sūtras* should not be definitively dated to Nāgārjuna based on this alone. However, it is important to note that the section cited by the *Sūtrasamuccaya*, possibly as early as the second century CE by the enormously influential Nāgārjuna, is from the very section on royal ethics which is not included in Guṇabhadra's fifth-century Chinese translation. This could mean that the section is not an interpolation into the later version of the *sūtra* and may have been deliberately excluded by Guṇabhadra. On the other hand, it could be taken as evidence that the *Sūtrasamuccaya* itself contains later interpolations. Further, since the internal content of the *sūtra* was also likely changed, we do not know whether the rest of the chapter that may have been in Nāgārjuna's hands was the same as the one we have today.

When Nāgārjuna addresses royal ethics, as in the *Ratnāvalī*, he does not directly cite this *sūtra*.[9] However, this *sūtra* says many things about military policy and punishment, through the mouth of a manifestation that should not be addressed by an ordained monk such as Nāgārjuna. The citation in the *Śikṣāsamuccaya*, attributed to Śāntideva some 600 years later, also comes from the section on royal ethics.[10] In terms of evaluating the *sūtra*'s currency and influence, particularly the chapter on royal ethics, all we can say is that influential figures in the Mahāyāna tradition believed that its foundational figure, Nāgārjuna, had cited the *sūtra*. Even if the *sūtra* evolved and changed, it would have continued to carry this pedigree. Tsong-kha-pa's frequent citations and exhortation to study it seem to suggest that this is true at least in the Tibetan tradition and for the currents of Indian tradition that influenced it.[11] Considering that the extent of Indian Mahāyāna *sūtra* literature may have been almost as daunting to ancient scholars as it is to modern ones, citation catalogs, such as the *Sūtrasamuccaya* and *Śikṣāsamuccaya*, may have been more important in monastic education than the vast corpus of *sūtras* themselves. So the *Satyakaparivarta*'s presence there is especially significant. Having stated the qualifications, the best evidence is that this *sūtra*'s section on royal ethics was well known and influential since the second century through the influence of Nāgārjuna and that its absence from the earlier Chinese translation was a deliberate exclusion. However, as usual in Indian Buddhism, the best evidence in such matters is highly subject to doubt.

On the Setting

With apparent humor and irony, this *sūtra* describes a dialogue between an ascetic called Satyavaca Nirgranthaputra and a king. A character by this name also appears in two Pāli *suttas* as a clever and aggressive anti-Buddhist debater.[12] In this earlier account of Satyavaca, he makes the mistake of challenging the Buddha to debate with highly insulting language. Subsequently, when he hesitates to answer a key question during the debate, the Buddha's menacing armed bodyguard, Vajrapāṇi, threatens to split his head open with a blazing *vajra*. The *vajra* was a handheld weapon that would later become the primary symbol of the power of compassion. The key question put to Satyavaca by Śākyamuni Buddha shows a connection to the later Mahāyāna *sūtra*. The question is whether an anointed king may exercise the power in his own realm to execute those who should be executed. The Buddha's argument hinges on the fact that this is so. Satyavaca concedes that an anointed king could indeed exercise the power of capital punishment and he would be worthy (Pāli: *arahati*) to

FIGURE 2.1 The Buddha engages an ascetic in his hut; a muscular Vajrapāṇi, brandishing his sidearm, is nearby. Photo taken at the Peshawar Museum in Pakistan by Stephen Jenkins.

exercise it. He strengthens the point by saying that this is true even for groups and societies that do not have such kings. So the Buddha forces Satyavaca, under threat of death, to concede that an anointed king both has and merits the power to execute criminals.

The violence of Satyavaca's situation is typical and shows how dangerous the world of the Indian ascetics was imagined to be. Those who lost debates are often described as being swallowed up by the earth, drowning in the Gaṅga, or spitting up blood and dying. It was not uncommon for the stakes to be death or conversion. The threat to split someone's head was typical of intellectual challenges and occurs often both in the Upaniṣads and in early Buddhist literature.[13] The fact that the threat is taken very seriously is shown here by Satyavaca's terror and the presence of Vajrapāṇi, who often works violence on the Buddha's behalf from early mainstream Buddhist literature to late Tantric literature. The legends of such debates often end in the forfeit of the losing community's right to assemble, or even being forced to fund new monasteries for the opponent. The relations between groups of ascetics were seen as violently competitive, even involving espionage and assassination. The Buddha is depicted as an attempted murder victim on multiple occasions and even as the victim of a conspiracy to implicate him in a murderous sex scandal (Jātaka 285).[14] One thinks of the attempted assassinations of the Buddha, the murders of Āryadeva and Nāgārjuna, the wizardly battles of Śāntideva and Dignāga, Candrakīrti's involvement in warfare, etc. In the Pāli account of Satyavaca, the shadow of deadly force hangs over the Buddha's debate in the form of Vajrapāṇi. If legend and scripture are any indication, the violence of the Indian Buddhists' imagination, and probably the violence of their world, was extreme. It is no wonder that in Tibet debate has evolved into a highly physical, intellectual martial art.

In the much later Mahāyāna *sūtra*, which existed at least as early as the fifth century CE, Satyavaca is actually a manifestation of the Buddha, and the text frequently states that he both is a manifestation and teaches through many manifestations. Perhaps he does not manifest in this context as a Buddhist monk or deity, because he teaches on topics, such as military tactics, which are forbidden for monks to discuss. Here, he finds himself again in a potentially deadly situation for an ascetic, an audience with a vicious king. The king's Sanskrit name, Pradyota, means "Radiance," a typical name for a king suggesting that he has an overabundance of *rajas*, dynamism, a quality kings are supposed to embody. The epithet *Caṇḍa* means Pradyota the Cruel, just as the great Aśoka was called *Caṇḍa-Aśoka*. He is a stock character in Buddhist lore. Zimmermann tracked him down in the *Mūlasarvāstivāda Vinaya* and describes him as "a mean little bald guy" who would kill anyone "on the spot" who said the word "fat." He was also said to have massacred 80,000 *Brāhmaṇas*.[15] He appears elsewhere in Sarvāstivādin *avadāna* literature in ethical tales focused on violence. In one case, he threatens to kill a Buddhist teacher, and in another, he savagely beats a young novice monk who presumes to teach the women of his court.[16]

Zimmermann notes that the king is described as ruling according to dharma, even though he is also seen as dangerously violent. This illustrates the usual Buddhist attitude of ambiguity toward kings. Aśoka, according to Buddhist legend, slaughtered 18,000 Jains, among other atrocities, well after he became "Dharma-Aśoka."[17] Some note that he renounces such violence after this pogrom takes the life of his own brother; nevertheless, Aśoka continues to commit horrible acts of violence even after this episode. In the literary accounts, dangerous Buddhist kings have a disturbing tendency for mass violence against non-Buddhists. The Buddhist historian Tāranātha records, for instance, that the great King Harṣa trapped and burned alive "12,000 experts of the doctrine of the *mlecchas* [foreigners]."[18]

It is not entirely clear, but the irony and absurdity of Satyavaca's encounter suggest a comical aspect. After Satyavaca advises him against capital punishment, the king calls for a public assembly with the Buddha and proclaims that anyone who does not show up will be executed. When Satyavaca criticizes him for being excessively wrathful, Pradyota comes very close to killing him. Satyavaca escapes execution by apologizing for criticizing the king in the presence of others. The situation is perhaps too dangerous and too commonly attested to be humorous. In the *Milindapañha*, the monk Nāgasena tactfully tells King Milinda that he will only speak to him as a fellow scholar, because disputing with a king can result in punishment.[19] In another case, Śākyamuni is described as avoiding directly confronting even the favorable King Pasenadi, who was fresh from impaling his enemies, for fear of alienating him.[20]

On Punishment

Satyavaca advises *Caṇḍapradyota* on criminal justice and military violence. In regard to criminal justice, the ascetic warns the king against excessive compassion. This is the point cited by Śāntideva in the *Śikṣāsamuccaya*.[21] Sentimental reluctance to act with harsh violence is a downfall of a king and leads to general criminal mischief. As in Buddhist thought in general, compassion should not be mistaken for sentimentality. While manifesting *maitrī* and *karuṇā*, the king should "bind, imprison, terrorize [or hurt/whip], beat, and harm uncivilized people." Harming, terrorizing, and beating clearly fit the modern definition of torture. On the other hand, the king should not mutilate criminals, deprive them of their senses, or execute them. Although historically "Buddhist polities have nearly always maintained capital punishment,"[22] capital punishment is ruled out. This is in direct contrast with the *dharmaśāstras*, compendiums of Hindu ethical thought, which generally advocate all three acts of violence. Permanent physical damage should be avoided in such harsh treatment, and such violence should be done with the intention of training the victim. Violence is a tool of both prevention and rehabilitation. Likewise, in the case of tax collection, a king should discern between those who are unable to pay by no fault of their own and those who evade taxes or squander their wealth.

The *Milindapañha*, a highly authoritative Theravādin text framed as a dialogue between a king and a monk, offers an interesting contrast by arguing that punitive violence should be understood as the fruition of the victim's own karma. How, the monk Nāgasena is asked, is a king to reconcile the Buddha's apparently contradictory injunctions not to harm anyone, on the one hand, and to punish those who deserve it, on the other? King Milinda pointedly reminds him that punishment includes amputation, mutilation, torture, and execution. Nāgasena affirms both teachings. If a robber deserves death, he should be put to death. Is, then, the execution of criminals part of the dharma laid down by the Tathāgatas? No, it is the robber's own karma that causes the execution, not the *Buddhadharma*.[23] The king merely facilitates this fruition. This concept of the king facilitating the fruition of negative karma is also prominent in the Hindu *dharmaśāstras*, which are based more on the logic of ascetic expiation of karma. In Hindu sources, the king functions as Yama, lord of death and dispenser of karmic outcomes.[24] Even the death penalty can be seen as a benefit from this perspective. The victim is benefited through relief of a karmic burden. The *Satyakaparivarta* argues instead that compassionate torture that does not result in permanent physical damage may have a beneficial influence on the character of the victim. The death penalty is not allowed, perhaps partly because it disallows the possibility of reform. Although the royal use of deadly force in battle is not explicitly described as an enactment of karmic outcomes, the *sūtra* says that weapons cannot harm a warrior protected by good karma. The unstated implications are that one's victims must be ripe for their own destruction, and losing suggests moral failure on the part of the loser.

The domination of vassals is spoken of in much the same terms as controlling criminals, and the *sūtra*'s arguments for the benevolent treatment of vassals are more pragmatic than naïvely idealistic. Compassion is generally understood in Buddhism as having a magical power to protect. The common description of bodhisattvas putting on the armor of compassion is more than metaphorical. One can cite many cases of saints being protected from assassins or vicious animals by manifesting compassion. Even today, the *Mettā Sutta* is recited to protect from snakebite and other dangers. The *Milindapañha* tells of a prince, renowned for his compassion, who was struck by an arrow only precisely when he allowed his concentration on compassion to lapse.[25]

The *Seyya Jātaka*, a story about one of the Buddha's previous rebirths, portrays an extreme example of a king who refuses to fight to protect his kingdom, because it will require him to do harm. While imprisoned by the victor, he pities his conqueror for the karmic outcomes of his actions. His captor is then attacked by great physical pain through the power of his victim's compassion. As a result, the king is released and his kingdom is returned (Jātaka 282). The implication is that compassion magically serves to sustain a king's power. Similarly, it is believed in this *sūtra* that the weather, public health, and agricultural productivity are enhanced by the power of compassion.[26] When we consider the rhetorical and political value of what may be regarded as merely magical perspectives, it must be remembered that in their cultural context these were not supernatural, but reflected concrete concerns for the forces at work in their world. It is also true that sometimes what initially appear to be mere formulations of magical thinking may be informed by practical insight. In a 2008 presentation on the moral reasoning of *avadāna* literature, Rotman showed how Buddhists viewed moral qualities and karmic merit as quantifiable forms of capital.[27] This is a somewhat magical form of what we would characterize in terms of intangible qualities such as political capital, moral bankruptcy, or the value of consumer confidence, institutional morale, work ethics, or creativity. There is a sense that the benefits of moral values may be entrepreneurially accumulated and developed. The store of those values is a fundamental source of the well-being of a people. The concern with karmic merit goes beyond the impact of ascetic values on popular culture to a highly pragmatic and self-interested concern for community well-being. In the same way, the Buddhist ethics of violence represents more than a simple allegiance to the values of ascetics. They are part of a comprehensive view of human thriving that values worldly abundance.

But in this *sūtra*, as even in the brutally pragmatic Hindu *Arthaśāstra*, there are also practical arguments for the protective power of justice and benevolence that go beyond the usual magical sense. A king must recognize that his own policies are a substantial cause of hostile relations and that his own virtue is his first defense, reasoning that has currently been used in regard to the rise of terrorism. In an argument reminiscent of the *Aggañña Sutta*'s claim that crime arises from poverty, it is stated here that enemy attacks and insurrections arise from unhappiness and dissatisfaction. A king is therefore indirectly protected by his benevolent cultivation of the well-being of his subjects, vassals, and neighbors. It is emphasized that, if they are happy and secure then, instead of becoming enemies, they will be allies when enemies do arise. In the same way, a benevolent king will successfully enrich his treasury through gifts and the general prosperity of his realm, while a rapacious and exploitive king will fail.[28] Compassion serves the purposes of domination, pacification, security, and enrichment.

On Warfare

Although the *sūtra* allows for war, it does so only under special conditions and with special restrictions on its conduct. In a graded series of skillful means, a king must first try to befriend, then to help, and then to intimidate his potential enemy before resorting to war. This set of four stratagems diverges from an ancient and pervasive set only by substituting "intimidation" for "fomenting dissension."[29] In Hindu sources, this common argument that war should be a last resort is grounded on the practical point that battle is highly unreliable and unpredictable. So we cannot simply assume, in this Buddhist context, that using war as a last resort is a moral issue. In Hindu contexts, the preliminary techniques are often not attempts to avoid conflict, but to win by safer means. It is not clear in this *sūtra* whether wars of aggression are acceptable or not. There is no explicit rejection of campaigns of conquest. It should be remembered that, in the *dharmaśāstra* literature, all of the activities of kings are regarded and referred to as "protection." So, references to protection do not necessarily refer to defensive activity.

Should attempts to succeed without armed conflict fail, the king is then instructed in how to assemble and deploy the various divisions of an army. He is to go to war with three intentions: to care for life, to win, and to capture the enemy alive. Only Zimmermann, based on the Chinese version, correctly translated the phrase for capturing the enemy alive. This is not immediately convincing because the Chinese translation often strives to soften the impact of the violent aspects of the text. However, the Sanskrit phrase corresponding to the Tibetan *srog gzung ba*, *jīvagrāham*, occurs often with this meaning in the *jātakas* (stories about the Buddha's previous rebirths), perhaps the most important Buddhist source for statecraft (Jātaka 23, 24, 282, 283). The *jātakas* frequently valorize intentions to capture the enemy alive or to win without bloodshed through intimidation (Jātaka 229, 230, 181). In comparing this *sūtra* to the *Arthaśāstra* literature, which for him includes the *Manusmṛti* and the *dharmaśāstras*, Zimmermann states, "There can be hardly any doubt that the main effort of the warrior must have been directed towards annihilation of the enemy."[30] However, the *Arthaśāstra*, *Manusmṛti*, Dharmasūtras, and *Śāntiparvan* of the *Mahābhārata* all agree that noncombatants, or those surrendering, fallen, disarmed, fleeing, or petrified by fear, shall not be harmed.[31] Bhīṣma, the great *kṣatriya* guru of the *Mahābhārata*, proclaims that a warrior should only fight for the sake of conquest, not out of wrath.[32]

The concern to care for life in the *sūtra* also includes the well-being of all innocents, including animals and the spirits that dwell in trees and water. In contrast to most Hindu *dharmaśāstras*, the *sūtra* forbids burning homes or cities, destroying reservoirs or orchards, or confiscating the harvest. This condition is extended to what might be called infrastructure in general, i.e., "all things well developed and constructed."

On Karma

Having come to war with these preconditions and restrictions, the king still faces a problem that plagued the imagination of Indian warriors: how to reconcile the necessity of battle with the horrific karmic repercussions of killing. It is well known that the Buddha denied the idea that those who die in battle automatically go to heaven.[33] However, the *jātaka* tales are full of stories of Buddhist warriors, often the Buddha himself in a past life, and occasionally romanticize their heroic deaths in battle (Jātaka 23, 24, 182, 226, 283, etc.). This *sūtra* gives the same answer for the warrior that is found for bodhisattvas elsewhere:

> A king, who is well prepared for battle, having used skillful means in this way, even if he kills or wounds opposing troops, has little moral fault or demerit and there will certainly be no bad karmic result. Why is that? It is because that action was conjoined with intentions of compassion and not abandoning. On the basis of having sacrificed himself and his wealth to protect living things and for the sake of his family, wife and children, there is immeasurable merit; it even strongly increases.[34]

If he does so with compassionate intentions, a king may make great merit through warfare, so warfare becomes auspicious. The same argument was made earlier in relation to torture, and the *sūtra* now proceeds to make commonsense analogies to doctors and to parents who compassionately inflict pain in order to discipline and heal without intending harm. Zimmermann expresses surprise at the reference to compassion here and describes it as an irrelevant "sporadic addition," out of keeping with the context. The *sūtra*, he says, fails to address the "obvious contradiction between his obligation to protect sentient beings . . . and his warfare activities." He states that "the pair 'killing with compassion' was incompatible with the basic Buddhist ethics."[35]

Based on a similar perspective, Davidson argues that Buddhists were ultimately unable to find a satisfactory answer to the conundrum of how to uncompromisingly stand by their pacifist values without alienating or disempowering the kings upon whom they depended for endowment and protection.[36] He refers to a much-discussed passage from the *Bodhisattvabhūmi*, supporting compassionate killing, as an example of the fact that Buddhism was "not unequivocal" in its pacifism.[37] He sees this as an equivocation based on two assumptions which have been common to the field of Buddhist studies. The first is that this is an isolated passage representing an exceptional view. It has also been more expansively asserted, "Needless to say, this stance is particularly favored by the Consciousness-Only school and in esoteric Buddhism."[38] However, the Mādhyamika thinkers Bhāviveka, Candrakīrti, and Śāntideva all agree on the basic point that bodhisattvas may do what is ordinarily forbidden or inauspicious, including killing, and make merit as long as they remain compassionate.[39] In the *Śikṣāsamuccaya*, Śāntideva says that the very things that send others to hell send a bodhisattva to the heavenly Brahmalokas, a traditional result of generating compassion.[40] The validation of compassionate violence made by Asaṇga here is found across Mahāyāna traditions and is common to its ethics, not an unusual exception to normative pacifism.

Second, Asaṅga's passage is misread as an ethic of self-sacrifice which "allows the bodhisattva to engage in the slaughter of thieves or brigands... so that the bodhisattva could go to hell instead of the criminals"; "the bodhisattva replaces himself for the other and suffers in his stead."[41] Obviously, this would be a problematic model for a king. First, it should be noted that Asaṅga recommends stealing from thieves. Killing is for the purpose of preventing crimes, with similar karmic results. It is true that Asaṅga says that the bodhisattva killer is compassionately freeing his victim from the karmic outcome of great crimes and has the wish that he, rather than the criminal, should be born in hell. However, he goes on to explain that the result of killing with this intention, far from going to hell, is that the bodhisattva actually becomes blameless and produces great merit (Skt. *anāpattiko bhavati bahu ca puṇyaṃ prasūyate*) exactly as in the *Satyakaparivarta*.[42] One could say that the more willing bodhisattvas are to go to hell, the more certain it is that they will not.

Asaṅga's conception of compassionate violence validates not only the prevention of terrible crimes, but also the aggressive removal of vicious rulers from power, a motivation that could be very important for kings:

> Likewise, the [karmic] outcome for a bodhisattva established in compassionate intentions for benefit and happiness, who removes from power kings or ministers who are excessively fierce, merciless and solely set out to afflict others, is that they generate great merit.[43]

Davidson goes on to say, "This same rubric allows wide latitude in questionable behavior," and "evidently this doctrinal basis was used to justify belligerence on the part of their favorite monarchs."[44] He gives the example of the Chinese pilgrim Hsüan-tsang's depiction of King Harṣa. However, Hsüan-tsang records neither Asaṅga's actual argument that Harṣa should invoke compassion toward his enemy, nor the argument based on the reading that he should willingly enter hell. The story depicts Harṣa as oppressed by a vicious anti-Buddhist enemy who killed his father. In his distress, Harṣa supplicates the celestial bodhisattva Avalokiteśvara with prayers and offerings.[45] In return for a promise to overthrow the anti-Buddhist king, restore the influence of Buddhism, and rule compassionately, Avalokiteśvara lends his power to Harṣa's campaign of military conquest. In fact, although Harṣa's general motivation is compassion, the ethics in the example of Harṣa is far more unapologetically open to violence and free from conditions than in Asaṅga's thought or in the *sūtra*. His war of conquest is not regarded as at all questionable in the legend. In fact, it has the sanction of Avalokiteśvara, the divine personification of compassion. This also belies the idea that Buddhist kings did not go to war to spread Buddhism.

Davidson intends to support the argument that there was a fundamental conflict in Buddhist support for violence. But Asaṅga's argument for compassionate violence is broadly and authoritatively attested in Mahāyāna literature. It is not an ethics of self-sacrifice, but one that offers merit for killing. This *sūtra* is somewhat more expansive in explicitly making compassionate killing an option not just for bodhisattvas, but also for kings. There is no sign that the kings addressed by this *sūtra* were regarded as bodhisattvas, quite the opposite; and one has to assume that the king's entire army, and those who enforced his punishments, would be implicated in his karmic situation and the logic of making merit through compassionate killing. Tantric literature, which was used in the royal cult in later Indian Buddhism, supplemented the basic Mahāyāna ethic of compassionate killing with hyperbolic exhortations and deadly ritual technologies.

Davidson notes inscriptions in Nālandā, the great North Indian monastic university, that glorify the gore-smeared swords of widow-making Buddhist kings, but finds their grisly language weaker and less common than comparable Śaivite inscriptions.[46] There can be no question that, in terms of both warfare and harsh penal codes, Hindu literature and inscriptions are far more robust and unreserved in their enthusiasm for violent imagery. Davidson makes an important argument here that Buddhist values were much more suited to periods of pacification and stability than to the violent instability of the last centuries of Indian Buddhism, and so Buddhist kings were ideologically disadvantaged. However, the force of the argument needs to be reconsidered to the degree that it is based on the normative perception of exaggerated Buddhist pacifism. The location of such inscriptions in a monastic university of vast international prestige suggests that Buddhists, rather than being conflicted or duplicitous, found it appropriate to publicly honor, and so validate, military violence. The relationship between rhetoric and action is complex. For instance, despite idealizing an ethic of compassion, Buddhist polities have historically done all of the things forbidden in the *Satyakaparivarta*, from aggressive warfare to blinding and capital punishment. On the other hand, despite their violent rhetoric, the Hindu ethics of violence are deeply intertwined with ideals of dharma and *ahiṃsā*. Considering the broad success of Buddhism with a remarkable variety of patrons, including Indian kings, Mongol khans, samurai warlords, and Chinese emperors in diverse political circumstances over several millennia, it seems dubious to attribute the downfall of Buddhism in India to the inability to ideologically support the violence of its protectors.[47]

Conclusions

General conceptions of a basic Buddhist ethics broadly conceived as unqualified pacifism are problematic. Compassionate violence is at the very heart of the sensibility of this *sūtra*. Buddhist kings had sophisticated and practical conceptual resources to support their use of force, which show a concern for defense, political stability, and social order through a combination of harshness and benevolence. These resources offer techniques for removing and preventing the causes of hostility, but fully empower the use of warfare when it is deemed appropriate and necessary. Military readiness and intimidation are important elements of a king's responsibilities. Violence is an important tool for criminal rehabilitation, social stability, and military defense. Torture, but not mutilation or execution, is approved as a means, and in battle a king should seek to capture the enemy alive. A king may avert fear of karmic retribution by establishing proper intentions, making efforts to avoid conflict, and limiting modes of waging war. The only killing compatible with Buddhist ethics is killing with compassion. Moreover, if a king makes war or tortures with compassionate intentions, even those acts can result in the accumulation of vast karmic merit. Values of compassion were not necessarily in conflict with the political necessities of Indian statecraft. Rather than an awkward extension of ascetic values into the realm of power politics, there was a recognized symmetry among dharmic rule, compassion, and the acquisition and retention of power.

In the course of orally presenting this research at conferences and in university lecture series, I have experienced how distressing it can be for Buddhists that compassionate warfare and torture could be advocated in Buddhist scriptures. I would ask those who find this disturbing to also consider that these texts advocate that warfare should only be pursued when all other means have failed; that benevolence is a state's first defense; that we must take responsibility for exploitation, which creates our enemies; that physical punishment may only be undertaken from a compassionate intention to benefit the recipient; that the destruction of infrastructure and the natural environment is a mistaken policy; and, above all, that a nation will thrive or fall based upon its capacity for compassion, rather than on the ethics of self- or national interest.

NOTES

1. The word *parivarta* normally indicates a chapter title. However, Indian Buddhist sources cite from multiple chapters of the *Bodhisattva-gocara-upāyaviśaya-vikurvaṇa-nirdeśa Sūtra* under the title, *Satyakaparivarta*.

2. Zimmermann renders "*vikurvaṇa-nirdeśa-sūtra*" as *Sūtra Which Expounds Supernatural Manifestations.* Michael Zimmermann, "A Mahāyānist Criticism of *Arthaśāstra*, the Chapter on Royal Ethics in the *Bodhisattva-gocaropāya-viṣaya-vikurvaṇa[sic]-nirdeśa-sūtra*," *Annual Report of the International Research Institute for Advanced Buddhology at Soka University for the Academic Year 1999* (2000). In my understanding, Satyavaca is the manifestation that expounds the *sūtra*. Regarding the spelling of the title, some sources and catalogues have "*vikurvāṇa*" rather than "*vikurvaṇa*." All the Tibetan editions I have seen give a phonetic rendering of "*vikurvaṇa*."

3. Zimmermann, "A Mahāyānist Criticism of Arthaśāstra". Zimmermann at the time of his study was apparently unaware of Jamspal's dissertation, and I became aware of both only after doing my own translation work. See also "Only a Fool Becomes a King: Buddhist Stances on Punishment," in *Buddhism and Violence*, ed. Michael Zimmermann (Kathmandu: Lumbini International Research Institute, 2006).

4. Lambert Schmithausen, "Aspects of the Buddhist Attitude towards War," in *Violence Denied: Violence, Non-Violence and the Rationalization of Violence in South Asian Cultural History*, ed. E. M. Houben and K. R. Van Kooij (Leiden: Brill, 1999).

5. Zimmermann, "A Mahāyānist Criticism of *Arthaśāstra*," 179. According to Tatz, passages related to compassionate killing were omitted from three out of four Chinese translations of the *Bodhisattva-bhūmi*. Mark Tatz, *Asaṅga's Chapter on Ethics with the Commentary of Tsong-kha-pa* (New York: Edwin Mellen Press, 1986), 296, note 396.

6. Lozang Jamspal, *The Range of the Bodhisattva: A Study of an Early Mahāyānasūtra, "Āryasatyakaparivarta," Discourse of Truth Teller*, Ph.D. dissertation (Columbia University, 1991), 4.

7. Ibid., 210.

8. Chr. Lindtner, *Nāgārjuniana: Studies in the Writings and Philosophy of Nāgārjuna* (Delhi: Motilal Banarsidass, 1987), 172.

9. Jamspal points out numerous examples from Nāgārjuna's *Ratnāvalī* and *Suhṛllekha* that suggest the *sūtra*'s influences. Candrakīrti's *Catuḥśatakaṭīkā* also makes a number of arguments that could have been drawn from this *sūtra*, rather than the *Aggañña Sutta*, particularly in the discussion of the king as an employee of the people. See Karen Lang, "Āryadeva and Candrakīrti on the Dharma of Kings," *Asiatische Studien: Zeitschrift der Schweizerischen Gesellschaft für Asienkunde/Études Asiatiques: Revue de la Société Suisse d'Études Asiatiques* 46.1 (1992): 232–243.

10. See Śāntideva, *Śikṣāsamuccaya: A Compendium of Buddhist Teaching Compiled by Śāntideva Chiefly from Earlier Mahāyāna Sūtras*, ed. Cecil Bendall (The Hague: Moutons, 1957), 165; and Jamspal, "The Range of the Bodhisattva," 228.

11. Tsong-kha-pa, *The Great Treatise on the Stages of the Path to Enlightenment: Lam Rim Chen Mo*, trans. Lamrim Chenmo Translation Committee (Ithaca, N.Y.: Snow Lion, 2000), 1:184, 236, 250, 256.

12. Majjhima.i.229; 239; *The Middle Length Discourses of the Buddha*, trans. Bhikkhu Ñāṇamoli and Bhikkhu Bodhi (Boston: Wisdom, 1995).

13. See Michael Witzel, "The Case of the Shattered Head," *Studien zur Indologie und Iranistik* 13–14 (1984): 363–415; and A. Syrkin, "Notes on the Buddha's Threats in the Dīgha Nikāya," *Journal of the International Association of Buddhist Studies* 7 (1984): 147–158. This model of menacing the insolent and rude with Vajrapāṇi can be seen among the commentators of the Bodhisattva-bhūmi. Tatz, *Asaṅga's Chapter on Ethics with the Commentary of Tsong-kha-pa, 130, 326.*

14. All Jātaka references refer to the Pali Text Society numbering as in *The Jātaka or Stories of the Buddha's Former Births,* 6 vols., trans. E.B. Cowell et. al (London: Pali Text Society, 1895–1907.

15. Zimmermann, "A Mahāyānist Criticism of Arthaśāstra," 180.

16. Charles Willemen, trans., *The Storehouse of Sundry Valuables* (*Tsa-pao-tsang ching/Kṣudrakāgama*) (Berkeley, Calif.: Numata Center for Translation and Research, 2004), 59–62, 210–219.

17. John S. Strong, *The Legend of King Aśoka: A Study and Translation of the Aśokāvadāna* (Princeton, N.J.: Princeton University Press, 1983), 232.

18. Lama Chimpa, trans.,*Tāranātha's History of Buddhism in India* (Delhi: Motilal Banarsidass, 1970), 178.

19. T. W. Rhys Davids, trans., *The Questions of King Milinda* (New York: Dover, 1963), vol. 1, 46.

20. Bhikkhu Bodhi, trans., *The Connected Discourses of the Buddha: A New Translation of the Saṃyutta Nikāya* (Boston: Wisdom, 2000), 410, note 257.

21. Śāntideva, *Śikṣāsamuccaya*, ed. Bendall, 162; and Jamspal, "The Range of the Bodhisattva," 228.

22. Robert Florida, *Human Rights and the World's Major Religions*: vol. 5, *The Buddhist Tradition* (Westport, Conn.: Praeger, 2005), 57.

23. T. W. Rhys Davids, trans., *The Questions of King Milinda*, vol. 1, 254–257.

24. Terence P. Day, *The Conception of Punishment in Early Indian Literature* (Waterloo, Ont., Canada: Wilfrid Laurier University Press, 1982), 38–39, 200–205.

25. T. W. Rhys Davids, trans., *The Questions of King Milinda*, vol. 1, 280–281.

26. Jamspal, "The Range of the Bodhisattva," 211.

27. Andy Rotman, "Marketing Morality: The Economy of Faith in Early Indian Buddhism," *International Association of Buddhist Studies Meeting*, Atlanta, GA, June 23–25, 2008.

28. Jamspal, "The Range of the Bodhisattva," 211.

29. Kautilya, *The Arthaśāstra,* tr. L. N. Rangarajan (New York: Penguin, 1992), 637–639; *The Law Code of Manu,* tr. Patrick Olivelle (Oxford: Oxford University Press, 2004), 200; Saṃyutta.i.100–102.

30. Zimmermann, "A Mahāyānist Criticism of Arthaśāstra," 202.

31. *Arthaśāstra* 739; *Law Code of Manu* 113; *The Mahābhārata: Book 11, The Book of the Women; Book 12, The Book of Peace, Part One,* Volume 7, trans. James L. Fitzgerald (Chicago: University of Chicago Press, 2004), 412; *Dharmasūtra of Baudhāyana,* 18.11–12, in *Dharmasūtras: The Law Codes of Āpastamba, Gautama, Baudhāyana, and Vasiṣṭha,* trans. Patrick Olivelle (Oxford: Oxford University Press, 1999), 159; *Dharmasūtra of Āpastamba,* 2.10.10–11, in *Dharmasūtras* 53; *Dharmasūtra of Gautama,* 10.17–18, in *Dharmasūtras,* 94).

32. *The Mahābhārata*, 410.

33. Rupert Gethin, "Can Killing a Living Being Ever Be an Act of Compassion? The Analysis of the Act of Killing in the Abhidhamma and Pali Commentaries," *Journal of Buddhist Ethics* (2004): 62.

34. Tib. *de ltar thabs mkhas shing gyul legs par shom pa'i rgyal pos ni pha rol gyi dpung bkum mam | rma phyung yang des rygal po la kha na ma tho ba chung zhing bsod nams ma lags pa chung ba dang | 'bras bu myong ba yang nges pa ma mchis par 'gyur'o | | de ci'i slad du zhe na | 'di ltar des snying rje ba dang | yongs su mi gtang ba'i sems kyis las de mngon bar 'du bgyis pa'i slad du'o | | gang des skye dgu yongs su bskyang ba dang | bu dang chung ma dang | rigs kyi don du bdag dang longs spyod yongs su btang ste las de bgyis pas | gzhi de las bsod nams tshad ma mchis pa yang rab tu 'phel lo | |* Derge, mDo-sde, Volume Pa, 110.b.2–4.

35. Zimmermann, "A Mahāyānist Criticism of Arthaśāstra," 203–205.

36. Ronald M. Davidson, *Indian Esoteric Buddhism: A Social History of the Tantric Movement* (New York: Columbia University Press, 2002), 24, 90.

37. Ibid., 88.

38. Christoph Kleine, "Evil Monks with Good Intentions," in *Buddhism and Violence*, 80.

39. Malcom David Eckel, *Bhāviveka and His Buddhist Opponents* (Cambridge: Harvard University, 2008), 183–189; See Candrakīrti's commentary on Āryadeva's *Catuḥśatakam*, Chapter V, verse 105. Āryadeva supports compassionate transgression and Candrakīrti extends this to compassionate killing. *Catuḥśatakam: Candrakīrtipraṇītaṭīkayā Sahitam*, Sanskrit and Tibetan edited with Hindi translation, Gurucharan Singh Negi, Ph.D. dissertation (Sarnath: Central Institute Higher Tibetan Studies, 2005) 250–253; Śāntideva, *Śikṣāsamuccaya*, ed. Bendall, 167–169; In *Ratnāvalī* verse 264, Nāgārjuna makes the analogy of a doctor cutting off a finger bitten by a poisonous snake in advising a king that it may be his duty to compassionately inflict pain. *Ratnāvalī of Ācārya Nāgārjuna with the Commentary of Ajitamitra*, ed. Ācārya Ngawang Samten (Sarnath: Central Institute Higher Tibetan Studies, 1990), 181–182. A comparative analysis of these sources will be offered in separate publication.

40. Śāntideva, *Śikṣāsamuccaya*, ed. Bendall, 165.

41. Davidson, *Indian Esoteric Buddhism*, 88. See also Michael Zimmermann, "War," in *Encyclopedia of Buddhism*, ed. Robert Buswell Jr. (New York: Macmillan, 2003), 2:893–897.

42. Asaṅga, *Bodhisattva-bhūmi*, Sanskrit Ed. Nalinaksha Dutt, K. P. (Patna: Jayasawal Research Institute, 1978), 114.2.

43. Asaṅga, *Bodhisattva-bhūmi*, 114.3; Tatz, *Asaṅga's Chapter on Ethics with the Commentary of Tsong-kha-pa*, 70–1.

44. Davidson, *Indian Esoteric Buddhism*, 88. According to legend, Guṇaprabha, the iconic seventh century vinaya master who wrote a commentary on the *Bodhisattva-bhūmi*, was the tutor to King Harṣa. Historically this is questionable, but it does suggest the kind of political influence such figures may have had on Buddhist kings. Tatz, *Asaṅga's Chapter on Ethics with the Commentary of Tsong-kha-pa*, 29; 43, note 36.

45. Samuel Beal, *Si-Yu Ki: Buddhist Records of the Western World* (London, 1884; reprint, Delhi: Motilal Banarsidass, 1981), 2:210; and D. Devahuti, *Harṣa: A Political Study* (Delhi: Oxford University Press, 1998), 92–94.

46. Davidson, *Indian Esoteric Buddhism*, 88.

47. I specially thank Ronald Davidson who, despite his disagreement with my conclusions, generously read an earlier draft of this chapter and shared his criticism.

3

Sacralized Warfare: The Fifth Dalai Lama and the Discourse of Religious Violence

Derek F. Maher

It is a truism that history is written by the winners. A correlate to that axiom of power and the control of rhetoric is less well noted. In many cases, the last battle of a war, the one that finally secures the victory, occurs when one party manages to represent the history of the war in its own terms, deploying its own account to justify its martial successes and representing itself in a light that is sensible, acceptable, and meaningful to the relevant audience. Wars, according to Michel Foucault, reveal disequilibriums between contending parties, and the subsequent political forms that arise in the wake of such conflicts both sanction and uphold those disparities in forces. By means of an ongoing subsequent "unspoken war," such disequlibriums are inscribed by political means in social institutions, economic inequalities, language, and the very bodies of the citizenry.[1]

In a companion lecture, Foucault describes how such power is seized and maintained through the successful deployment of a particular discourse, a set of declarations that frame and define a moment in time. He argues that it is not possible "to exercise power except through the production of truth," and he observes, "[t]hese relations of power cannot themselves be established, consolidated nor implemented without the production, accumulation, circulation and functioning of a discourse."[2] Foucault maintains that a given historical moment calls into existence a discourse that configures power and summons a narrative that makes sense of how power is to be arranged. A shift in a religious or political reality, for example, only becomes possible when the prevailing narrative is supplanted by a new account of the past and the present, an alternative vision with new or refurbished symbolic connections that arrange people and events in a pattern justifying the new paradigm. This, he suggests, is one of the most significant engagements of a war.

In this chapter, I will explore the evolution of discourses of power in seventeenth-century Tibet, a period of great turmoil and flux. I will focus on the ways the discourse that emerged in the middle of that century was elaborated in Buddhist terms and the ways that the discourse employed narrative accounts of warfare and other forms of violence. I will concentrate on the religious justifications and associations of violence in an effort to problematize the generally accepted notions of Buddhism as an entirely pacifistic religion and of Tibet as a place where Buddhism "turned their society from a fierce grim world of war and intrigue into a peaceful, colorful, cheerful realm of pleasant and meaningful living."[3] It is precisely because such enduring—but superficial and limiting—notions of Buddhism and Tibet have some bases in historical and doctrinal truth that problems of religious violence have been at the center of Buddhist efforts to create meaningful discourses for themselves. This is particularly true in historical periods when Buddhist actors were endeavoring to create and maintain political structures. It is not just contemporary scholars who must struggle to place Buddhist violence in a nuanced context, but theoreticians throughout Buddhist history have contended with the polyvocal foundations of their own tradition.

My objective is to probe the ways in which rhetoric is employed to justify warfare and other forms of violence; how these arguments are couched in specifically Buddhist terms; and how these efforts are embedded in discourses that seem to have answered the evolving needs of the time period. In Foucault's terms, I will examine the ways in which discourses of truth are deployed to secure and express power.

This chapter focuses on the writings of the Fifth Dalai Lama, Ngag dbang blo bzang rgya mtsho (1617–1682), a key figure who not only distinguished himself as one of the more important historians of the seventeenth century, but who also ended up at the center of a war that served as a significant pivot point in Tibetan history. This war culminated in the unification of a large portion of Tibet, the defeat of his opponents, and his own ascent to political power. His religious sect, the dGe lugs school, simultaneously underwent a dramatic elevation in prestige, importance, and influence.

The Fifth Dalai Lama's attitudes toward warfare and violence can be fathomed by exploring how he describes such incidents in Tibetan history. Fortunately, he was a prolific author and wrote a wide range of historical, biographical, and autobiographical material; he thereby provided many examples for analysis. In particular, his highly motivated history of Tibet, *Song of the Queen of Spring: A Dynastic History*, provides insights into his thinking on Buddhist justifications for violence.[4]

That text was published in 1643, a critical time when the twenty-six-year-old reincarnate lama was working to fortify the gains his Mongolian allies had recently made on the battlefield. Beginning in 1635, pro–dGe lugs pa forces battled opponents of the Dalai Lama from far eastern Tibet to the edge of the Himalayas in the west. By 1642, they had subdued most of the outright opposition. In the view of dGe lugs partisans, the seeds of that war were sown in the latter part of the sixteenth century, when a period of disharmony began to manifest between the well-established rival bKa' brgyud school and the Dalai Lamas' own nascent dGe lugs school.[5] The two schools were increasingly in competition for patronage and adherents, particularly as the dGe lugs pas extended their influence into the gTsang region in western Tibet, a traditional stronghold of the bKa' brgyud school.

The dGe lugs pas perceived themselves as subject to systematic patterns of persecution at the hands of the bKa' brgyud pas. For example, the patronage tours of both the Second Dalai Lama, dGe 'dun rgya mtsho (1476–1542), and the Fourth Dalai Lama, Yon tan rgya mtsho (1589–1617), in gTsang and mNga' ris in western Tibet, were perceived as being hindered by pro–bKa' brgyud allies in gTsang. More significantly, in 1613, a bKa' brgyud monastery was built on the hillside above bKra shis lhun po monastery, which had been founded near Shigatse by the First Dalai Lama, dGe 'dun grub (1391–1474), in 1447. The words "Suppressor of bKra shis lhun po" were written above the gate, and boulders were rolled down from the hillside, damaging the dGe lugs monastery below. When Mongols retaliated by stealing livestock from the Karmapa (the most prominent incarnate lama in the bKa' brgyud school), forces allied with him attacked 'Bras spungs monastery. This was the home of the Dalai Lama, and the attack killed hundreds of dGe lugs pa monks.[6] Simultaneously, non-Buddhist religious rivals of the dGe lugs who were members of the indigenous religion of Tibet, Bon, were perceived to be persecuting the latter school in eastern Tibet. These Bon opponents were thought to be in alliance with the dGe lugs pas' bKa' brgyud enemies.[7]

Surviving the lifetime of the Fourth Dalai Lama, these violent trends emerged in a more virulent form during the Fifth Dalai Lama's youth. According to dGe lugs sources, many of their monasteries were forcibly converted to the bKa' brgyud school. Such grievances festered over a period of decades while new complaints accumulated, continuing to animate dGe lugs imaginations. New provocations from Bon opponents in eastern Tibet finally compelled pro–dGe lugs Mongols to act.[8]

In 1635, a Mongolian army under the leadership of the tribal chief Gushri Khan (1582–1654/1655) was assembled and launched with the objective of rectifying all of these perceived wrongs to the Dalai Lamas' school. Before we turn to the Fifth Dalai Lama's presentation of these events in the *Song of the Queen of Spring: A Dynastic History*, it will be illuminating to get a preview of how he comments on these events in his autobiography, the *Good Silk Cloth*, written decades later. There, he describes a meeting he held in the Potala Palace prior to the war with his own first regent, bSod nams Chos 'phel (1595–1657/1658), and with dKa' bcu dGe bsnyen don grub, the envoy from Gushri Khan, his Mongolian patron. The three men discussed how the Mongols would protect the Dalai Lama's dGe lugs interests in eastern Tibet from the persecution of the Bon chieftain from Be ri, whereupon the Mongolian military force would withdraw. The Fifth Dalai Lama writes:

> That night in the camp, Zhal ngo gave instructions to the messenger, dKa' bcu dge bsnyen don grub, in my presence. He said that Be ri should be cut at the root by all necessary means. Thereafter, Gushri Khan himself should return to the Blue Lake [on the northeastern frontier with Mongolia]. His two queens and a group of pilgrims were invited to come to Lhasa. I gave extensive advice against fomenting any sort of civil conflict. The next day, when dKa' bcu dge bsnyen don grub was departing, Zhal ngo rode out to dGa' ldan Khang gsar to give him provisions. Just the two of them rode along speaking for the time it takes to prepare tea twice. However, it hadn't occurred to me that the trill of the flute had changed into the whistle of an arrow.[9]

In other words, the Dalai Lama is claiming that his regent freelanced and changed the instructions that were conveyed to Gushri Khan and that this deception was responsible for launching a war that the Dalai Lama himself did not anticipate or authorize. In the event, the Mongolian forces did not return to northeastern Tibet after defeating the Be ri chieftain in eastern Tibet. Instead, they progressed to Lhasa and moved throughout dbU and gTsang in the west, where a broad-ranging war resulted in the defeat of most of the Dalai Lama's other Buddhist opponents, the deaths of many soldiers and civilians, and the establishment of dGe lugs hegemony.

In the wake of these bloody battles, members of the dGe lugs pa alliance were compelled to develop a discourse that configured events in a meaningful way, in order to satisfy public opinion and to contribute to a stable new social organization. This multipronged effort needed to justify and legitimize the recent warfare by placing it in the context of acceptable Buddhist values and recognizable narratives. The approach that evolved over a period of decades consisted of a new symbolic system, with the institution of the Dalai Lama at its apex. In its mature form, it had historical, ritual, narrative, architectural, and biographical components. In short, as Foucault would have it, the development of this discourse enabled the Dalai Lama and his cohorts "to exercise power... through the production of truth."

One of he first steps in creating this discourse was taken by the Fifth Dalai Lama with his composition of the *Song of the Queen of Spring*. In it, by retelling the history of Tibet, he did more than exercise the prerogative of the victor. In a sense, he was prosecuting the last battle of the war by placing the recently concluded conflict within a framework that made it meaningful and that exonerated him and justified his rule. The Dalai Lama's autobiography, *Good Silk Cloth*, was compiled throughout his life in three volumes, and supplemented by an additional three volumes which were composed by his last regent, sDe srid Sangs rgyas rgya mtsho (1653–1705). *Good Silk Cloth* was not published until 1692, a full decade after the former's death in 1682 and half a century after the pivotal events of 1642. With the fullness of time, these two authors knew how events had turned out and that they had been able to create a stable environment. From the comfortable vantage point of their fully articulated—and by then successful—mythology, they seem to have decided to distance the Dalai Lama from responsibility for the warfare of the 1630s and 1640s, denying that he had approved of the most consequential bloodshed. It may also be that, by that time, the elderly Dalai Lama had come to have second thoughts about the violence that had been unleashed in his name. It is evident, for example, that the Dalai Lama remained troubled by the human impact of the battles. A wide variety of the dreams and visions reported in the Fifth Dalai Lama's *Sealed and Secret Biography* demonstrate that he was often disturbed by specters of violence and war.[10]

However that may be, it is clear that, in contrast to his more seasoned reflections on the warfare of his younger years, he took great care to glorify Gushri Khan and to justify his war in the *Song of the Queen of Spring*, written just a year after the cessation of hostilities. In that text, he unequivocally trumpets his endorsement of his Mongolian patron's endeavors. He begins the description of Gushri Khan's exploits by identifying him as an emanation of Vajrapāni, the bodhisattva representing perfect yogic power.[11] He writes that, out of compassion for humanity, the bodhisattva "would take birth as a religious king, whereupon he would radiate a hundred rays of light in the ten directions." He goes on to say that even hearing the name of the dGe lugs school made the young khan happy, and he prostrated in the direction of Lhasa so often that his forehead became swollen. He is praised as having realized emptiness [107b–108a].[12]

Still in his twenties, before the wars that concern us came to fruition, Gushri Khan is described in the text as having settled a terrible conflict between rival Mongolian factions. As the Dalai Lama phrases it, the young warrior—moved by great compassion for other beings—plunged into "an overgrown forest of dissension between limitless numbers of people born in bad transmigration due to their murderous ways." As a sign of his transcendent status, Gushri Khan managed to sort out that quarrel, seemingly all by himself. Thereupon, the Dalai Lama cites a prophecy saying, "A dharma-protecting king, the second Srong btsan sgam po, has come" [108b]. King Srong btsan sgam po (617–649), a luminary of Tibet's imperial period, is credited with bringing Buddhism to Tibet in the seventh century. His significance in the Tibetan mind can hardly be overemphasized. In part, by suggesting that Gushri Khan was a latter-day echo of that seventh-century king, the Dalai Lama was evoking King Srong btsan sgam po's symbolic resonance as a protector and promoter of Buddhism. Below, we will discuss the symbolic assignment given to that king in the more sophisticated discourse of the Dalai Lama's later years.

If there is a more potent royal symbol to evoke in Tibet than King Srong btsan sgam po, it would be the legendary King Ge Sar of Ling, the paradigmatic martial hero, savior of Tibet, and exemplar of wise rule. Thus, it comes as no surprise that the Dalai Lama likens Gushri Khan to King Ge Sar [3b]. Leaving no symbolic opportunity unexploited, he also likens Gushri Khan to Buddha in the prologue verses [2a]. All of these rhetorical maneuvers are directed toward legitimizing Gushri Khan as a sanctified, righteous warrior in the cause of Buddhism.

But the Dalai Lama does not stop there. He also endeavors to frame the particular events of the wars leading up to 1642 in Buddhist terms. He provides a discourse that enables his audience to understand those events as pious actions, embedded in a righteous quest. For example, one of his primary antagonists, Hal ha Chog thu, was a Mongolian chieftain who had come from western Mongolia to the Blue Lake region in northeastern Tibet. It is said that "his mind was possessed by malevolent black spirits, due to which he implemented plans to undermine Buddhism in general and the teachings of Tsong kha pa[13] in particular." The Dalai Lama goes on to say that, as a result, Gushri Khan "gathered an army from his own region, with Buddhism as his only concern, and went to the Blue Lake in the first month of 1637." Here, the Dalai Lama evokes the resonant literary paradigm of the Indian epic the *Rāmāyaṇa*:

> Just as the powerful King Rāma dispatched the lord of Lanka, so [Gushri Khan] destroyed Chog thu and 40,000 troops, until only the name remained. He took control of the region up to the eastern edge of the lake and protected his subjects in happiness by way of

> a religio-political government. Gradually, the sun dawned in the domain of central Tibet, and Gushri Khan established a festival in which the stores of merit were enhanced. At the vajra seat of the Tibetan land in the Ra sa 'phrul snang Temple, he received the title and assumed the responsibilities of a great *dharmarāja* such that he came to stand above all other kingdoms. [108b–109a]

Here, the Dalai Lama not only embeds Gushri Khan's military exploits within a Buddhist narrative, but he intends to evoke, once again, an identity between Buddha and the khan with the analogy between the *vajra* seat of Bodhgaya and the Ra sa 'phrul snang Temple. Additionally, the khan is depicted as a *dharmarāja*, or a religious king (*chos rgyal*), a class of sovereign that is regarded as particularly just and righteous because they dedicate their rule to promoting the interests of Buddhism.

In 1639, Gushri Khan battled the Bon chieftain from Be ri, who is represented as oppressing Buddhism and only permitting the Bon religion to grow in Kham. "In the fifth Hor month of the Earth-Hare year of 1639," we are told, "Gushri Khan brought his forces down on top of Be ri, whereupon he seized most of the latter's subjects" [109a]. The Be ri coalition fell apart, and many of the principals were imprisoned. Now that the danger to Buddhism was overcome, according to the Dalai Lama, the lamas and leaders of the Sa skya, dGe lugs, Kar ma bKa' brgyud, 'Brug pa bKa' brgyud, sTag lung, and so forth were liberated from a dungeon and sent home. In this terse account of a very complex situation, Gushri Khan is depicted as an impartial supporter of a broad array of Tibetan Buddhist schools.

This interpretive move seems to be required by the general tenor of the Fifth Dalai Lama's argument justifying violence and warfare. It is one thing to deploy Buddhist imagery and narratives to justify the defense of the interests of Buddhists being persecuted by some malevolent non-Buddhist oppressor; it is quite another to legitimize sectarian conflicts between Buddhists. The Dalai Lama has a heightened sensitivity to this question, and he downplays the intrareligious basis of the most substantial warfare that took place leading up to the culmination of events in 1642. The battle against Chog thu and the Be ri chief were minor sideshows compared to the decisive battles that took place in dbU and gTsang between partisans of the Buddhist dGe lugs and bKa' brgyud schools. When the Dalai Lama reaches this part of the story, he merely mentions that Gushri deployed billions of troops and subjugated the land, but he makes no mention of who was defeated. He further obfuscates matters when he concludes by remarking that the kings and ministers of Tibet had to learn to bow humbly to Gushri Khan in 1642 [109b].

The Dalai Lama attempts to convey a tone of neutrality among Buddhists. This tone is in stark contrast to the manner in which this series of events was perceived by others at the time and in the decades and centuries that followed. In the eyes of non–dGe lugs pas, Gushri Khan's conquests and the ascendancy of the Dalai Lama as the paramount political force in the country were both permeated with sectarian agendas. Monasteries were seized and converted, land estates were reassigned to support dGe lugs institutions, the Karmapa was driven into exile, and the entire symbolic universe was reconfigured to feature the institution of the Dalai Lama at its core.

The Fifth Dalai Lama wrote *Song of the Queen of Spring* in an attempt to influence the way people perceived these conquests soon after they took place. It would do no good for the dGe lugs pa alliance to win on the battlefield but then be unable to legitimize that victory, thus the imperative to fashion a narrative that would be compelling in the court of public opinion. This fact goes a long way in explaining why the Dalai Lama rushed this historical work into print within a year of the 1642 victory. With an almost journalistic timeliness, he was compelled to shape perceptions in order to alter the course of events.

Yet the ideological split that the Dalai Lama was attempting to knit together remains in his text. He finds that he must address the essential partisan question. In the closing pages of the text, he comments fleetingly on the relationship between members of the dGe lugs and bKa' brgyud lineages:

> Gushri Khan became king over the three regions of Tibet.... Even though he had a strong commitment to maintaining an earnest respect for all tenet systems without distinction, the Karmapa's functionaries were unskilled in their behavior due to which the khan forcefully deployed forces up to the Kong po region in the east. [110a]

The Dalai Lama is careful not to blame the Karmapa himself, a figure as prestigious in the bKa' brgyud school as the Dalai Lama was then for the dGe lugs pas. But he does try to legitimize Gushri Khan's military action by portraying the people who surrounded the Karmapa as having behaved badly. The language is indirect and glosses over the real tensions, but he then attempts to fortify the notion that the khan is in the right by citing two additional prophecies legitimizing the Mongol.

In the concluding lines to the body of the text, he returns to a more explicitly pro–dGe lugs tone:

> Because of taking birth as the receptacle of the three secrets, imbued with the nectar of compassion of the great Conqueror Tsong kha pa, [Gushri Khan] fulfills the qualities of a king who transforms with a golden wheel all aspects of religio-political government. [110a]

The Fifth Dalai Lama skillfully narrates these events, shaping them to serve his own emerging agenda.

In the portions of the *Song of the Queen of Spring* examined here, the Dalai Lama does not explicitly employ the justification that particular acts of violence ought to be understood as beneficial and compassionate toward their target, but he makes such arguments elsewhere in the text.[14] Thus, the reader of the text would have felt that there was some implication that Gushri Khan's violence could be understood as a case of that sort. Still, the main thrust of the language surrounding the khan is directed toward justifying his warfare by virtue of his identity as a righteous religious-warrior king, a man who is rhetorically connected to many of the most potent emblematic figures in the Indo-Tibetan symbolic universe: Śākyamuni Buddha, King Srong btsan sgam po, King Ge sar, and others. Each of these figures is a sovereign on a religious mission and a transcendent agent intent on furthering Buddhism. As such, each is committed to promoting Buddhism even if it involves the commission of sanctified violence. In other words, because of who Gushri Khan is, his violence is justified.

As Rupert Gethin argues, the reason that violence is forbidden for conventional Buddhists is that it harms the agent mentally, fostering the very cognitive states that the practitioner seeks to overcome.[15] Yet, in this text, the Dalai Lama is suggesting that highly advanced Buddhist yogins may be able to undertake acts of violence that serve salutary ends without themselves experiencing afflictive emotions. Under certain circumstances, cases of murder, suicide, self-sacrifice, warfare, and other types of violence may be regarded as legitimate within Buddhist discourse so long as they are carried out by people capable of undertaking them without generating harmful mental attitudes. The Dalai Lama seems to have something of this sort in mind when he glorifies the many deeds of Gushri Khan that would, in another circumstance, be regarded as dreadful sins violating core Buddhist values. In the immediate aftermath of 1642, this may be as much as the Dalai Lama felt he could achieve with this history.

As the fully articulated discourse took shape in the following decades, the Dalai Lama and his regent sDe srid Sangs rgyas rgya mtsho endeavored to create a stable social structure through their exertion of power; a significant part of that effort was conducted through formulating a coherent paradigm. As Foucault points out:

> What makes power hold good, what makes it accepted, is simply the fact that it doesn't only weigh on us as a force that says no, but that it traverses and produces things, it induces pleasure, forms knowledge,

> produces discourse. It needs to be considered as a productive network which runs through the whole social body, much more than as a negative instance whose function is repression.[16]

The discourse they eventually created went far beyond what could have been accomplished in 1643, when the *Song of the Queen of Spring* was written. In the more mature mythology that was to develop over the coming decades, the Dalai Lama and his last regent placed great emphasis on an identification between the Dalai Lama lineage and Avalokiteśvara, the bodhisattva representing perfect compassion, whose special responsibility it is to protect and nurture Tibet. King Srong btsan sgam po, mentioned above as the sovereign responsible for introducing Buddhism to Tibet, is particularly important for followers of the oldest lineage of Tibetan Buddhism, the rNying ma school. He also stands as an icon of the religious and political unity of the Tibetan people that prevailed in the seventh century. It is little wonder then that King Srong btsan sgam po was seen as an emanation of the bodhisattva Avalokiteśvara.

Thus, Srong btsan sgam po and other supposed incarnations are repeatedly associated with the Dalai Lama lineage. This connection is most notable in the fourth volume of the Fifth Dalai Lama's biography, *Good Silk Cloth*, authored by the regent sDe srid Sangs rgyas rgya mtsho. The entirety of that volume is occupied with describing scores of previous incarnations of Avalokiteśvara in India and Tibet, leading up to and including accounts of the previous Dalai Lamas and culminating with a description of the last years of the fifth member of that lineage. The tone of this text is magical and miraculous, and it is meant to transport the reader with tales of the continual kindness and perpetual protection of the compassionate bodhisattva Avalokiteśvara, all in an effort to attribute the most beneficent associations to the Fifth Dalai Lama himself.[17]

Likewise, in the Fifth Dalai Lama's *Sealed and Secret Biography*, there are dozens of references to his visionary encounters with both King Srong btsan sgam po and Avalokiteśvara. In addition, he records frequent dreams and apparitions of Padmasaṃbhava (eighth century), the great shamanic yogin from India who is credited with subduing the indigenous spiritual forces in Tibet and turning them to the protection and support of Buddhism.[18] Like King Srong btsan sgam po, Padmasaṃbhava is a tremendously significant figure from the imperial period of Tibet, an era when Tibet was both powerful and united. The Fifth Dalai Lama's interest in Padmasaṃbhava was a consequence of the Indian's symbolic value, arising from his role in establishing Buddhism in Tibet. Additionally, the Dalai Lama was preoccupied with Padmasaṃbhava because of his personal devotional interest in the rNying ma school, with which that guru is most closely associated. The Dalai Lama had a variety of notable rNying ma teachers, and he incorporated many rNying ma teachings into his own personal practice. In addition, he employed a broad range of rNying ma symbols, rituals, and narratives from the imperial period in the discourse he developed to justify his own evolving political role in post-1642 Tibet. That imagery was particularly potent for him because it harked back to a time that Tibetans regarded as religiously and politically unified, when just and righteous religious kings (*chos rgyal, dharmarāja*) ruled, and the rNying ma doctrine taught by Padmasaṃbhava prevailed.[19]

The appropriation of Avalokiteśvara was perhaps the most consequential dimension of the Dalai Lama's evolving discourse. In the immediate aftermath of Gushri Khan's military victory of 1642, the Dalai Lama seems to have had less political authority than either his regent bSod nams Chos 'phel or Gushri Khan. Yet, this began to shift as the mythology began to take hold:

> One reason that between 1642 and 1653 the political power of only the Dalai Lama grew at the expense of the regent and the king may be considered to lie in the fact that this belief identifying the Dalai Lama as Avalokiteśvara gradually spread and gained wide acceptance.[20]

During the intervening period, the Dalai Lama frequently gave empowerments in the practice of Avalokiteśvara; he wrote biographies of the Third and Fourth Dalai Lamas, emphasizing themes that would fortify their identity as emanations of that bodhisattva; and he sponsored the restoration of monasteries and temples connected with King Srong btsan sgam po.[21]

In 1645, construction was begun on the Potala Palace, the most compelling architectural dimension of the emerging discourse. Named after Avalokiteśvara's mountain home in South India, the hillside location was particularly meaningful for the narrative being developed because King Srong btsan sgam po had constructed a small palace there nine centuries before. The Potala was sanctified to a degree by the restoration of an image said to have been used by the king in his devotions. This image had in the meanwhile made its way through the hands of many notables, including a period of time in Mongolian royal households. Gushri Khan arranged to have it returned to Tibet and to the hillside where Srong btsan sgam po had once dwelled.[22] As intended, the literally awe-inspiring visage of the Potala Palace, which dominates the Lhasa Valley, would have struck visitors as an otherworldly and arresting expression of power, particularly once phase two of the construction was completed by the regent in the 1690s.[23] The Dalai Lama fortified his position of power also by insinuating his mythology into the ancient geomantic ideology of the valley,[24] by configuring "a clearly defined group of guardian deities that protect the lineage,"[25] and by projecting authority in the international arena.[26] All of these efforts were directed toward creating a discourse with the broadest appeal possible throughout Tibet.

These dimensions of the mature discourse took years to conceive, deploy, and implement before they had the effect of placating resentments and winning allegiance. In the short term, just after the war, the Dalai Lama needed a way to soothe the most immediate opposition to the dGe lugs ascent to power. As the upstart and recently successful usurper of a stable government, the dGe lugs pas of the 1640s had an interest in representing the violence authored in their name as spiritually legitimized through the status of Gushri Khan as a bodhisattva. However, the dGe lugs pas of the 1670s and 1680s, by then in control of power themselves, were more concerned with promoting stability. Consequently, within this elaborate paradigm, the warfare that brought the dGe lugs pas to power began to be described in a new way. The later discourse pays greater attention to the types of concerns that are encountered in standard just-war theory, elaborated by both Christians and Muslims once they found a need to create governments. That is to say, the Dalai Lama and sDe srid Sangs rgyas rgya mtsho expended considerable efforts to represent the battles as being responsible reactions to others' improper actions. Hence, it is asserted and forcefully argued that the bKa' brgyud pas were oppressing the dGe lugs pas, the gTsang pas were obstructing the Dalai Lamas, the Bon pos were attacking dGe lugs interests, and so forth. These types of arguments are entirely absent from *Song of the Queen of Spring*. As the new dGe lugs discourse became a comprehensive legitimizing ideology, there would be no violence authorized merely by the charismatic identity of the agent performing it. Now, violence would be legitimized only if it were a response to just causes.

In the Dalai Lama's earliest efforts to configure the warfare that had been prosecuted in his name, he tried to legitimize the disparities in power the war had revealed, and he tried to embed those disequlibriums in a political discourse that created new religious, social, and economic forms. In the mature discourse that he and his regent developed subsequently, they found that their initial successes had fashioned a new reality. This in turn summoned a new narrative about how power would be arranged. This new production of truth would occupy the balance of his life and would preoccupy his regent thereafter. With efforts that were architectural, linguistic, ritual, symbolic, and otherwise, they worked to solidify a new pattern of power relations that had been initiated by the war. Unfortunately for them, the very things they did to concretize this new narrative also set in motion forces that would eventually displace and overturn the pattern that the Dalai Lama had envisioned; thus, this account is just a snapshot in a genealogy of power.

NOTES

1. Michel Foucault, "Two Lectures," in *Power/Knowledge: Selected Interviews and Other Writings 1972–1977* (New York: Pantheon, 1980), 89–90.

2. Ibid., 93.

3. Robert Thurman offers these romantic notions in Marylin M. Rhie and Robert A. F. Thurman, *Wisdom and Compassion: The Sacred Art of Tibet* (New York: Abrams, 1991), 22:

> From the 7th century on, Tibetans became more and more interested in Buddhism. Their own histories credit the Buddhist movement with giving them a whole new way of thinking, feeling, and acting that eventually transformed their personal and social lives. It turned their society from a fierce grim world of war and intrigue into a peaceful, colorful, cheerful realm of pleasant and meaningful living.

4. Ngag dbang blo bzang rgya mtsho (Fifth Dalai Lama), *rgyal rabs dpyid kyi rgyal mo'i glu dbyangs/Song of the Queen of Spring: A Dynastic History* (Lhasa, 1643; reprint, Gangtok, Sikkim, India: Sikkim Research Institute of Tibetology, 1991).

5. Unless otherwise noted, the outline of the events leading up to Gushri Khan's 1642 victory is drawn from chapters 6 and 7 of volume 1 of Tsepon W. D. Shakabpa, *bod kyi srid don rgyal rabs* (Kalimpong, India: Shakabpa House, 1976). My annotated translation of this comprehensive work is *One Hundred Thousand Moons: An Advanced Political History of Tibet* (Leiden: Brill, 2009). Hereafter, this title is referred to as Shakabpa, *One Hundred Thousand Moons.*

6. Shakabpa, *One Hundred Thousand Moons,* 1:361.

7. Ngag dbang blo bzang rgya mtsho (Fifth Dalai Lama), *za hor gyi bande ngag dbang blo bzang rgya mtsho'i 'di snang 'khrul pa'i rol rtsed rtogs brjod kyi tshul du bkod pa du kU la'i gos bzang/The Good Silk Cloth, the Play of Illusion, Setting Forth the Biography of Ngag dbang blo bzang rgya mtsho, the Monk of Za hor* (Lhasa: Tibetan People's Printing Press, 1991), 1:155ff. Hereafter, this title is referred to as Fifth Dalai Lama, *Good Silk Cloth.*

8. Fifth Dalai Lama, *Good Silk Cloth,* 1:197–198.

9. Ibid., 1:194.4–11.

10. The author would like to thank Janet Gyatso for raising this provocative point. For a thorough analysis of this text, see Samten Karmay, *Secret Visions of the Fifth Dalai Lama: The Gold Manuscript in the Fournier Collection* (London: Serindia, 1988).

11. A bodhisattva is an advanced practitioner of Buddhism who has approached the level of a buddha's insight without actually completing the soteriological objective of liberation. Such a figure is thought to reincarnate repeatedly in order to serve other sentient beings. Such altruistically motivated spiritual heroes populate the imagination of Mahāyāna Buddhism, particularly in Tibet. The Dalai Lamas are regarded as emanations of the bodhisattva Avalokiteśvara, the embodiment of perfect compassion.

12. Hereafter, I will use square brackets to indicate page numbers in the Fifth Dalai Lama's *Song of the Queen of Spring.*

13. Tsong kha pa (1357–1419) is regarded as the founder of the dGe lugs school.

14. I explore acts of compassionate violence found in the Fifth Dalai Lama's *Song of the Queen of Spring* in an earlier and overlapping version of this chapter: Derek F. Maher, "The Rhetoric of War in Tibet: Toward a Buddhist Just War Theory," *Journal of Political Theology* 9:2, 2008, 179–191. In that article, I argue that the Dalai Lama is playing off canonical narratives about sanctified violence committed by the Buddha in his previous lives, a paradigm that is elaborated in a variety of *jātaka* tales about the Buddha's previous births and in *sūtras* taught by the Buddha.

15. Rupert Gethin, "Buddhist Monks, Buddhist Kings, Buddhist Violence: On the Early Buddhist Attitudes to Violence," in *Religion and Violence in South Asia: Theory and Practice*, ed. J. R. Hinnells and Richard King (London: Routledge, 2007).

16. Foucault, "Truth and Power," in *Power/Knowledge*, 119.

17. *Sans-rGyas rGya-mTSHo: Life of the Fifth Dalai Lama*, vol. 4, pt. 1: *The Fourth Volume Continuing the Third Volume of the Ordinary, Outer Life Entitled "The Fine Silken Dress," of My Own Gracious Lama, Ńag-dBan Blo-bZan rGya-mTSHo*, trans. Zahiruddin Ahmad (New Delhi: International Academy of Indian Culture, 1999).

18. Karmay, *Secret Visions of the Fifth Dalai Lama.*

19. The Fifth Dalai Lama's connections to the rNying ma lineage have been deftly elaborated by Georges B. J. Dreyfus in his article "The Shuk-den Affair: History and Nature of a Quarrel," *Journal of the International Association of Buddhist Studies* 21.2 (1998): 227–270.

20. Ishihama Yumiko, "On the Dissemination of the Belief in the Dalai Lama as a Manifestation of the Bodhisattva Avalokiteśvara," *Acta Asiatica* 64 (1993): 44.

21. Karmay, *Secret Visions of the Fifth Dalai Lama*; and Yumiko, "Dissemination of the Belief in the Dalai Lama as a Manifestation of the Bodhisattva Avalokiteśvara."

22. Shakabpa, *One Hundred Thousand Moons*, 1:429–430.

23. Anne Chayet, "The Potala, Symbol of the Power of the Dalai Lamas," in *Lhasa in the Seventeenth Century: The Capital of the Dalai Lamas*, ed. Francoise Pommaret (Leiden: Brill, 2003), 39–52.

24. Anne-Marie Blondeau and Yonten Gyatso, "Lhasa: Legend and History," in *Lhasa in the Seventeenth Century*, ed. Pommaret, 15–38.

25. Amy Heller, "The Great Protector Deities of the Dalai Lamas," in *Lhasa in the Seventeenth Century*, ed. Pommaret, 81–98.

26. Fifth Dalai Lama, *Good Silk Cloth*, 1:343–416; Shakabpa, *One Hundred Thousand Moons*, 1:433–440; and Zahiruddin Ahmad, *Sino-Tibetan Relations in the Seventeenth Century* (Rome: Instituto Italiano per il Medio ed Estremo Oriente, 1970), 166–191.

4

Legalized Violence: Punitive Measures of Buddhist Khans in Mongolia

Vesna A. Wallace

The second conversion of the Mongols to Buddhism took place in the latter part of the sixteenth century. Since then until the first decades of the twentieth century, Mongolian Buddhist khans, nobles, and Buddhist monastics engaged more than once in acts of violence on behalf of their Buddhist faith. Their acts of violence manifested in various ways: the forceful replacement of Shamanism with Buddhism as a state religion, engagement in Buddhist sectarian wars, the implementation of harsh penal systems, and so on. The first violent action took place when the Khutukhtu Setsen Khung Taiji (1540–1586), the ruler of the Ordos Mongols, along with his relative Altan Khan (1508–1582), the ruler of Tümeds, initiated the Mongols' conversion to Tibetan dGe lugs pa Buddhism and then attempted to institutionalize it among the southwestern Mongols. He did this by mercilessly vanquishing Mongolian shamans, burning shamanic spirit figurines (*onghons*), and introducing severe penalties, ranging from the confiscation of people's entire property to exile or execution.

Those who demonstrated irreverence for Buddhist monks or who continued to perform the native funerary practices of blood sacrifice, to sponsor shamanic performances, or to make shamanic blood offerings on the first, eighth, and fifteenth days of a month were subjected to brutal punishments or executed. Setsen Khung Taiji published decrees requiring that, in every household, shamanic spirit figurines be replaced with six-armed Mahākālas and animal sacrifices be replaced with bloodless offerings, fasting, and alms giving. His use of harsh force in implementing this exclusivist policy was based on his political aspirations. He sought to reestablish the dual governance of the Buddhist church and the state as it once existed in the relations between Qubilai Khan (1215–1294) and his imperial preceptor (*guoshi*), 'Phags pa Bla ma of the Tibetan Sakya order.

To revive this principle of dual governance, which had pervaded the Mongolian political mentality of the earlier dynasty, Setsen Khung Taiji initiated Altan Khan's conversion to Tibetan Buddhism and Altan Khan's meeting with the high-ranking Tibetan dGe lugs pa *lama*, bSod nams rGya mtsho, who conferred upon Altan Khan the title of "universal emperor" (Skt. *cakravartin*). He also declared Altan Khan to be an incarnation of Qubilai Khan. Due to these two acts, bSod nams rGya mtsho was able to link Altan Khan (who lacked genealogical connection with the Golden Clan of Chinggis Khan) to Chinggis's lineage and to legitimize Altan Khan's power.

Likewise, in order to sanction the dual political enterprise by means of the imperial Mongolian past, Khutukhtu Setsen Khung Taiji brought to light and edited the *White History of the Tenfold Virtuous Dharma* (*Arban Buyantu Nom-un Chaγaan Teükei*), which he dated to the late thirteenth century and attributed to Qubilai Khan. The *White History* gives an account of the policy of dual law as initially implemented in India, then brought into Tibet, and ultimately introduced in Mongolia in the thirteenth century by Qubilai Khan on the initiative of his imperial preceptor, 'Phags pa Bla ma. It traces the Buddhist governance based on the principle of dual law among the Mongols to Chinggis Khan himself, whom it characterizes as a consummate follower of the *Buddha* Dharma. This characterization illustrated the desire of the newly converted Mongolian Buddhist nobility for the unification of the church and state, which viewed Qubilai Khan and 'Phags pa Bla ma as personifications of the unified civil and religious rules. In advocating governance based on the principle of dual law, *The White History* points to the indestructibility of the dual law by comparing Buddhist teachings to a silken knot that cannot be loosened and the laws of the khan to a golden yoke that cannot be crushed. Thus, where the law is enduring, the Dharma and the State will be lasting. Urging rulers to eradicate those antagonistic to the Dharma, the *White History* provided Khutukhtu Setsen Khung Taiji and Altan Khan with justification for eliminating the shamans who performed forbidden blood rituals, as well as those who sponsored them. While justifying his violence against those engaging in shamanic practices in light of 'Phags pa's guidance on building an empire based upon firm Buddhist principles, Setsen Khung Taiji conveniently ignored 'Phags pa's instructions, provided in *Explanation of the Subject of Cognition* (*Shes bya rab gsal*). *Explanation of the Subject of Cognition* was composed in 1278 at the request of

Qubilai Khan's son Jingim. In *Advice to the Prince Jibigtemür, the So-called Jewel Rosary* (Tib. *rGyal bu ji big de mur la gdam du byas nor bu'i phren ba*),[1] 'Phags pa appealed for the abolishment of capital punishment. He asserted: "He who washes out dirt from his cloth is wise, but not he who burns it along with the dirt."[2] In addition, *Explanation of the Subject of Cognition* encouraged Qubilai Khan not to resort to violence, on the grounds that violence is never effective in strengthening royal power.[3]

By ignoring this advice and implementing the aforementioned measures, Setsen Khung Taiji and Altan Khan set an example for other Mongol rulers. Appropriating the titles of *cakravartins* and *dharmarājas,* they subsequently attempted to restore the principle of dual governance whenever they saw a need to consolidate their power, because the principle enabled them to justify using violent methods in their struggle for political centralization and religious unification. Indeed, the *White History* advises state administrators to protect the Dharma and the state by implementing harsh measures when needed:

> If a monk breaks his precepts, disrobe him. Tie his hands tightly and paint his face with ink. Place a black flag on his head. Put a rope around him and beat him with a golden stick on his buttocks. Then take him around the temple clockwise three times. Afterwards, banish him to a faraway place.
>
> If one steals, blind his eyes. If one tells a lie, cut his tongue. If one injures the state, take his life.
>
> For a common person, a kingdom is like a black sword. When a khan passes away, free all prisoners as [a sign of] mercy. Afterwards, if someone commits a crime, imprison him. There are three kinds of prisoners who will not be set free: one who killed his spiritual mentor, one who drew blood from the Buddha's body out of harmful intention, and one who harmed the state out of poisonous intentions. Those who committed any of these [crimes] will not have room in, this and another world.[4]

While the author of the *White History* perceived punishment for unforgivable crimes as deserved retribution, he considered other forms of punishment to be preventive measures—means of facilitating the prosperity of the *Buddha* Dharma and the state.

The ideas expounded in the *White History* echoed in the first Mongol law, the *Altan Khan's Law* (*Altan Khany Tsaaz*). The *Altan Khan's* praises the khan as the victorious, supreme ruler, an incarnation of the bodhisattva Āryabala

(Avalokiteśvara), and a protector and pacifier of all beings within the six realms of existence. It speaks of Altan Khan's implementation of the dual law as a unification of the indestructible *vajra* and the Golden Yoke. The *Altan Khan's Law* regards this unification as the khan's means of facilitating the invincibility of the state and as his method of revealing and teaching the path of peace to the beings living in the deep darkness of ignorance, who are acquiring sin and neglecting virtue. This view served Altan Khan in two ways: first, it justified the forceful conversion of his Tümeds to Buddhism; second, it justified implementing harsh penalties upon administrative leaders (and anyone else) who failed to uphold the dual law within his administrative unit. Altan Khan saw these penalties to be in conformity with those imposed by the *dharmarāja*, lord Yama himself.[5]

The later Mongolian author Tserenjav justified this stand on punishment in his *Notes on Important Words Selected for the Ordained and the Laity* (early twentieth century).[6] In this work, Tserenjav mentions a dialogue between a teacher and a disciple. The disciple asks the question, "How does one distinguish the teaching of the Buddha from that of the king's State?" The teacher replies that the principle of abandoning one's own ten non-virtues is the teaching of the Buddha, while causing others to abandon the ten non-virtues is the teaching of the state. Hence, both strive for the same goal but use different methods. For this reason, dual governance is to be understood as a sharp double-edged sword, whose two edges are the integrated state and religious laws that cut through the faults of a mundane life. It is evident that, for those who supported the principle of dual law, this type of integrated governance (one utilizing the methods of inner, spiritual development and those of civil improvement) was indispensable. It accomplished both the strengthening of the state and the spiritual purification of the nation.

This view is also advocated in the work entitled *The Pure Morality of People* (*Ard Tümnii Ariun Yoson*), composed in 1923 by Darpa Pandita of Ar Khalkha. It is further expanded upon in the text composed by Miggiddorj (Mi bsKyod rDo rJe) called *The Mirror That Perfects the Pure Morality of People* (Tib. *Sa mtha'i btzun gzugs ban snyoms las pa*). According to these two texts, the public principles of state governance promote the moral discipline of the individual and of the nation as a whole; the two texts complement and support private religious practice, which aims at the elimination of one's own mental afflictions and the root of all social evils. Thus, the Buddhist principle of dual governance presumes that the pursuit of happiness depends as much on the common welfare as on individual happiness; it thereby depends on the policies of the state. In lieu of this, it sees itself as a tool for achieving the social purpose of personal and common welfare. In accordance with these views on dual governance,

Buddhist legal theorists viewed punishment as having two principal aims: the moral regeneration of the person and the prevention of crime. If the aim of law is to make people virtuous, then it is permissible for the state to legislate against potentially dangerous or harmful actions, for the benefit of those being coerced.

Khutukhtu Setsen Khung Taiji's extreme measures against indigenous Mongolian practices conveyed the message that at times it is necessary for a Buddhist ruler to sanction acts of violence for the sake of establishing the Dharma and for securing the inner stability of the state. As attested in the codes of law instituted by later Mongolian rulers, this message echoed for a long time in the minds of Buddhist legislators and in the penal systems they established. Following the instructions given in the *White History*, which endorses the institutionalization of the Buddha Dharma and the enactment of firm laws by the khan, the Mongol rulers severely punished those who disobeyed their religious and secular ordinances.

This inculcation of virtue through legislation seems to contradict the view expressed in early Buddhist texts that laws come into existence when virtue among the people is in decline and when the Dharma deteriorates. For example, in the *Bhaddali sutta* of the *Majjhima Nikāya*, the Buddha states that when the basis for moral defilements manifests, it is time to lay down rules to ward off those taints—but not before an event occurs that requires the formulation of an appropriate rule.[7] Similarly, the later originators of Mongolian legal codes that inculcate virtue either implicitly or explicitly justified their legislation and harsh punitive measures on the basis of moral degeneration among the Mongols.

Although a prohibition of shamanic practices continued into subsequent centuries, as evidenced in the *Mongol-Oirat Code* enacted in 1640, the earlier harsh penalties for those practices were reduced to more reasonable fines of animals. However, other brutal and gruesome punishments, either inherited from the past or introduced by Manchu rulers into the Mongolian penal system, continued until 1921, when the Mongolian revolutionary government was formed. Most violent punishments were dispensed primarily for civil crimes, but brutal beatings were also legislated by the state for breaching Buddhist practices and etiquette. The harsh punishments prescribed in various penal codes were often justified indirectly with opening eulogies to legislators, many of whom were recognized as high, incarnate lamas (*khutukhtus*) and living buddhas (*khuvilgans*); they were praised for being accomplished in virtue and wisdom and for being endowed with unbiased compassion.

The punitive statutes instituted by Tüshetü Khan and other dignitaries of Khalkha in 1728 were inserted in the earlier version of "The Khalkha Regulations of the Western Khüree" (*Baruun Khüreenii Khalkh Juram*). These statutes end with an explanation of the pure motivation and virtuous mindset in which they were enacted. The penal codes also often begin with prayers to the buddhas and bodhisattvas for the spiritual and social well-being of the nation because their authors intended to point out the virtue-centered character of the contents of the penal codes and of those who enacted them.[8] There is a strong resemblance of these opening salutations and prayers to those in the more pronouncedly religious works of Buddhist literature dealing with subjects of philosophy, ritual, and the like. This resemblance suggests that the authors of these penal systems considered their work to be their sacred duty and their codes an exclusive type of religious Buddhist text. Another possible reason behind this is that a virtue-centered punitive system requires trust in the ethical capacities of the khans and legislators dedicated to the Buddha Dharma, regardless of how cruel they may appear. Its virtuous character renders it as a just law; it also explains and justifies the khan's use of coercive and uncompromising power.

Mongol lawmakers assumed the role of protectors of the Buddha Dharma and the state, instituted measures that protected monastic properties, defined the positions and privileges of Buddhist clergy in society, and regulated the conduct of ordained Buddhists and their interactions with lay communities and state authorities. For example, according to the "Khalkha Regulations," attacks on monasteries were punishable by exile and the confiscation of serfs if the offender was a nobleman. If the attacker was a commoner, however, punishments included the death penalty and confiscation of property. By legislating social and ritual practices that were in accordance with Buddhist teachings and monastic rules and by introducing penal measures for the infractions of both monks and laypeople, Mongolian legislators converted Buddhist teachings and practices into state law.

Similarly, when the Manchu Qing dynasty conquered Mongolia in the seventeenth century, the Manchu rulers identified their roles as Tantric *cakravartins* and emanations of the dark-blue bodhisattva Mañjuśrı (whose iconographic presentation appears in a semi-ferocious form). The Manchu rulers declared themselves to be the fervent guardians of Mongolian Buddhism. Under this pretense, they instituted the *Mongolian Code of Laws* (Mong. *Mongol Tsaazyn Bichig*, or *Menggu Luli*) in 1643, which underwent several revisions. It became increasingly harsh in regulating both secular and religious matters; under Emperor Qianlong's rule (1736–1796), capital sentences and penal exiles increased and corporal punishments became widespread.

The traditional Mongolian form of bloodless execution consisted of breaking the person's spine by bending it backward in the shape of a bow (*khövchdön alakh*) and subsequently strangling the person from behind. In addition, the

Manchu rulers applied two other forms of the death penalty not previously practiced among the Mongols: decapitation (*tsavchin alakh*) and cutting the culprit's body into pieces (*ogtchin alakh*). The property of those lawbreakers who were sentenced to one of these forms of execution would also be confiscated and their families enslaved and given as awards to others. The crimes for which the aforementioned death penalties were dispensed ranged from illegal sable hunting and illegal collecting or purchasing of ginseng, to intentional murder, robbery, the theft of large herds, arson, the desecration of graves, a commoner's intimate relations with a wife of a nobleman, and so on. In all cases that resulted in the death penalty, the final decision was made by the imperial emanation of Mañjuśrı himself. His function in this matter resembled that of the lord Yama, who is depicted in the *Saddharmasmṛtyupasthāna Sūtra* as ordering his servants to mutilate and hack to pieces the body of the guilty party, who was destined to this type of karmic retribution. An appeal for a pardon or for a change of the capital sentence was successful only if the person sentenced to capital punishment was a wealthy nobleman; he could replace his death sentence with a large fine, such as a herd of horses. During this period, juridical standardization of punitive measures was introduced into the Mongolian legal system. Two extant documents from this period, "Having the Red Cheek" (*Ulaan Khatsart*) and "Having the Broken Face" (*Khugarkhai Nüürt*), contain records of cases that attest to this fact and to the cruelty of the penal system at that time.

Following the fall of the Qing dynasty, the autonomous Mongolian Bogd Khan State was established in 1911. The Eighth Jebtsundamba Bogdo Gegeen ascended to the throne as absolute monarch and as the "Holder of the Power of the Church and State." As the embodiment of dual governance, he held two seals: one for religious affairs and one for state affairs. The inscription on his seals for religious affairs read: "The Golden Seal of Jebtsundamba, the Disseminator of Dharma, the Bestower of Happiness to Sentient Beings, the Omniscient, and the Most Sublime." *The Laws and Regulations to Actually Follow* (Mong. *Jinkhene Yavakh Dagaj Khuuly Dürem*)[9] were inaugurated by the order of the Eighth Jebtsundamba Khutukhtu in 1913. Under his auspices, the two types of execution previously introduced by Manchu rulers were replaced with execution by gun. However, armed attacks on monasteries and robberies in which the number of stolen animals exceeded twenty or thirty were still punishable by breaking the spine of the person who orchestrated the attack or robbery. Likewise, other forms of legalized brutality continued in various forms of interrogation methods and punitive actions. For instance, there were nine types of torture inherited from the Qing period as legally sanctioned means of extracting a confession from the accused: (1) flogging with a stick for up to fifty times, (2) beating with a long club for up to a hundred times, (3) beating the face with shoe soles for up to forty times, (4) tying the hands together with a narrow and wet rope, (5) trampling on the accused as he knelt on sharp pieces of wood or broken stones with a round stick placed behind his knees, (6) tying the hands with a rope and suspending him from a ceiling, (7) bolting his arms and legs to a thick and long piece of wood, (8) burning designated areas of his back and thighs with a large stick of burning incense, and (9) crushing his hands and feet in a special device until they were permanently damaged. The extent of these tortures was carefully orchestrated to ensure that the accused would suffer enough to confess but would not die during the interrogation. However, oral histories and well-kept archives from this period inform us that it was not uncommon for a person subjected to these interrogation methods to die within a week after the tortures ended.[10]

In the case of litigations in which it was difficult to determine which of the contesting parties was telling the truth, both parties were subjected to the humiliating ritual called *shakhaa*, in which they were stripped naked and forced to crawl beneath objects considered by the Mongols to be inauspicious, such as women's underwear stained by menstrual blood, filthy socks and other dirty clothing, discarded animal bones, and old, used ropes hanging on a string. The person whose body did not touch any of these objects was declared truthful; the other contestant was punished in accordance with the degree of his offense.

During this period of theocratic monarchy, other punishments for civil and religious infractions ranged from religious penances and fines in animals to harsh beatings and floggings, shackling in a cangue for up two years, burying a criminal in the ground while still alive, the exile of his entire family to southern China, the death penalty, forced labor, slavery, and so on. Recorded judicial cases from this period reveal that the judiciary administration, which consisted of lay and monastic nobles, was becoming increasingly biased in favor of the Mongolian nobility, whose punishments tended to be much lighter than those of commoners. They could be fined in animals, receive temporary salary cuts, and be demoted from official posts in lieu of execution, beatings, and exile. The Russian ethnographer Pozdneyev, who visited Mongolia in the late nineteenth century, mentions a case in which a Mongol noble (*taiji*) punished one of his serf's sons for not making adequate progress in his studies as a Buddhist novice by tying him naked outside the tent during a winter night. When the boy died as a consequence, the nobleman was merely fined eighteen animals.[11] The same class-based bias was also common among ordained monks within monasteries. When, in the year 1920, lamas of Amarbayasgalant monastery filed a collective complaint against their proctor for his cruel beatings, breaking lamas' heads, drawing their blood, and penalizing them with unrealistic fines for any trivial infraction, their complaints were ignored. After many lamas left the monastery, the proctor was merely demoted from his post.[12]

Other recorded cases reveal similar stories of high-ranking lamas from the families of nobles causing the deaths of lower-ranking monks who had been implicated in a theft. Lower-ranking monks were severely beaten or delivered to the Ministry of Affairs for execution if they stole an object belonging to the Jebtsundamba's private treasury. Those who publicly showed their irreverence for the Jebtsundamba were put to death. The Jebtsundamba was already losing the respect of Mongols of all classes because of his vices and extravagant lifestyle. As reported by Boryn Jambal, a lower-ranking monk at that time, the last such case occurred in 1921, just before the overthrow of the theocratic government. A lama by the name of Damdinsüren was executed for calling the Eighth Jebtsundamba "a wretched Tibetan beggar who has wandered here."[13] Since in all cases of the death penalty, the final decision was made by the Eighth Jebtsundamba, the Bestower of Happiness to All Sentient Beings, himself, it is safe to conclude that Damdinsüren's death sentence was authorized by the Jebtsundamba as well.

Grigorri Efimovich, who visited Mongolia in the late nineteenth century, noticed that ordinary, lower-ranking monks were drafted into the military and border guard services while still wearing their monastic robes.[14] The legal employment of monks in services requiring the use of weapons attests to the dual standard of the theocratic government. In 1913, the government enacted a state law that required monks to strictly follow monastic discipline; the government authorized penalties for monks that included beatings, shackling into a cangue, and animal fines for such "crimes" as letting their hair grow, wearing layman's clothing, consuming alcohol, gambling, leaving their monastic quarters without a designated permit, receiving women into their living quarters, and so forth.

All of the aforementioned cruel policies and unfair judicial practices of the theocratic government became crucial factors in its demise. Newly emerging political forces in the country were able to use these cruel and unfair practices as propaganda against the current theocratic form of governance. During the Eighth Jebtsundamba's lifetime, as soon as the provisional people's government was formed, it implemented the separation of the Buddhist church from the state; in addition, it abolished corporal tortures and punishments, serfdom, slavery, and the institution of a standing army.

The extremely harsh punitive measures that the Mongolian and Manchu *cakravartins* implemented made them quite dissimilar to the Indian Mahāyāna ideal of righteous and merciful kings of Dharma, custodians of the peaceful Dharma-*cakra*. They were more similar to Indra of the Vedas, the irresistible warrior and monarch who dispensed his authority by fierce means. Indra attained universal sovereignty by might and power, uncompromisingly annihilating his enemies with his dreadful *cakra*. Like Ge Sar (Mong. Geser), who was considered an incarnation of the god Indra in one of the Mongolian versions of the Ge Sar epic, Mongols and Manchus were intent on annihilating those whom they regarded as enemies of good.

By implementing fierce penal systems in order to maintain inner stability in their kingdoms and empires, the Mongol and Manchu methods of ruling strongly resembled that of the Indian Brahmanic conception of kingship, which was often argued against and was contrasted with the Buddhist concept of kingship in Indian Buddhist Pāli and Sanskrit sources. However, it was not the teachings of the *dharmaśāstras* that Mongol or Manchu rulers tried to emulate, but the *Golden Light Sūtra* (Skt. *Saddharma Prabhāsottama Sūtra*), which attributes divine origins to earthly kings and insists on the loyalty of their subjects. This means of legitimating their sovereignty appealed to the Manchu and Mongol rulers. Therefore, it was not by accident that Altan Khan, when he initiated the conversion of southern Mongols to Buddhism, ordered the first block printing of this *sūtra* in Mongolia; he was the first Mongol khan to ritually sanctify it in the manner that Buddhist statues were sanctified.

Certain *sūtras* of the Nikāyas[15] merely endorsed the attempts made by secular authorities to prevent crime by economic measures and to rehabilitate criminals. In contrast, the *Golden Light Sūtra*, like several other Mahāyāna sources, encourages a king not to overlook evil deeds but to punish the wrongdoers. However, among the Mahāyāna sources dealing with the topic of kingship, *The Golden Light Sūtra* is perhaps the most adamant about the king's duty to destroy evil deeds and inflict penalties on the evildoers in conformity with their crimes. If a king were to ignore any evil deed and neglect his royal duty, lawlessness and wickedness would increase, unfavorable asterisms and planets would rule, meteor showers would fall, evil demons would arise, and natural disasters, diseases, and foreign armies would ruin his kingdom. Likewise, the chief gods in the Trayaṃstriṃśa heaven would become wrathful, because the king's neglect of duty would cause their dwellings to burn. Therefore, the king would be separated from his loved ones and eventually become lawless himself. A king's duty to punish evildoers and to reward those who do well exemplifies the consequences of good and bad actions; therefore, a king's lawlessness would undermine the universal law of karma and consequently disturb the laws of nature in the cosmos.[16] Thus, the *Golden Light Sūtra* advocates a conceptual overlap between law and morality—the idea that there are necessary moral constraints on the content of the law, which makes the law just.

It is unlike certain Mahāyāna sources (such as *Daśacakra Mahāyāna Sūtra*, Nāgārjuna's *Rājaparikathāratnamālā*, and others), which argue for a fair and compassionate penal system based on the king's paternal sentiments for his subjects, one that excludes capital punishment, mutilation, or injury to the offender's sense faculties.[17] Rather, the *Golden Light Sūtra* does not specify the punishments that a Buddhist king may or may not apply; it leaves room for multiple interpretations concerning the degrees of punishments the ruler may implement in his task of upholding the law. It indirectly suggests that punishment enforces not only the law of a given society but also the laws of nature. For these reasons, the Inner Mongolian author Rashipuntsag (Rashipungsug) referred to the *Golden Light Sūtra* in his work *Crystal Rosary* (*Bolor Erikhe*, 1774–1775), declaring that Dharma laws do not prevent one from punishing criminals. He argued against Confucians who claimed that the state could be ruled only by means of secular laws because the law of Dharma was too weak to punish criminals, because it advocates compassion.[18]

In many ways, the *Golden Light Sūtra*'s description of the consequences of a king's failure to uphold the law resembles those provided in the *dharmaśāstras* and the *Mahābhārata*. This resemblance suggests a possible common inspiration for these texts, one whose influence extended as far as Inner Asia and which facilitated the justification of various forms of penal violence by Mongol and Manchu khans.

In conclusion, one could say that the justification for various forms of penal violence on the part of Mongolian Buddhist lawmakers and their apologists rests in part on the presupposition that the offender (to some extent) had the freedom to make moral decisions to commit his offense and was therefore morally responsible for breaking the law. If the offender did not have freedom in making moral decisions, it would be impossible to prevent his future crimes through deterrence based on fear of punishment or through moral rehabilitation—in which case, a penal system would be useless. Thus, Mongolian Buddhist lawmakers and their apologists implicitly suggest that the Buddhist view of an individual's actions, antecedent choices, and decisions (as the effects of particular causal chains) does not entail that the individual's actions are determined by their causes and conditions, but are only made probable by them.

NOTES

1. In these two texts, 'Phags pa elevates Mongol khans, beginning with Chinggis Khan, to the status of Buddhist universal emperors (*cakravartin*). Similarly, in his *Counsels to the Emperor* (*rGyal po la gdams pa'i rab byed*), written in 1275, 'Phags pa extols Qubilai Khan as "the King of Dharma, the defender of the spiritual power of the All-Mighty Buddha."

2. A. I. Vostrikov, *Tibetskaya tibetoyazychnaya istoricheskaya literatura* (Ulaanbaatar, 1960), XVII–XIX.

3. "Khublai Khan and Phags-a Bla-ma," *in Studies in Mongolian History, Culture and Historiography.* Collected and edited by Ts. Ishdorji and Kh. Purevtogtokh. Ulaanbaatar: International Association for Mongol Studies. Mongolian Academy of Sciences, Institute of History. International Institute for the Study of Nomadic Civilization, 2001, 3:312.

4. *Mongol Ulsyn Arvan Buyant Nomyn Tsagaan Tüükh Nert Sudar Orshivoi,* in Mongolyn Tör, Erkh Züin Tüükh (Ulaanbaatar: University of Mongolia, 2006), 1:13.

5. *Altan Khany Tsaaz,* in *Mongolyn Tör, Erkh Züin Tüükh,* trans. B. Bayarsaikhan into modern Mongolian (Ulaanbaatar: University of Mongolia, 2006), 1:15.

6. *Sngags ram pa ngag dbang tse ring skyabs lser skya byings la ma grags pa nye bar mkho ba'i gtam brjed thor bskod pa bzhugs so drin can bla ma sngags ram pa ngag dbang tse ring kyis bsgrigs pa'i brjed bzhugs so.* 2 Vols, pp. 7b4/218–8a/219.

7. Bhikkhu Ñānamoli and Bhikkhu Bodhi, trans., *The Middle Length Discourses of the Buddha: A Translation of the Majjhima Nikāya* (Boston: Wisdom, 1995), 548.

8. For example, the "The Khalkha Regulations of the Yamen" (*Yaamny Khalkh Jurmyn Dürem*) and "The Khalkha Regulations of the Western Khüree" (*Baruun Khüreenii Khalkh Juram*), which were enacted in 1709 as customary laws of the Khalkha Mongols, both begin with the following prayer:

> Homage to the Guru! May the Dharma blaze strongly, like the *vajra*-feet of the supreme Lama, the crown-pendant of living beings. May the lives of benefactors who support it be lengthened. May the state and nation prosper! May there not be even the slightest mention of the name of a bad deed! May the mind be peaceful! May pure and good conduct thrive, infinitely flowing forth.

See *Mongolyn Tör, Erkh Züin Tüükh,* trans. Bayarsaikhan B., 1:53, 88.

9. This legal text was a part of the records of the Ministry of the All-Governing Court of the Bogdo Khan State, entitled *The Records of Actions Followed by All According to Special Orders and Established by Many Ministries, Starting from the First Year of the State Supported by All,* which consisted of sixty documents.

10. See Charles Bawden, trans., *Tales of an Old Lama* (Tring: Institute of Buddhist Studies, 1997).

11. Pozdneyev, A. M. Edited by J. R. Krueger. *Mongolia and the Mongols.* Vols. 1–2. Uralic and Altaic Series, Vol. 61 and 6 1/2. Bloomington: Indiana University Publications, 1971–1977.

12. Bawden, Charles, R. *Tales of an Old Lama.* Buddhica Britannica Series Continua, Vol. 8. Tring, U.K.: The Institute of Buddhist Studies, 1997.

13. Charles Bawden, *The Modern History of Mongolia* (London: Kegan Paul International, 1989), 166, 167.

14. Cited from Aleksei M. Pozdneyev's *Sketches of Life of Buddhist Monasteries and Buddhist Clergy in Mongolia,* 1887 in Bayarsaikhan, B. *Khalkh juram, manjiin tsaazyn bichgüüd, tedgeeriin khoorondyn khamaaral."* Erkh züi, 2–3, 2001.

15. *Aggaa Sutta, Cakkavattisinhanada Sutta, Dhammapada*, etc.

16. R. E. Emmerick, trans., *The Sūtra of Golden Light* (*Suvarṇaprabhāsottamasūtra*) (Oxford: The Pali Text Society, 2004, 59–65.

17. See *Buddhāvataṃsaka-mahāvaipulyasūtra, Mahāsatyanirgranthavyākaraṇa-sūtra, Bodhisattva-gocaryaviṣayavikramanirdeśasūtra, Daśacakrakṣītigarbhanāmamahā-yānasūtra, Bodhisattvabhūmi of the Yogācārabhūmi, Nāgārjuna's Ratnāvāli, Mātṛceta's Mahārājakaṇikalekhā.*

18. Sh. Bira, "The Worship of Suvarṇaprabhāsottama-sūtra in Mongolia," in *Studies in Mongolian History, Culture, and Historiography* (Ulaanbaatar, 2001), 2:322–331.

5

A Buddhological Critique of "Soldier-Zen" in Wartime Japan

Brian Daizen Victoria

This chapter marks a significant departure in approach from those of my colleagues. That is to say, in addition to introducing yet another example of Buddhist involvement in war and violence, in this case the concept of "soldier-Zen" in Japan during the Asia-Pacific War, I critique this involvement on the basis of what are generally recognized as the core teachings of Buddhism. Controversially to be sure, I come to the conclusion that, by virtue of its fervent if not fanatical support of Japanese militarism, the Zen school, both Rinzai and Sōtō, so grievously violated Buddhism's fundamental tenets that the school was no longer an authentic expression of the *Buddhadharma*.

I am well aware that, in adopting such a stance, I expose myself to the charge that I have left the realm of "objective scholarship" to pursue a partisan agenda. In one sense, that charge is accurate: I do indeed seek to provoke debate among Buddhist scholars and practitioners as to what the Buddhist position is with regard to the use of violence. Should I seem to adopt an extreme position in what follows, it is not for the purpose of establishing some form of "pure" Buddhism. Rather, it is my hope that those who disagree will subsequently put forth their own understandings of the narrowly focused, yet critically important, issues I raise.

As this book makes abundantly clear, the historic connection between Buddhism and violence is not limited to any one time or country. As in the case of other world religions, it is, sadly, an evergreen phenomenon. How many, if any, of the world's major religions can be said to have seriously reflected on, let alone overcome, their long-standing connection to religiously sanctioned violence?

As for Buddhism, I am reminded of an academic conference I attended where a presentation was made on the alleged faith-healing powers of a contemporary female Zen master. When the question was subsequently raised as to whether faith healing was an authentic expression of the *Buddhadharma*, the presenter stated that, inasmuch as the beneficiary of the healing was a Buddhist layperson who believed it to be so, who are we, as scholars, to question its authenticity?

If the claim is made that whatever those who identify themselves as Buddhists believe or do is in fact Buddhism, then Buddhological critiques such as this one have no place in the academy. That is to say, because those Buddhist believers in faith healing (or Japanese militarism) were convinced that their actions were in full accord with the *Buddhadharma*, what right do scholars have to question their claim?

In stark contrast to the preceding is the following statement made by Hakamaya Noriaki, a Sōtō Zen scholar at Komazawa University: "[True Buddhists] must draw a sharp distinction between Buddhist teachings and anti-Buddhist teachings, using both intellect and language to denounce the latter."[1] Hakamaya and his colleague Matsumoto Shirō are leaders of the Critical Buddhism (*Hihan Bukkyō*) movement. Hakamaya goes on to critique institutional Buddhism's collaboration with Japanese militarism:

> One must never allow oneself to be reduced to a mere physical entity. Instead, the intellect must be used to its utmost to clearly distinguish what is right, and words used to their utmost to criticize what is wrong. I believe this is the way in which faith becomes an activity opposed to war.[2]

This chapter is based on the premise that there are indeed times when it is necessary for scholars as well as practitioners to "draw a sharp distinction between Buddhist teachings and anti-Buddhist teachings." Once again, I invite those who disagree with this premise to put forth their own arguments to the contrary. My only request or hope is that, when counterarguments are made, they are grounded in core Buddhist beliefs rather than in the personal prejudices of the author.

Background to Soldier-Zen

In seeking to understand soldier-Zen, it is important to recognize that this term is but one historical expression of a much broader phenomenon, i.e., the fanatically pro-militarist ideology of numerous leading Zen masters and scholars, as well as their lay and clerical disciples, prior to and during the Asia-Pacific War. I have chosen the term *soldier-Zen* to represent this much larger body of discourse although, due to limited space, I can but introduce a small fraction of the ideology associated with this term. Those readers wishing a more detailed description are advised to read my two books *Zen at War* and *Zen War Stories*.[3] On the other hand, those who have already read *Zen at War* may wish to skip over this section.

Soldier-Zen is most closely associated with Lt. Col. Sugimoto Gorō (1900–1937). According to Rinzai Zen master Yamazaki Ekijū (1882–1961), Sugimoto once said:

> The Zen that I do is . . . soldier-Zen [*gunjin-Zen*]. The reason that Zen is important for soldiers is that all Japanese, especially soldiers, must live in the spirit of the unity of sovereign and subjects, eliminating their ego and getting rid of their self. It is exactly the awakening to the nothingness [*mu*] of Zen that is the fundamental spirit of the unity of sovereign and subjects. Through my practice of Zen I am able to get rid of my ego. In facilitating the accomplishment of this, Zen becomes, as it is, the true spirit of the Imperial military.[4]

On September 14, 1937, Sugimoto was mortally wounded on the battlefield in China's Shanxi province. While Sugimoto was in every sense a good soldier and officer, what made him stand out from his peers were three elements: (1) his total and absolute reverence and loyalty to the emperor, (2) his many years of Zen practice, and (3) his writings, posthumously published under the title *Taigi* (*Great Duty*), describing the same sentiments.

What is of interest here is Sugimoto and his Zen master's understanding of (Zen) Buddhism. As Sugimoto's following comments on the emperor make clear, his understanding of Zen "selflessness" was at the heart of his entire ideology:

> The emperor is identical with the Great [Sun] Goddess Amaterasu. He is the supreme and only God of the universe, the supreme sovereign of the universe. All of the many components [of a country] including such things as its laws and constitution, its religion, ethics, learning, art, etc. are expedient means by which to promote unity with the emperor. That is to say, the greatest mission of these components is to promote an awareness of the non-existence of the self and the absolute nature of the emperor. Because of the non-existence of the self everything in the universe is a manifestation of

> the emperor...including even the insect chirping in the hedge, or the gentle spring breeze....
>
> This great awareness will clearly manifest itself at the time you discard secular values and recognize that the emperor is the highest supreme value for all eternity. If, on the other hand, your ultimate goal is eternal happiness for yourself and salvation of your soul, the emperor becomes a means to an end and is no longer the highest being. If there is a difference in the degree of your reverence for the emperor based on your learning, occupation, or living conditions, then you are a self-centered person. Seeking nothing at all, you should simply completely discard both body and mind, and unite with the emperor.[5]

According to Sugimoto, even Buddha Śākyamuni was a model for emperor worship:

> When Śākyamuni sat in meditation beneath the Bodhi tree in order to see into his true nature, he had to fight with an army of innumerable demons. Those who rush forward to save the empire are truly great men as he was, pathfinders who sacrifice themselves for the emperor.[6]

Sugimoto went on to quote the *Nirvāṇa Sūtra* on the importance of "protecting the true Dharma by grasping swords and other weapons." He claimed, "The highest and only true Dharma in the world exists within the emperor." Likewise, he quoted the same *sūtra* on the need to "keep the [Buddhist] precepts." Putting this all together, he concluded, "Everyone in the world should grasp swords and other weapons to reverently protect the emperor. This is the world's highest keeping of the precepts, the highest morality, and the highest religion."[7]

And what of Buddhist compassion? According to Sugimoto:

> The wars of the empire are sacred wars. They are holy wars. They are the [Buddhist] practice [*gyō*] of great compassion [*daijihishin*]. Therefore the Imperial military must consist of holy officers and holy soldiers.[8]

As for Zen, Sugimoto said:

> If you wish to penetrate the true meaning of "Great Duty," the first thing you should do is to embrace the teachings of Zen and discard self-attachment.[9]

As to why self-attachment should be discarded, Sugimoto explained:

> War is moral training for not only the individual but for the entire world. It consists of the extinction of self-seeking and the destruction of self-preservation. It is only those without self-attachment who are able to revere the emperor absolutely.[10]

Sugimoto also found inspiration for his beliefs in the teachings of some of Zen's greatest masters. For example, he wrote about Dōgen, the thirteenth-century founder of the Sōtō Zen sect in Japan, as follows:

> Zen Master Dōgen said, "To study the Buddha Dharma is to study the self. To study the self is to forget the self." To forget the self means to discard both body and mind. To discard beyond discarding, to discard until there is nothing left to discard.... This is called reaching the Great Way in which there is no doubt. This is the Great Law of the universe. In this way the great spirit of the highest righteousness and the purest of the pure manifests itself in the individual. This is the unity of the Sovereign and his subjects, the origin of faith in the emperor.[11]

Sugimoto was equally ready to enlist one of the greatest Chinese Chan (Zen) masters in his cause. About Nan-ch'üan P'u-yüan (748–834), he wrote:

> An ancient master [Nan-ch'üan] said, "One's ordinary mind is the Way."... In the spring there are hundreds of flowers, and in the fall, the moon. In the summer there are cool breezes, and in the winter, snow. Laying down one's life in order to destroy the rebels is one's ordinary mind. If one does not fall victim to an idle mind, this is truly the practice of Great Duty. It is this that must be called the essence of faith in the emperor.[12]

Sugimoto subsequently went on to add that "sacrificing oneself for the emperor is one's ordinary mind." Further, those who possess this mind are "true Imperial subjects."[13]

Sugimoto devoted an entire chapter (chapter 20) to the question of "life and death." In the best Zen fashion, he noted, "Life and death are identical." As to how one comes to this realization, he stated, "It is achieved by abandoning both body and mind, by extinguishing the self."[14] While the preceding appears to be orthodox Zen teaching, Sugimoto added:

> Warriors who sacrifice their lives for the emperor will not die, but live forever. Truly, they should be called gods and Buddhas for whom there

FIGURE 5.1 Zen-trained Lt. Col. Sugimoto Gorō, a "god of war." Photo provided by Brian D. Victoria.

> is no life or death.... Where there is absolute loyalty there is no life or death. Where there is life and death there is no absolute loyalty. When a person talks of his view of life and death, that person has not yet become pure in heart. He has not yet abandoned body and mind. In pure loyalty there is no life or death. Simply live in pure loyalty![15]

While it might be argued that Sugimoto's understanding of Buddhism and Zen was no more than one ultranationalist's willful distortion of these traditions, the same cannot be as easily said of Yamazaki Ekijū, chief abbot of the Buttsūji branch of the Rinzai Zen sect and head of the entire sect at war's end (1945–1946). In one sense, it is hardly surprising to find Yamazaki lending his support to Sugimoto inasmuch as the latter had long been his lay disciple. Concretely, Yamazaki's support took the form of a 104-page eulogy attached to the end of Sugimoto's book. It began as follows:

> I once said at a lecture I gave, "The faith of the Japanese people is a faith that should be centered on His Imperial Majesty, the emperor." At that time Sugimoto said that he was in complete agreement with me. He then went on to add, "I had felt exactly as you do, but I had been unable to find the right words to express it. Present-day religionists raise a fuss about the need for faith, but their faith is mistaken. Buddhists say that one should have faith in the Buddha, or Mahāvairocana, or Buddha Amita, but such faith is one that has been captured by religion. Japanese Buddhism must be centered on the emperor; for were it not, it would have no place in Japan, it would not be living Buddhism. Even Buddhism must conform to the national structure of Japan. The same holds true for Śākyamuni's teachings."

Sugimoto continued:

> The Buddhist statues that are enshrined in temples should, properly speaking, have the emperor reverently enshrined in the center and such figures as Buddha Amita or Mahāvairocana at his sides. It is only the various branches of the Zen sect in Japan who have His Majesty enshrined in the center.... All of Japanese Buddhism should have His Majesty, the emperor, as their central object of worship.[16]

Yamazaki then proceeded to compare Sugimoto's feelings of reverence for the emperor with his own. About himself, he stated:

> For Japanese there is no such thing as sacrifice. Sacrifice means to totally annihilate one's body on behalf of the Imperial state. The Japanese people, however, have been one with the emperor from

FIGURE 5.2 A 1937 cartoon of a farmer pouring a bucket of nourishment entitled "religious spirit" on a tree entitled "Great Empire of Japan." A symbol representing the Japanese emperor can be seen shining in the upper part of the tree. Photo provided by Brian D. Victoria.

> the beginning. In this place of absoluteness there is no sacrifice. In Japan, the relationship between His Majesty and the people is not relative but absolute.[17]

In comparing Sugimoto's and Yamazaki's attitudes toward the emperor, it can be said that they are absolutely identical in their absoluteness. It is hardly surprising to learn that Sugimoto, already a seasoned Zen practitioner when he first met Yamazaki, went on to train an additional nine years under the latter's guidance. With evident satisfaction in the level of realization of his lay disciple, Yamazaki quoted Sugimoto as once having said:

> The national structure of Japan and Buddhism are identical with each other. In Buddhism, especially the Zen sect, there is repeated reference to the identity of body and mind. In order to realize this identity of the two it is necessary to undergo training with all one's might and regardless of the sacrifice.
>
> Furthermore, the essence of the unity of body and mind is to be found in egolessness. Japan is a country where the Sovereign and the people are identical. When Imperial subjects meld themselves into one with the August Mind [of the emperor], their original countenance shines forth. The essence of the unity of the sovereign and the people is egolessness. Egolessness and self-extinction are most definitely not separate states. On the contrary, one comes to realize that they are identical with one other.[18]

The "egolessness" of which Sugimoto spoke is the well-known Japanese Zen term *muga* (lit. no-self). In his book *Zen and Japanese Culture*, D. T. Suzuki identified *muga* as being identical with not only *musō* (no-reflection) and *munen* (no-thought), but also *mushin* (no-mind).[19] About these latter terms, Suzuki had this to say:

> *Mushin* [*wu-hsin*] or *munen* [*wu-nien*] is one of the most important ideas in Zen. It corresponds to the state of innocence enjoyed by the first inhabitants of the Garden of Eden, or even to the mind of God when he was about to utter his fiat, "Let there be light." Enō (Hui-neng), the sixth patriarch of Zen, emphasizes *munen* (or *mushin*) as the most essential element in the study of Zen. When it is attained, a man becomes a Zen-man, and... also a perfect swordsman.[20]

Was Sugimoto, then, the "Zen-man" of whom Suzuki wrote? It is clear that Yamazaki believed he was. This master wrote:

> As far as the power of his practice of the Way is concerned, I believe he [Sugimoto] reached the point where there was no difference between him and the chief abbot of this or that branch [of Zen]. I think that when a person esteems practice, respects the Way, and thoroughly penetrates the self as he did, he could have become the teacher of other Zen practitioners. That is how accomplished he was. In my opinion his practice was complete.[21]

Further, as the following quote makes clear, Sugimoto was, for Yamazaki, the modern equivalent of Bodhidharma, the traditional, perhaps legendary, fifth-century founder of the Zen sect in China: "Altogether Sugimoto practiced Zen for nearly twenty years. Bodhidharma practiced [meditation] facing the wall for nine years. Sugimoto's penetrating *zazen* [seated meditation] was as excellent as that."[22]

With all of his Zen training, what kind of soldier did Sugimoto actually become? Was he the "perfect swordsman" to whom Suzuki referred? About Sugimoto's military prowess on the battlefield, Yamazaki wrote:

> I don't know what degree [of attainment] he had in *Kendō* [Way of the Sword], but it appears he was quite accomplished.... When he went to the battlefield it appears that he used the sword with consummate skill.... I believe he demonstrated the action that derives from the unity of Zen and the sword.[23]

Yamazaki also recorded the following conversation the two men had shortly before Sugimoto went off to fight in China for the first time in 1931:

> Sugimoto asked, "Master, what kind of understanding should I have in going over there?" I answered, "You are strong, and your unit is strong. Thus I think you will not fear a strong enemy. However, in the event you face a [numerically] small enemy, you must not despise them. You should recite the *Prajñāparamitā Hṛdaya* [Heart] *Sūtra* every day. This will insure good fortune on the battlefield for the Imperial military."[24]

Yamazaki added that, when Sugimoto eventually returned safely from China, he reported, "I died once while I was in Tianjin." About this, Yamazaki commented, "Through the awareness Sugimoto achieved in becoming one with death, there was, I think, nothing he couldn't achieve."[25]

Finally, there is the question of Sugimoto's death on the battlefield in 1937. Based on reports he received, Yamazaki described how Sugimoto had been leading his troops into battle when an enemy hand grenade landed behind him and exploded:

> A grenade fragment hit him in the left shoulder. He seemed to have fallen down but then got up again. Although he was standing, one could not hear his commands. He was no longer able to issue commands with that husky voice of his.... Yet he was still standing, holding his sword in one hand as a prop. Both legs were slightly bent, and he was facing in an easterly direction [toward the imperial palace]. It appeared that he had saluted though his hand was now lowered to about the level of his mouth. The blood flowing from his mouth covered his watch.[26]

In Yamazaki's mind, at least, this was his lay disciple's finest moment—the moment when he most clearly displayed the power that is to be gained by those who practice Zen. That is to say, Sugimoto had died standing up. As the master explained:

> In the past it was considered to be the true appearance of a Zen priest to pass away while doing *zazen*. Those who were completely and thoroughly enlightened, however,... could die calmly in a standing position.... The reason this was possible was due to *samādhi* power [*jōriki*].[27]

The technical term *samādhi* refers to the concentrated state of mind, i.e., the mental one-pointedness, that is achieved through the practice of *zazen*. It was about this meditation-derived power that D. T. Suzuki and other Zen leaders had written so often. Together with Yamazaki, they were all in agreement that Zen was the fountainhead of this power, a power that was available to Japanese warriors both past and present. Sugimoto's life and, most especially, his death were living proof of its effectiveness in battle.

At last, Yamazaki was ready to complete his eulogy of Sugimoto. He did so as follows:

> To the last second Sugimoto was a man whose speech and actions were at one with each other. When he saluted and faced the east, there is no doubt that he also shouted, "May His Majesty, the emperor, live for 10,000 years!" [*Tennō-heika Banzai*]. It is for this reason that his was the radiant ending of an Imperial soldier. Not only that, but his excellent appearance should be a model for future generations of someone who lived in Zen....
>
> Although it can be said that his life of thirty-eight years was all too short, for someone who has truly obtained *samādhi* power, there is no question of a long or short period. The great, true appearance of

> Sugimoto Gorō was of someone who had united with emptiness, embodying total loyalty [to the emperor] and service to the state. I am convinced he is one of those who should he be reborn seven times over, would reverently work to destroy the enemies of the emperor. (Written on the 11th of February of the 2,598th year of the imperial reign) [i.e., 1938][28]

Although the preceding words mark the end of Sugimoto's book *Taigi*, these words by no means mark the end of the influence that his writings (and those of his Zen master) were to have on the Japanese people, especially its youth. As Yamazaki hoped, Sugimoto was celebrated in both the Rinzai and Sōtō sects as the model of a military figure thoroughly imbued with the Zen spirit. That is to say, he had become a "military god" (*gunshin*).

But was this (Zen) Buddhism?

Where Did the Zen School "Go Wrong"?

The siren call of soldier-Zen, like its predecessor "samurai-Zen," was the promise it offered of self-transcendence. This was the goal that Sugimoto had in mind when he identified Zen as "the true spirit of the Imperial military," for his practice of Zen had enabled him, or so he believed, to rid himself of, i.e., transcend, his own ego.

On the surface, such transcendence *appeared* to be Buddhist in nature because it called on the warrior or soldier to transcend attachment to his personal well-being. Having accomplished this, he was next called upon to sacrifice himself for the well-being of the ruler(s) of his fiefdom (in premodern Japan) or of the nation-state (in modern Japan). Is this not the stuff of which "heroes" are made in any culture? Is this not fundamentally the same value system that underlies the West Point Military Academy's creed of "Duty, Honor, Country"?

In the *Buddhadharma*, however, inherent compassion is not limited to one's own group or nation, no matter how small or large that may be. In the *Buddhadharma*, there is ultimately only *one* group—the group of all beings up to and including the very cosmos itself. To purposely inflict pain and suffering, let alone death, on one segment of beings under the guise of benefiting another part, however defined, can *never* be part of a Buddhism rooted in the teachings of its founder. In explaining the four practices of a bodhisattva, Dōgen wrote:

> The foolish believe that their own interests will suffer if they put the benefit of others first. They are wrong, however. Benevolence is

all-encompassing, equally benefiting oneself and others.... With the passage of time both self and others become one.[29]

A bodhisattva in the Mahāyāna tradition knows full well the difficulties of practicing, or implementing, the Buddha way even in the best of worlds. Furthermore, a bodhisattva is deeply aware (or *ought* to be aware) that a nation represents nothing more (or less) than the *collective ego* of its citizens. The engaged Buddhist scholar David Loy coined the word "wego" to refer to this latter entity, noting that "nationalism is a powerful institutional version of such a group wego-self."[30] Taking advantage of wego, a nation's leaders constantly seek to utilize the patriotic and altruistic feelings of its citizens in the pursuit of policies of aggrandizement that they claim to be "in the national interest."

In a world that is today dominated by nations, corporations, and individuals, each looking out for number one, it can be argued that "put[ting] the benefit of others first" is anachronistic at best, if not impossible or even downright suicidal. Nevertheless, a bodhisattva vows to do so. Foolishness? Perhaps. But foolish or not, this does not alter the fact that this is the teaching of the *Buddhadharma*, at least according to the Mahāyāna school.

Should there be Zen adherents like Sugimoto, Yamazaki, and their like who are unwilling or unable to adhere to this foolishness, they have every right to start a religion of their own, with all the war-affirming doctrines and practices they care to have. But at the very least, intellectual honesty and personal integrity should demand that they acknowledge that such a faith would have nothing to do with Buddhism—that such a faith would, in fact, be a clear denial of its core teachings.

The Non-Self in Action

Sugimoto was not content with using his practice of Zen merely to rid himself of his ego. As a corollary, he further strived to embrace the state of egolessness (J. *muga*). As the reader will recall, Sugimoto asserted, "The essence of the unity of the sovereign and the people is egolessness. Egolessness and self-extinction are most definitely not separate states. On the contrary, one comes to realize that they are identical with one other." Here the question must be asked, is *muga* (at least as understood in the Zen school) Buddhist? At first glance, the answer appears self-evident, for wasn't the doctrine of *anātman* one of Buddha Śākyamuni's core teachings? While this is undeniable, the question must still be asked whether *muga* or even the typical English translations, "no-self" or "non-self," are accurate translations of the Sanskrit term.

Controversially to be sure, I suggest that these translations are fundamentally flawed, for *ātman* does not simply mean "self" but an *eternal, unchanging* self or *soul*. Buddha Śākyamuni sought to deny the belief that the self was eternal, *not* that you and I, as *temporary* psychophysical personalities, don't exist in the conventional sense. As the well-known Buddhist scholar-priest Walpola Rahula noted:

> According to the Buddha's teaching, it is as wrong to hold the opinion "I have no self" (which is the annihilationist theory) as to hold the opinion "I have a self." Why? What we call "I," or "being" is only a combination of physical and mental aggregates, which are working together interdependently in a flux of momentary change within the law of cause and effect.... there is nothing permanent, everlasting, unchanging and eternal in the whole of existence.[31]

If the above comments seem obvious to even beginning students of Buddhism, they were, sadly, not obvious to proponents of samurai-Zen like the famous Rinzai Zen master Takuan (1573–1645). Addressing his patron, the highly accomplished swordsman Yagyū Tajima no Kami Munenori (1571–1646), Takuan wrote:

> The uplifted sword has no will of its own, it is all of emptiness. It is like a flash of lightning. The man who is about to be struck down is also of emptiness, and so is the one who wields the sword. None of them are possessed of a mind that has any substantiality. As each of them is of emptiness and has no "mind" [*kokoro*], the striking man is not a man, the sword in his hands is not a sword, and the "I" who is about to be struck down is like the splitting of the spring breeze in a flash of lightning.[32]

In Takuan, we have a priest, who even today epitomizes Zen "enlightenment" in Japan, telling us that the killing of a human being is of no more consequence than "the splitting of the spring breeze in a flash of lightning." Compare these words with those attributed to Buddha Śākyamuni in the *Dhammapada*, a work dating back to the oldest stratum of the Buddhist *sūtras*:

> All men tremble at punishment, all men fear death; remembering that thou are like unto them, do not strike or slay.
>
> All men tremble at punishment, all men love life; remembering that thou are like unto them, do not strike or slay.[33]

In comparing these two quotations, one by the faith's founder and the other by a disciple allegedly sharing the founder's enlightenment, it is difficult to accept that both could be members of the same faith. I assert that they are not, for if ever there were a case when a teaching ought to be unequivocally rejected as "not Buddhism," it is that of Takuan. Furthermore, many other noted Zen masters and scholars, up to and including D. T. Suzuki, have given their unqualified support for what has been traditionally expressed as the "unity of Zen and the sword" (J. *zenken ichinyo*). And a close (and deadly) corollary in their hands is the Zen teaching of the "unity of life and death" (J. *shōji ichinyo*).

As is well known, the Zen sect has been deeply influenced by the Mādhyamika school of Mahāyāna Buddhism, with its teaching of two levels of truth, conventional and ultimate. However, by placing an exclusive emphasis on ultimate truth (Skt. *paramārtha-satya*), Takuan and the like devalued and delegitimized conventional truth to the point that human life effectively became worthless. Consciously or not, such Zen exponents failed to recognize that, as Bernard Faure noted, the Middle Way advocated by the Mādhyamika school insists on "the 'simultaneous vision of the two truths,' wherein each extreme *keeps its distinct status*. It does not always try to collapse them into one undifferentiated reality" (italics mine).[34] In other words, while the self is indeed ultimately "empty" in that it is, like all phenomena, impermanent, the pain and suffering each one of us experiences are simultaneously all too real. Buddhist compassion must never be blind to addressing that pain, let alone serve to increase it.

Nevertheless, Zen leaders in Japan effectively collapsed these two truths into one undifferentiated reality, thereby providing Bushidō with a corrupted metaphysical foundation. This foundation not only sanctioned killing, it also valorized the Zen-trained warrior's willingness to die—in the process of taking life, in loyal service to his feudal lord—as the antinomian expression of full enlightenment. And should there be any doubt that Takuan's teachings were subsequently incorporated into Zen support for Japanese militarism, we need look no further than wartime Sōtō Zen leader Ishihara Shummyō, who said in March 1937:

> Zen master Takuan taught that in essence Zen and Bushidō were one.... I believe that if one is called upon to die, one should not be the least bit agitated. On the contrary, one should be in a realm where something called "oneself" does not intrude even slightly. Such a realm is no different from that derived from the practice of Zen.[35]

Imperial Army major Ōkubo Kōichi responded in enthusiastic agreement with Ishihara's comments:

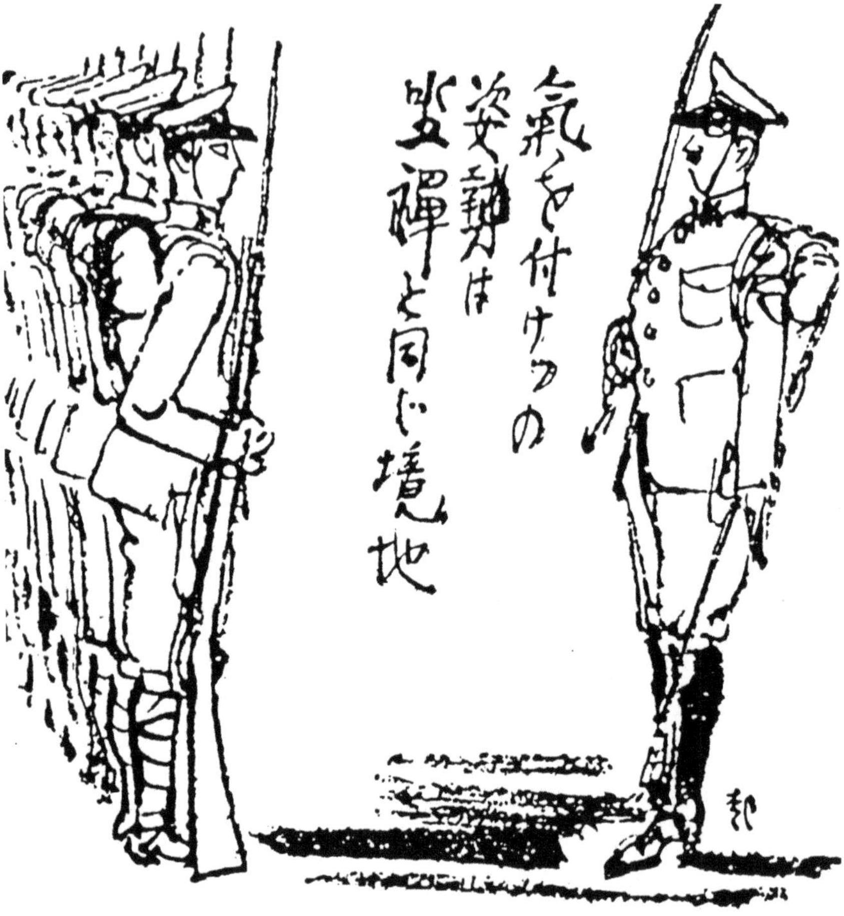

FIGURE 5.3 A 1937 cartoon stating, "Standing at attention is the same state of mind as Zen meditation." Photo provided by Brian D. Victoria.

> The soldier must become one with his superior. He must actually become his superior. Similarly, he must become the order he receives. That is to say, *his self must disappear.* In so doing, when he eventually goes onto the battlefield, he will advance when told to advance.... On the other hand, should he believe that he is going to die and act accordingly; he will be unable to fight well. What is necessary, then, is that he be able to act freely and without [mental] hindrance. (italics mine)[36]

During the Asia-Pacific War (1937–1945), Japanese soldiers of all ranks were indoctrinated with a program of Bushidō-promoting "spiritual education" (J. *seishin kyōiku*). This spiritual education was based on the metaphysical foundation of the unities of Zen and the sword, life and death. Once trained, Japanese soldiers were dispatched to the battlefield where nearly 3 million of them died "selflessly" even as they killed more than 20 million Chinese and other "selfless" enemies in the process.

The fact that, even in the twenty-first century (both in Japan and the West), this corrupted Zen understanding of selflessness has remained unchallenged (with only a few exceptions) cannot but be regarded as one of the world's most successful religious deceptions. Although omitting the specifics, the Buddhist scholar and translator Thomas Cleary noted:

> [M]ilitarism has distorted Zen along with the rest of Japanese culture.... Japanese people today are just as susceptible to being deceived by deviant Zen as are Westerners, with the result that the various conflicting elements in modern Zen are generally not analyzed for what they really are.[37]

Having asserted this, the question can now be asked, is there any major faith whose adherents have *never* employed illegitimate doctrinal interpretations to justify the slaughter of their fellow human beings? For example, are words like "crusade" and *jihad* unconnected to religiously inspired violence if not fanaticism? Nevertheless, I maintain that, even though all major religions (or their leaders) have acted similarly, this does not excuse samurai- and soldier-Zen's gross betrayal of the *Buddhadharma*.

Samādhi Power

The application of *samādhi* power to the battlefield was closely connected with the militaristic use of Zen selflessness. This application, dedicated as it was to the destruction of others, should be unequivocally repudiated; for the only legitimate Buddhist use of *samādhi* power is the facilitation of true spiritual growth and understanding.

In this context, Zen adherents should be open to an insight from the Theravāda school of Buddhism. The Pāli Buddhist *suttas* (Skt. *sūtras*) clearly warn against the misuse of *samādhi*, i.e., *miccha-samādhi*. In the *Gopaka Moggallana Sutta*, for example, Ananda, one of Buddha Śākyamuni's chief disciples, points out to Vassakara (the chief minister of the country of Magadha), that Śākyamuni did *not* praise every form of meditation:

> What kind of meditation, Brahman, did the Lord [Śākyamuni] not praise?... He [who] dwells with his thought obsessed by *ill-will*, and

FIGURE 5.4 A 1937 cartoon depicting Imperial Japanese Army officers practicing Zen meditation. Photo provided by Brian D. Victoria.

> does not comprehend as it really is the escape from the ill-will that has arisen; he, having made ill-will the main thing, meditates on it, meditates absorbed, meditates more absorbed, meditates quite absorbed. . . . The Lord does not praise this kind of meditation, Brahman.[38]

Meditating "obsessed by ill-will" is not, of course, the only misuse to which *samādhi* can be put. Meditative obsession with "the pleasures of the senses," "sloth and torpor," "restlessness and doubt," etc., are also condemned. But as anyone who has actually been in battle will tell you, the slaughter of one's fellow human beings inevitably, and inescapably, requires a *great deal* of ill will.

Experienced meditators know that the one-pointedness of mind arising out of meditation is a very powerful force indeed, whether used for good or ill. Yet it appears that Zen, perhaps even the entire Mahāyāna school, has failed to recognize the danger of *misusing* meditation power, a singular misunderstanding of the *Buddhadharma*. Fortunately, this danger is recognized in the Theravāda tradition and is furthermore entirely consistent with Buddha Śākyamuni's fundamental teachings of compassion and nonviolence.

Viewed in terms of its historical development, it can be argued that Zen (and, as this book reveals, Buddhism as a whole) was the victim of something akin to a hijacking. This particular hijacking occurred over such a long period of time, however, that the victims were seldom conscious of being taken for a ride, let alone taken against their will. To give but one example, a full millennium prior to the advent of soldier-Zen, a famous Chinese writer by the name of Liang Su (753–793) criticized Chan's lack of ethical standards:

> Nowadays, few men have true faith. Those who travel the path of Ch'an go so far as to teach the people that there is neither Buddha nor Dharma, and that *neither good nor evil has any significance.* When they preach these doctrines to the average man, or men below average, they are believed by all those who live their lives of worldly desires. Such ideas are accepted as great truths that sound so pleasing to the ear. And the people are attracted to them just as *moths in the night are drawn to their burning death by the candle light* (italics mine).[39]

In reading this, one is tempted to believe that Liang was also a prophet, able to foresee that, over a thousand years later, millions of young Japanese men would be drawn to their own burning deaths by the Zen-influenced "light" of Bushidō. And we must never forget the many more millions of innocent men, women, and children who burned with (or because of) them.

Even more to the point, the French scholar Paul Demiéville notes that, according to the seventh-century Chan text "Treatise on Absolute Contemplation," killing is evil only in the event the killer fails to recognize his victim as empty and dream-like. On the contrary, if one no longer sees his opponent as a living being separate from emptiness, then he is free to kill him at will.[40] This early antinomian license to kill with moral impunity reveals that soldier-Zen was not some medieval invention of the Zen school in Japan. Nor was it a more recent aberration resulting from the advent of Japanese militarism in the 1930s. Instead, its roots can be traced back to the very emergence of Chan in China.

In addition to being stripped early of its ethical moorings, Chan was also hijacked by a syncretism that identified Buddhism with both Confucianism and Taoism. As Dōgen, who was a direct observer, discovered when he visited China from 1223 to 1227:

> Among present-day Chinese monks there is not even one who is aware that the teachings of Confucius and Lao-tzu [legendary founder of Taoism] are inferior to those of the Buddha. Although it is true that, throughout China, those who call themselves descendants of the

> Buddhas and [Zen] Patriarchs are now as numerous as rice plants, hemp, bamboo, and reeds, not one of them, not even half of one of them, has understood that the Buddha's teachings are superior to [those of] the other two. It was only Ju-ching, my late master, who understood this fact and proclaimed it ceaselessly day and night.[41]

If Dōgen sounds somewhat polemical here, it should be remembered that, like Hakamaya and Matsumoto of the present day, he, too, was attempting to establish in Japan what is "not Buddhism." Significantly, Dōgen based one part of his critique of Taoism on a Taoist work, the *Lieh-ch'uan*, which stated that Lao-tzu had required a would-be disciple by the name of Kuan-ling Yin-hsi to kill seven people, including the latter's own mother and father. About this incident, Dōgen wrote: "The Tathāgata, for his part, based his teachings on [the need for] great compassion. Where, then, did Lao-tzu find the basis for his treacherous teachings?"[42]

Within the context of this chapter, Dōgen's further critique of both Lao-tzu and Confucius is even more telling:

> [Lao-tzu and Confucius] were also quite ignorant of causality in the three stages of time [i.e., past, present, and future]. *They merely taught loyal service to the emperor and filial piety*, the latter seen as a method of regulating one's household. Their teachings concerned the present world only, ignoring the future, and therefore were one form of the denial of causality.[43]

In Dōgen's comments, we once again encounter a prophetic voice. When wartime Zen practitioners like Sugimoto and his master fervently advocated loyalty to the emperor, they were clearly concerned with the immediacy of the world around them. But in terms of the subsequent untold millions of deaths that this loyalty produced, they, too, were equally guilty of "ignoring the future."

Be that as it may, Dōgen's critique of these two Chinese philosophies, especially Confucianism, was no more successful or long lasting in Japan than it had been in China. Less than a hundred years after Dōgen's death, Gidō Shūshin (1325–1388), Rinzai abbot first of Enkakuji in Kamakura and later of Nanzenji in Kyoto, confidently taught Shōgun Ashikaga Yoshimitsu (1358–1408) that, while it was impossible for Confucian teachings to contain Buddhism, it was quite possible for Buddhism to contain Confucianism. To his credit, Gidō did employ his Buddhist faith to speak out against the almost continuous civil warfare that characterized his age. Nevertheless, he failed to recognize that the price of "containing Confucianism" would, over the long term, be the wholesale incorporation into Zen of the hierarchically based Confucian ethical system. This system is centered on the creation of "social harmony" through inculcating subordinates with feelings of absolute and unquestioning loyalty toward their superiors, be they feudal lord, military superior, emperor, or, today, the corporate leaders who collectively constitute "Japan, Inc."

Violence and the Bodhisattva

Bearing this in mind, let me address the issue that is, for me as a Mahāyāna Buddhist in the Sōtō Zen tradition, the most difficult one of all. I refer to the question of whether a bodhisattva can, under any circumstances, legitimately employ violence to the point of actually taking the life of another human being? I also ask my readers, what do you think about this crucial question?

My own position is to make a flat denial, identifying *sūtras* to the contrary as later Mahāyāna accretions to the *Buddhadharma* having as one of their aims the transformation of the absolute prohibition of killing (in early Buddhism) into something more acceptable to Buddhism's later patrons—the empire-building monarchs and the war-prone states they headed. In support of my denial, I would point out that I find no evidence in what are generally considered to be the fundamental tenets of Buddhism (i.e., the Four Noble Truths and Holy Eightfold Path) that would condone an adherent's participation in violence against other human beings for any reason whatsoever.

Furthermore, it should not be forgotten that even lay Buddhists, let along male and female clerics, are expected to follow the Five Precepts (Pāli. *pañca-sīla;* Skt. *pañca-śīla*). These precepts constitute the very core of Buddhist ethics and followers of Buddha Śākyamuni in both the Theravāda and Mahāyāna traditions pledge to adhere to them unconditionally. The importance placed on abstention from killing can be seen in the fact that it is the very first of the Five Precepts followed only then by abstention from stealing, sexual misconduct, lying and intoxication. Thus Buddhism, from its earliest formulation up through today, should be considered to take the position of nonviolence as its normative standard of conduct.

That said, there does exist in Mahāyāna Buddhism a doctrine known as "skillful/expedient means" (Skt. *upāya* aka *upāya-kauśalya*). Skillful means is a concept that encourages Buddhist teachers to adapt their message to the needs and capacities of their audience, i.e. to use language, methods or techniques leading to the cessation of suffering and spiritual liberation based on individual needs and abilities.

In the *Lotus Sūtra* the use of skillful means is illustrated by the story of a father who comes home to find his house on fire and his children still inside unaware of the danger. The man calls out to his children to leave the house, but not believing it to be on fire they continue playing with their toys. Thinking about how he may use skillful means, the father tells his children that he has brought home gilded carts and toy oxen for them to play with, but they must first come outside to get them. Hearing this, the children run from the burning house and are saved. In employing skillful means the father broke the Buddhist precept against lying but in the service of saving his children from death.

In Mahāyāna Buddhism the use of skillful means has particular reference to the actions of a bodhisattva. The idea is that a bodhisattva may use any expedient methods in order to help ease the suffering of people, introduce them to the Dharma, or aid them in their quest for Nirvana. While this doctrine seems benign enough on the surface, it has nevertheless been used over the centuries to justify the unorthodox or even precept-breaking behavior engaged in by Buddhist teachers in certain extreme cases, including the use of non-life threatening violence.

There is, for example, the famous Zen story about a ninth-century Chinese priest known in Japanese as Gutei Isshi. Gutei is said to have raised his finger whenever he was asked a question about Zen. Observing Gutei's behavior, a boy attendant began imitating his master by raising his own finger when anyone asked him what his master taught. When Gutei heard about this conduct, he seized the boy and cut off the offending finger. The boy cried and started to run away, but Gutei called and stopped him. Turning his head toward Gutei, Gutei raised up his own finger and in that instant the boy was said to have realized enlightenment.

Invented or not, this story illustrates that under certain extreme cases, the use of non-life threatening violence may have a certain didactic viability. Nevertheless, the most important concept in skillful means is that its use be guided by the duel qualities of wisdom and compassion. Would anyone suggest that the mass slaughter associated with modern warfare could ever be an expression of these qualities?

Finally, when looking at records of Buddha Śākyamuni's life, we find his actions to be totally consistent with his earliest teachings. Śākyamuni peacefully sought to prevent war, as can be seen in his initial successful attempt to prevent an attack on his own country. Further, he successfully dissuaded King Ajātasattu from attacking the Vajjians. Still further, even when the very existence of his own homeland was at stake, he did not mobilize the members of the *sangha* as monk-soldiers to defend his country, nor did he use force to enlarge the power and landholdings of the *sangha* itself (as was later done in medieval Japan).

In light of the above, the question that contemporary Buddhists must ask themselves is: "Am I really willing to make nonviolence the standard for my own personal conduct and, to the extent I can individually influence it, the standard of conduct for the nation (and world) to which I belong?"

Conclusion

As this book reveals, over the centuries those calling themselves Buddhists have all too frequently ignored the pacific aspect of their faith. And as amply demonstrated in this chapter, they have done so at the cost of their own physical and spiritual welfare (let alone the physical and spiritual welfare of others).

When one seeks to understand why this has happened, the answer (at least as far as the state is concerned) is not difficult to discover. In the first instance, it derives from the fact that the state represents the collective ego, i.e., the wego of those who identify with it. In turn, patriotism becomes no more or less than *attachment to this collective ego.*

This said, it is important to recognize that some parts of the collective ego exercise far more power over the state's actions than do others. Thus, the "national interests" that governments today so vigorously seek to defend are typically congruent with, if not derived from, the *financial* interests of its richest and most powerful (corporate) citizens. In this context, the phrase "What's good for General Motors is good for the nation" typifies this reality and goes far in explaining why, in the midst of the current economic crisis, it is the rich and powerful who are the major beneficiaries of government bailouts (including, of course, General Motors itself).

As contemporary Buddhists look upon today's violence-filled, poverty-stricken world, are the socially engaged, violence-forswearing teachings of Buddha Śākyamuni any less true, any less relevant than they were 2,500 years ago? When we recall the great compassion and active concern that Buddha Śākyamuni showed toward both the individual and society as a whole, should modern-day disciples be any less concerned about the monumental suffering in the world around us?

How many of us (along with so-called Buddhist rulers, past or present) are truly able to live up to the social ideals advocated by Buddha Śākyamuni? As modern Buddhists look at the history of the twentieth century, I think most, if not all, would agree that one of the chief characteristics of this age has been the national and ethnic struggle of smaller nations and peoples to free themselves from foreign domination, especially the domination of Western and Japanese imperialism. The dissolution of the Soviet Union and the liberation, however flawed, of many of its captive peoples are but one further manifestation of this phenomenon. If this is true, are Buddhists going to continue to cling to empire-building personages like King Aśoka of India, Emperor Wen of China, or Emperor Shōmu of Japan as paradigms of Buddhist rule?[44]

My reading of Buddhist political history tells me that every time Buddhist leaders have closely aligned themselves with the political rulers of their day, the *sangha* has become corrupt and degenerate. The *sangha*'s often slavish subservience to and actions on behalf of political rulers have resulted in its becoming the de facto pimp and prostitute of the state. Nowhere was this reality more clearly manifested in the twentieth century than in the Japanese Zen school's fanatical embrace of soldier-Zen and its cohorts. But, as the other chapters of this book so graphically reveal, Buddhism's historic embrace of violence and war has by no means been limited to either the Zen school or Japan.

Note, too, that as important as the distortions in practice and doctrine noted in this chapter are, they are but the tip of the iceberg. For example, even were the Zen school to recognize that *samādhi* power can be misused, or that the doctrine of non-self does not confer an antinomian license to kill, this would not affect those contemporary Singhalese Buddhists who maintain that their government's recent military actions directed against the non-Buddhist Tamil minority were done "in defense of the *Buddhadharma*."

This illustrates the reality: the root causes of the historic connection between violence and Buddhism are far more complex than a misunderstanding of this or that doctrine or practice. This is as true for other world religions as it is for Buddhism. For example, the sociologist Peter Berger notes:

> Whenever a society must motivate its members to kill or to risk their lives, thus consenting to being placed in extreme marginal situations, religious legitimations become important.... Killing under the auspices of the legitimate authorities has, for this reason, been accompanied from ancient times to today by religious paraphernalia and ritualism. Men go to war and men are put to death amid prayers, blessings, and incantations.[45]

If Berger is correct (as ample evidence indicates he is), no amount of doctrinal tinkering, no matter how important, will in and of itself change phenomena that are so deeply rooted that they relate to the very nature of religion and its role in society and transcend any one faith. Questions like these demand investigation not only by Buddhists but by all who would free their faiths from the scourge of sacralized violence.

Yet, while recognizing this, my research leads me to the conclusion that one of the principal causes of the general decline in the influence of Buddhism in Asian countries today lies in the *sangha*'s past subservience to and identification with the aggressive, violence-prone rulers of their day. The *sangha,* both lay and clerical, ignores at its peril its teachings of the fundamental equality and identity of all sentient beings and its concern for *all* aspects of their well-being. As Buddhism continues its spread in an easterly direction (i.e., to the "West"), one critically important question is, how much of Buddhism's historic proclivity to condone warfare as a function of the *Buddhadharma* will spread with it?

NOTES

1. Hakamaya Noriaki, *Hihan Bukkyō* (Tokyo: Daizō Shuppan, 1990), 297–298.
2. Ibid., 294.
3. *Zen at War* was published first by Weatherhill in 1997. It is currently available in a second, enlarged, 2006 edition from Rowman & Littlefield. *Zen War Stories* was published in 2003 by Routledge Curzon.
4. Sugimoto Gorō, *Taigi* (Tokyo: Heibonsha, 1938), 178.
5. Ibid., 23–25.
6. Ibid., 62.
7. Ibid., 53.
8. Ibid., 139.
9. Ibid., 19.
10. Ibid., 140.
11. Ibid., 101.
12. Ibid., 99.
13. Ibid., 143.
14. Ibid., 152.
15. Ibid., 153–154.
16. Ibid., 160–161.
17. Ibid., 164.
18. Ibid., 167.
19. D. T. Suzuki, *Zen and Japanese Culture* (Princeton, N.J.: Princeton University Press, 1959), 111–127.
20. Ibid., 111.
21. Sugimoto, *Taigi*, 192.
22. Ibid., 219.
23. Ibid., 195.
24. Ibid., 182.
25. Ibid., 182–183.
26. Ibid., 254.
27. Ibid., 255–256.
28. Ibid., 256–257.
29. Quoted in Yokoi and Victoria, *Zen Master Dōgen: An Introduction with Selected Writings* (New York: Weatherhill, 1976), 62. The four bodhisattva practices as explained by Dōgen are (1) "giving offerings," i.e., sharing both material and spiritual

wealth with others, (2) "loving words," i.e., addressing all beings with compassion and affection, (3) "benevolence," i.e., devising ways to help others, and (4) "identification," i.e., making no distinction between oneself and others. For further discussion, see Yokoi and Victoria, *Zen Master Dōgen*, 61–62.

30. David Loy, "What's Buddhist about Socially Engaged Buddhism?" available at http://www.zen-occidental.net/articles1/loy12-english.html, accessed March 29, 2007.

31. Rahula Walpola, *What the Buddha Taught*, 2nd ed. (New York: Grove Press, 1974), 66.

32. Quoted in Suzuki, *Zen and Japanese Culture*, 114.

33. Irving Babbitt, trans., *The Dhammapada* (New York: New Directions, 1965), 22.

34. Bernard Faure, *The Rhetoric of Immediacy* (Princeton, N.J.: Princeton University Press, 1991), 57.

35. Quoted in Victoria, *Zen at War*, 103. Note that Ishihara Shummyō was the editor in chief of the pan-Buddhist magazine *Daihōrin* (Great Dharma Wheel) and therefore exerted influence well beyond the Sōtō Zen sect with which he was affiliated.

36. Ibid.

37. Thomas Cleary, *The Japanese Art of War* (Boston: Shambhala, 1991), 119.

38. Maurice Walshe, trans., *Thus Have I Heard: The Long Discourses of the Buddha* (London: Wisdom, 1987), 63–64.

39. Quoted in Kenneth Chen, *Buddhism in China* (Princeton, N.J.: Princeton University Press, 1964), 357.

40. Demiéville, "Le bouddhisme et la guerre," *Choix d'études Bouddhiques (1929–1970)*, 296.

41. Quoted in Yokoi and Victoria, *Zen Master Dōgen*, 163.

42. Ibid., 165.

43. Ibid., 161.

44. For a brief critique of these three rulers, see the second edition of *Zen at War*, 196–199, 201, and 212.

45. Peter L. Berger, *The Social Reality of Religion* (New York: Penguin, 1973), 53.

6

Buddhists in China during the Korean War (1951–1953)

Xue Yu

On October 8, 1950, China decided to participate in the Korean war by supporting Communist North Korea against the United States of America and South Korea. Within a few days, the state machine had implemented the powerful propaganda campaign of "Resisting America and Assisting Korea, Protecting the Family and Safeguarding the Nation" (抗美援朝、保家衛國). The entire country was then mobilized and millions of Chinese volunteer soldiers crossed the Yalu River into Korea; at the same time, people remaining in China made sacrifices in order to support Chinese soldiers at the warfront. Under these circumstances, Chinese Buddhists, especially monks and nuns, became increasingly involved in war activities, providing material donations and spiritual support for the war.

This chapter examines the war-related activities of Chinese monks and nuns who had undertaken a series of transformative Marxist campaigns since the socialist liberation in 1949. Once again, the government expected their support in China's war efforts. They had to actively demonstrate themselves as "family" members of the Chinese nation under the Communist leadership. Some of them, as recorded in *Xiandai Foxue* (現代佛學), became deeply involved in war activities, such as political propaganda, demonstrative parades, patriotic pledges, and material donations. The phenomenon of monks and nuns campaigning for donations of a Chinese Buddhist airplane and their competition with each other in joining the

Volunteer Army are highlighted in this chapter. These examples demonstrate how monks and nuns, being Buddhists as well as citizens of a new China, attempted to demonstrate their nationalistic ideals and patriotic passions.

The roles of leading Buddhists, such as Ven. Juzan (巨贊), during this period are examined as they assisted the government in shaping its new policy on Buddhism. They reveal the impact of Buddhist activities during the war on the subsequent development of Buddhist institutions in China as a whole. One may conclude that a new form of Buddhism appeared in China during this period. This new form was reinvented largely by the Chinese Buddhists themselves, especially by leading figures who supported the Communist regime and encouraged its strict control over institutional Buddhism. First, however, let us examine the sociopolitical situation in which Buddhists underwent Marxist reeducation; only then will we be able to understand how the Communist government effectively transformed Chinese Buddhists into new patriotic citizens of socialist China.

Buddhism in the Early Communist Era (1949–1953)

The vicissitudes of Buddhism in China since its introduction demonstrate that institutional Buddhism (the *sangha*) could not avoid political influence. In fact, institutional Buddhism sometimes was completely manipulated by political powers. Buddhism would either flourish under the government's patronage or be persecuted mercilessly if the state turned against it. At the end of the Qing Dynasty and into the early Republic Period (1912–1949), Buddhist institutions throughout the country no longer received moral support and legal protection from the state. Instead, temples were destroyed in war or occupied by the military troops of warlords, and temple properties were confiscated for the establishment of public education. Under these circumstances, Master Taixu (太虛; 1898–1947) and others called for Buddhist reform (of doctrines, properties, and organizations) with the hope of mitigating external persecutions and strengthening inner spiritual energies. In the end, however, Master Taixu had to admit that reform efforts had failed. A number of reasons contributed to such failure, including the personal inability of Taixu to organize the Buddhist movements, his lack of the skills necessary to implement such reform ideas, and the powerful resistance of Buddhist conservatives. Perhaps the most important factor was the reform movement's inability to win political support from the Nationalist regime. This may have provided a lesson for Taixu's followers, such as Juzan and Zhao Puchu (趙朴初), who subsequently realized the vital importance of the Communist government's support. As a result,

Juzan and Zhao Puchu went to great lengths to collaborate with the regime; by collaborating, they hoped that a new Buddhist reform could be politically guaranteed, thus legally safeguarding the existence of institutional Buddhism.

Shortly after the founding of the People's Republic of China in 1949, a full-scale reconstruction of socialism in China was enforced under the leadership of the Communist Party. Buddhism, although faced with tremendous uncertainties and challenges, entered this new era with hopes for a better future. The Communists claimed credit for having overthrown or suppressed imperialism, feudalism, and bureaucratic capitalism. With great ambition, they endeavored to build a new and powerful China under the polity of the new democratic revolution. In the beginning, the government called for coexistence with religious communities within the framework of the United Front and patriotic ideology; a policy of freedom of religious belief was announced. As Holmes Welch observed, "Until the Cultural Revolution began in 1966, it was the policy of the Chinese Communist Party to protect Buddhism, while at the same time keeping it under control and utilizing it in foreign policy."[1] By announcing the freedom of religious belief, the government attempted to win support from various religious leaders so that they could effectively convey the government's policy to ordinary religious followers.

From September 21 to 30, 1949, the Chinese People's Political Consultative Conference (CPPCC) held its first meeting in Beijing and passed the Common Program. This served as the first constitution of the People's Republic of China. Of the 662 members who participated in the conference, seven were practitioners of Buddhism, Christianity, or Islam. Article 5 of the Common Program states, "[T]he citizens of the People's Republic of China enjoy the freedom of religious beliefs." In interpreting the statement, the government announced that people enjoyed the freedom to believe in a religion and the freedom to refuse to believe in a religion. Although the members of the Communist Party did not believe in any religion, they understood that religion would not disappear until the advanced development of science and the elimination of social classes. At the end of the conference, the seven members of the religious faction expressed their satisfaction with the religion policy and their appreciation of the government's protection for religions.[2]

It should be pointed out, however, that the religious leaders taking part in the CPPCC did so not because of their religious status but due to the political consideration of presenting "the united front" (統一戰線). On April 13, 1950, Premier Zhou Enlai delivered a speech at the National Conference on the United Front Works in Beijing in which he outlined the government's attitude toward the political participation of religionists:

> We have united democratic personages from religious groups just because they are democratic personages. Giving the permission to the freedom of religious belief is different from inviting the democratic personages from religious groups to participate in CPPCC or other representative meetings. The latter is done purely out of political consideration no matter they are priests or monks.[3]

The government deliberately minimized the religious significance of the religious leaders' presence in the political conference, stating that the participation of those leaders in the conference was not because of their religious professions but because they were democratic personages (民主人士) within the framework of the United Front. The United Front was one of three great resources necessary for the success of the Chinese Communist revolution that had secured the victory of the Communist Party over the Nationalist Party. (The other two were the Communist leadership and the People's Liberation Army.) The aim was to unite all Chinese people collectively to build a new China under the unique leadership of the Communist Party. The principle that guided the United Front at this period was patriotism against imperialism, feudalism, and bureaucratic capitalism.

Patriotism was one of the most inspiring ideas and complicated sentiments in modern history and deeply influenced the Chinese people's thinking and regulated their actions.[4] Although the meaning and content of patriotism changed with the changing political and social environments of different periods, it was always associated with the idea of nationalism. During the period shortly after the founding of the People's Republic of China, patriotism was interpreted to mean that the Chinese people (being proud of the Chinese nation and its long history of civilization) should firmly defend their national territory and integrity, even at the risk of their lives.[5] Being loyal to the nation-state, one should make heroic self-sacrifices for the sovereignty of the country under the leadership of the Communist Party.

Only the Communist Party, the propaganda declared, was able to expel the foreign invasion and counterrevolutionaries so that the Chinese people could become the true masters of their country. Within the framework of patriotism in connection with nationalism, the people's love for the nation was synonymous with their love for the party; such love could be manifested and implemented only through unconditional support for the Communist government. Because the party, the nation-state, and the government at the time were almost identical as a trinity, the Chinese people were urged to follow government policies without question and to respond positively to political movements launched by the state.[6] Only then could they be considered patriots and good citizens of the country. In order to implement such patriotic ideology, the state organized a series of political programs nationwide to reeducate the Chinese people with Marxism.

Shortly after the founding of the People's Republic of China, the government launched a number of political campaigns (such as land reform and three anti- movements), and virtually the entire nation followed the path directed by the Communist Party, without the slightest doubt or question. Most Buddhists seemed to have followed the contemporary social and political trends and expressed their support for the government. Some well-known Buddhists, having participated in and experienced these campaigns, became quite convinced that the Communist Party with its United Front could indeed lead them and other Chinese in the great cause of constructing a new and prosperous China. Although some ordinary monks and nuns may have continued to harbor doubts, uncertainties, and even fear toward the newly founded regime,[7] there was no public way for them to openly express their feelings. It was commonly believed among Buddhists, both lay and clergy, that they enjoyed religious freedom and were considered to be equal citizens of the new China, therefore it was their responsibility to make sacrifices and contributions to the nation.

Many Buddhists believed that, by positively responding to the government's call and undertaking socialist transformation, they would in return receive sympathy from the government, which would then protect Buddhist institutions. Yet, from the viewpoint of the Communist Party, Buddhists (as well as the followers of other religions who became fully engaged in the socialist transformation and construction) would divert their attention from their faith and eventually forget and abandon their religion altogether. Although the Common Program, which served as the constitution, permitted freedom of religious belief, it never clearly stated that people also enjoyed the freedom of religious practice. As Richard Bush has pointed out, religious activities outside the walls of temples were prohibited.[8] Communist documents often stated openly that religion would certainly decline and die with the development of science. The government was to make a great effort to educate people with Marxist materialism so that people would gradually give up their religious beliefs altogether:

> As the genesis and existence of religion is man's oppression by the forces of nature and society, therefore, only when class exploitation has been eliminated from human society and man's power to control nature has been greatly developed, and on this basis man's consciousness and scientific-cultural level have been greatly raised, may religion gradually die out.[9]

Yet, religion would not die quickly; the government needed a policy to facilitate people in abandoning their religion. Therefore, the Communist Party implemented a policy of Marxist education by categorizing religion as superstition, which was considered adverse to science. At the same time, it deterred Chinese people from religious practice, portraying it as backward and harmful to themselves as well as the nation. The result of such a policy and its forceful implementation was the destruction of Buddhist temples throughout China. As Welch reported:

> In the first years after Liberation there were places in China where monasteries were destroyed, monks were beaten or killed, copies of the Buddhist canon were burned, and sacred images were melted down for their metal. In these places the *sangha* or Buddhist clergy, already worried about the effects of land reform, was reduced to "a state of terror."[10]

The state never actually launched any campaign directly targeting the elimination of Buddhism, nor did it openly announce that Buddhist practice should be prohibited because it opposed Marxist ideology. Rather, in order to build a new China, the destruction of Buddhism was systematically implemented by other means, such as land reform and the three antis. The declared purpose was the transformation of all Chinese into new citizens who would build the new socialist China. Members of the *sangha* were requested to abandon their feudal ideology and superstitious practice, give up their temple lands, and demonstrate their hatred toward imperialists, feudalists, and bureaucratic capitalists. Only by doing so could they be qualified as socialist workers and not social parasites (those whose lives depended on laypeople and exploited their hard work). Monks and nuns were advised to closely follow government policies or be considered enemies of the people within the framework of the people's democratic dictatorship. To a large extent, these campaigns successfully transformed monks and nuns, physically as well as mentally. As the lands of temples were confiscated, the livelihoods of monks and nuns could no longer depend on land rents; they eventually became ordinary workers and farmers and readily prepared to follow whatever the Communist Party would advocate in the years to come. As a consequence, their religious identities disappeared, and their religious practices, such as observing Buddhist precepts and conducting ritual services, were abandoned. Monks and nuns who refused to undertake such transformation became the targets of class struggle. As victims of the campaigns, they were identified as the remainders of feudal society and condemned as enemies of the people.

Buddhism in Support of China's Effort for the War

After the Second World War, Korea was divided by the Thirty-eighth Parallel into the Communist North and the capitalist South. When the relationship between the two superpowers (the Soviet Union and the United States) began to deteriorate and the Cold War loomed, tension between the two sides of the Thirty-eighth Parallel intensified. Eventually, on June 25, 1950, war violently arrived. The exact cause for the war remains unclear, but within a few days,[11] North Korean troops advanced deep into the territory of the South. On July 7, the Security Council of the United Nations declared war against the North and established a unified command under the UN flag. The authority for the command was delegated to the United States. Due to the powerful military intervention of the United Nations (or, rather, the United States), the course of the war in Korea turned against the North. Coalition troops led by America successfully launched counterattacks and pushed the troops of the North back toward its border with China.

Meanwhile, on June 27, U.S. president Harry Truman had declared that the United States would do its best to deter China from taking over Taiwan; he ordered the Seventh Fleet to enter the Taiwan Strait. Suddenly, all military actions were perceived as posing an imminent threat to China's security. On October 8, China declared that it was entering the war to assist Korea in resisting America. The Volunteer Army immediately crossed the Yalu River with the rhetorical mission of defending the family and safeguarding the nation.[12] Due to China's involvement, the course of the war was again altered; this time, attacks by U.S. and South Korean troops were effectively halted. China's involvement exerted a tremendous impact not only on the lives of millions of Chinese solders but also on ordinary Chinese, including monks and nuns, who could no longer remain as they had been as they were forced to dedicate themselves to nationwide efforts supporting the war.

It is traditionally believed that the *sangha* may not be involved in social and political activities, and certainly not military campaigns. The earlier history of Chinese Buddhism had demonstrated that monks and nuns in general remained within the temple premises or inside mountain caves, unconcerned with outside worldly affairs. This situation, however, began to change after Master Taixu campaigned for Buddhist reform in the early 1920s. He urged monks and nuns to enter into society and take part in social and political activities. By doing so, it was hoped that Buddhism could better serve the needs of ordinary people in general and that the result would be Buddhism surviving and even reviving. As an example to his followers, Taixu became deeply engaged in Nationalist efforts and in resisting the Japanese invasion during the Anti-Japanese War (1937–1945); he was rewarded by the Nationalist government after the war. Taixu's legacy of political participation and involvement in war was later used by his followers and admirers, who believed that Buddhist reform (in accordance with contemporary social and political developments) was the only way for Chinese Buddhism to survive and be revived. One such follower was Ven. Juzan, well known in modern Chinese history for his vigorous campaign for Buddhist reform and his unswerving support of the Communist government.

When he was a student in Shanghai in the late 1920s, Juzan was an anti-government activist against the Nationalists; he became tonsured partially to escape arrest. He was ordained in Hanzhou and, with the recommendation of Master Taixu, pursued his Buddhist education at Mingnan Buddhist College in Xiamen. During the Anti-Japanese War, Juzan actively organized Buddhist propaganda as well as military campaigns against the Japanese invasion in Hunan and Jiangxi; thus, he became associated with well-known Communist leaders and intellectuals.[13]

In June 1949, Juzan was nominated by his Communist friends to be one of the two Buddhist delegates to attend the October CPPCC in Beijing. In February 1950, while proposing a plan for Buddhist reform, he wrote a letter to Chairman Mao with the signatures of twenty-one well-known Buddhists, expressing Buddhist support for the revolution of the people's democracy under the leadership of the Communist Party.[14] Having received no reply, Juzan then revised the proposal, highlighting Buddhist reform in conformance with the contemporary three anti- campaigns in China. The proposal was later discussed in a symposium held by the Religious Affairs Team of the central government. It was then concluded that Buddhist reform should not be implemented in haste, lest it jeopardize the government's efforts in dealing with religion and cause confusion among ordinary Buddhists.

China's decision to enter the Korean War in October 1950 provided Juzan with a new opportunity in his attempt to implement Buddhist reform. In line with the government's campaign, he quickly initiated a propaganda plan for Buddhists to criticize the U.S. invasion. He called upon all Chinese Buddhists to organize anti-American parades, make patriotic pledges, and establish the committee called Resisting the United States and Assisting Korea Campaign. In January 1951, Juzan and some leading monks in Beijing gathered in Zhongshan Park (中山公園) to discuss how Buddhists should respond to the government's call. Juzan presided over the meeting and delivered the keynote speech, which highlighted the importance of Buddhists' active commitment to the campaign and their preparation for participation in the war. He said:

> We Buddhists uphold peace, yet America is the deadly enemy of peace. Therefore, we must reject American imperialism in order to safeguard peace.... Now, the people of Korea have been severely tortured by imperialist America; assisting Korea will safeguard not only the nation and the world, but also Buddhism.[15]

At this meeting, it was decided to establish the Committee of Buddhist Circles in Beijing for Safeguarding the World Peace and Resisting American Invasion.[16] Juzan and eight other leading Buddhists were elected as members of the standing committee. The participants then discussed plans for various patriotic activities. On February 2, more than 600 monks and nuns, together with 2,000 other Buddhists (including lamas, laypeople, and students from Buddhist schools in Beijing), assembled in Zhongshan Park.[17] In his speech to the gathering, Juzan explained the significance of Buddhist participation in the campaign against the U.S. invasion of Korea:

> The Buddhist campaign as demonstrated today is not a miracle, but sincere responses to the call of Chairman Mao and the people's government. It indicates that Buddhists love their motherland as all other Chinese do.[18]

Juzan reported to the gathering that more than 1,300 monks and nuns in Seoul had joined the People's Army of North Korea. He highly praised the patriotic action of the North Korean monks and urged his Chinese counterparts to follow their example. The participants in the gathering then proceeded to the patriotic parade. Monks and nuns, dressed in gray and black robes with hoods, carried on their shoulders huge portraits of Mao, Stalin, Kim Il-sung, and other leaders of Communist states worldwide. Slogans such as "Resisting the American Invasion" and "Opposing the Remilitarization of Japan" could be heard from far away.

During the meeting before the parade, three separate telegrams were dispatched to Chairman Mao,[19] the Chinese Volunteer Army, and the Korean People's Army, with statements pronouncing the patriotic pledges on behalf of all Buddhists in Beijing:

1. All Buddhist circles are united together in resisting a U.S. invasion of the Taiwan Strait and the remilitarization of Japan, and in safeguarding world peace;
2. studying hard to update our consciousness, firmly opposing all counterrevolutionary and heterodox sects;
3. loving the fatherland, loving the people, and working hard in productive activities'

4. assisting the government to eliminate Nationalist bandits and dismiss rumors; and
5. supporting the people's government, the Communist Party, and Chairman Mao.

Buddhists in Beijing thus initiated nationwide Buddhist participation in the war as they set an example for others to follow. In Wuhan (武漢), more than 2,500 monks, nuns, and lay Buddhists took to the streets for a parade on January 22, 1951. A well-known lay Buddhist, Chen Mingshu (陳銘樞), delivered a speech in which he condemned the U.S. invaders as devils and urged all Buddhists to fight against these devils so that peace would prevail in the world.

In Hanzhou, Buddhist representatives participated in the Symposium of Representatives of All Walks of Life in Hanzhou for Resisting America and Assisting Korea. Ven. Tongyuan, a leading monk in the Buddhist community in the area, explained why monks and nuns, who had traditionally remained within the temple premises, should now take part in such political activities. He pointed out that great compassion, loving-kindness, and heroic strength are the fundamental morals and principles of Buddhism. Therefore, Ven. Tongyuan reasoned, to protect world peace, Buddhists should fight against the invaders who dared to violate the peace.[20]

Buddhist Patriotism during the War

Buddhist activities in China during this period changed with the development of the war in Korea, with international politics, and with the diplomatic policy of the Chinese government; however, one dominant theme of all these activities was always patriotism. Patriotism for Chinese Buddhists during this period implied that, as members of the new socialist China, they should make unconditional sacrifices for the sake of defending the nation, even at the expense of sacrificing their religious commitments. The government urged them to demonstrate the virtues of good citizenship and to manifest their patriotic sentiments. Various ceremonies were arranged at which monks and nuns would make resolute vows to support the Communist Party. Buddhists in China thus embarked on organizing patriotic activities, including disseminating propaganda, signing patriotic pledges, and contributing material donations.

Theoretically, Buddhists extend their compassion and loving-kindness toward all living beings, without showing discrimination or hatred toward anyone. This is especially true for monks and nuns; having once renounced the world, they were to have transcended individual nationalistic ideology with no attachment to the concept of "my country." Yet, it is quite difficult if not impossible (particularly during war) for Buddhists to apply such theories in practice, either because of their worldly inclinations or because of the contemporary political limitations.[21]

What is the just and righteous response for Buddhists, particularly monks and nuns, in responding to violence and war or to political and military calls for involvement in such violence and war? It is suggested in the *Dharmapada* that one should respond to violence with loving-kindness, as violence is never ceased by violence. The Buddha employed peaceful means to dissolve war, and his teachings of non-killing and compassion prevent Buddhists from engaging in violence. On the one hand, violent revenge for violence and waging war against war seems to have been the general practice throughout the history of humanity; only isolated incidents have confirmed that violence could be overcome by peace. On the other hand, it seems impossible for Buddhists to substitute their precepts of nonviolence for their individual responsibility to defend their nation—a principle often enacted into the constitution of a secular state, such as the People's Republic of China.

Being citizens of the Chinese nation, Buddhists were and are duty-bound to positively respond to their government's call to defend the nation. Thus, in the period being discussed, they needed to find some way to deal with the dilemma. To a large extent, ordinary monks and nuns had little influence on the political situation in China. They had virtually no power to dissuade the Communist government from involvement in war, nor to provide a peaceful solution at that time. It seemed that there was no choice for Chinese Buddhists but to follow their government's order. Otherwise, if they entertained doubts and voiced opposition against the war, they would be branded as traitors to their country. Instead of attempting to change the contemporary situation and government policy, most Chinese Buddhists, after about two years of Marxist reeducation, willingly accepted the concept of patriotism as defined at the time by publicly demonstrating their hatred toward the United States and openly calling for the killing of the U.S. invaders, while preparing themselves for participation in the war.

Several articles discussing Buddhism and patriotism appeared in *Xiandai Foxue* (現代佛學 Modern Buddhist Studies) shortly after the Korean War began. One of them, "On Buddhist Patriotism," was written by Juzan. Utilizing Buddhist literature and history, he concluded that, since the time of Śākyamuni Buddha, Buddhists had always been patriotic participants against foreign invasion, and the Buddha supported patriotic action against invaders.[22] Early one morning, Juzan related, a king came to the Buddha and informed him that his army had just successfully repelled an enemy invasion. The king further stated that the invaders would not have been captured had he not responded promptly by sending troops. The Buddha endorsed what the king had said.[23] Then, Juzan cited another example from the *Records of Eminent Monks*: Master Gunabhadra once urged King Vaisa to resist an invasion by a neighboring country with military force, explaining that "the evil invaders should be resisted."[24]

Referring to the Buddhist teachings of compassion and refraining from killing, Juzan insisted that tolerance, quite different from weakness, is a virtue in which one sustains hardship without surrendering; and he argued that compassion and killing are not necessarily contradictory but rather actions that dialectically complement each other. Juzan quoted a passage from the *Yogācāra* bodhisattva precepts text to demonstrate that one may kill others if the killing is for the sake of saving more lives. In connection with the current war, Juzan then said:

> American imperialists attempt to murder more people out of craving, they are robbing thieves. Due to our compassion, we may kill them. By doing so not only would we not violate the precept but also generate more merit.[25]

Chinese Buddhists, especially monks and nuns, always had been scrupulous and conscientious on the issue of killing. Yet in modern history some of them made efforts to reinterpret the precept of nonviolence, suggesting that they could kill others under certain circumstances—such as defending the nation, safeguarding the dharma, and saving more lives. By such reinterpretation, Buddhists might be able to escape from the dilemma of trying to observe the Buddhist precept against violence while fulfilling the constitutional duty of citizens to defend their nation against invasion.

This type of reinterpretation had occurred during the Anti-Japanese War, when progressive clergy vehemently called upon Buddhists to take military action against the Japanese.[26] Juzan, one such advocate, maintained a similar interpretation and spirit during the Korean War. He upheld the idea of compassionate killing as an act of patriotism. To Juzan, resisting America was the same as subduing evils, whereas assisting North Korea was a manifestation of compassion through skillful means. In replying to a question put forward by a reader of *Xiandai Foxue* as to how Buddhist compassion and skillful means would apply to the contemporary war, Juzan stated that the Korean people were at that time undergoing tremendous suffering caused by America. Chinese Buddhists, out of compassion, should therefore release the Koreans from their suffering by eliminating its cause, that is, the U.S. invaders, who were the enemies of world peace.[27] Juzan concluded:

> Buddhists should face the reality without shivering, standing firmly on the side of the anti-invasion. In other words, we should

> staunchly protect our nation without questioning. Therefore, we Buddhists set up an organization to participate in the activities of resisting America and assisting Korea, to safeguard... our own nation from invasion. By doing so, one does not violate Buddhist principles, rather one produces merit. This is the necessary path to releasing suffering for happiness, and Buddhists should take it up seriously. This is the reason why Buddhism and Buddhists resolutely uphold patriotism.[28]

Juzan urged Buddhists in various parts of China to become organized through the patriotic campaign sponsored by the Communist regime, so that they could also demonstrate their Buddhist patriotism. On August 3, 1951, Juzan responded to a letter from a readers inquiring about how Buddhists should be united and reorganized in the contemporary war effort. He advised them to set up a Committee of Buddhist Circles for Resisting America and Assisting Korea, which would have ten benefits:

1. It is in tune with the request of the government.
2. Such patriotic activities could rectify the feudal practice of the world escapism and world isolation of the *sangha*.
3. It demonstrates Buddhist compassion.
4. One cannot love the nation just by words without action; by setting up the committee, Buddhists might expand labor productivity.
5. It may show that Buddhists love their nation and religion.
6. It may solve all of the problems Buddhist institutions face within the framework of patriotism.
7. It may change traditional beliefs about Buddhism so that Buddhists may be respected.
8. At the end of the Korean War, the committee, after reshuffling, may be reorganized as a Buddhist society.
9. By obtaining regular supervision and instruction from the government, the committee may play a significant role in Buddhist affairs.
10. The committee could deal with individual persons and carry out its work with skillful means.[29]

On June 14, 1951, at the Conference of Young Christians held in Beijing, Zhao Puchu, a leading lay Buddhist in Beijing and Shanghai, delivered a speech that summarized the political task of religious believers. He emphasized the importance of religious followers expounding on the spirit of patriotism and actively participating in the struggles against the imperialist invasion. He then continued:

> It is required in all religions that their followers must love their nation and people, resisting invasion and safeguarding peace. Buddhists are duty-bound to repay the kindness of the nation and people, and always remind ourselves of this duty through reciting the scriptures everyday. Working for the benefit and happiness of people without considering even our lives is the vow of Buddhists.[30]

Zhao Puchu urged Buddhists to work for the Chinese people even at the risk of their lives. He reiterated the importance of a religious follower loving his nation (愛國) more than his religion (愛教). Loving one's nation is primary while loving one's religion is secondary in that the existence of one's religion *depends* on the existence of one's nation. Chinese Buddhists had no separate political standpoints, but always shared the same ideology that the Chinese people expressed under the leadership of the Communist Party. In other words, in demonstrating their patriotism, Chinese Buddhists should work hard for their country and stand firmly by their fellow citizens; only then could they be in a position to love their religion.

The patriotic sentiments of Buddhists at the time were also manifested in their eulogies for the greatness and nobility of Chairman Mao; only he, as they and other Chinese at the time commonly believed, could protect the nation and save them from suffering. Ven. Yiliang, a leading monk in Beijing, expressed his belief that Mao and the Communist Party had brought a new era to China, so that people could enjoy unprecedented happiness and freedom. During the forty years of revolution, the Communist Party had generated the superior merits of kindness, and all Chinese should repay these merits of kindness by following the instructions of the party leaders. Ven. Yiliang called upon all Buddhists to pay homage to the Communist regime and to eulogize the absolute rightness of its policy on culture. In order to repay these great kindnesses and merits of the party and Chairman Mao, Yiliang suggested that Buddhists put Buddhist compassion into practice within the context of patriotism, willingly making sacrifices for whatever cause the nation was undertaking.

It is generally understood among Buddhists that one who practices great compassion and loving-kindness shares happiness with all sentient beings and releases their sufferings without discrimination. Yet very few Buddhists practice such ideas in their daily activities. Some monks at this time believed that Buddhist compassion and loving-kindness should be guided by the principle of wisdom. "One has to be compassionate to good people, but if one is compassionate to bad people, it will indirectly help bad people to do evil things."[31] The standard criteria in making such distinctions between the bad and the good were those that were in accordance with the principles of the party and the sayings of Mao. The Buddha showed great compassion to his contemporary people, yet he also fought against Devadatta and other evil ones. Ven. Yiliang (一量) reminded Buddhists that they should make a clear distinction without the slightest ambiguity between good and bad, friends and enemies, and stand always on the side of the Volunteer Army and the People's Army; they should show no sympathy whatsoever but only hatred toward the U.S. troops and the puppet government of South Korea.[32]

On March 8, 1951, a Committee of Buddhist Circles in Nanchang for Resisting America and Assisting Korea was organized, and Ven. Xindao and 15 other leading monks were elected as committee members. On March 11, Xindao made the following address to a meeting of 187 monks and nuns from the Nanchang area:

> We know that the people's government surely guarantees the freedom of religious belief. We Buddhists must unite as quickly as possible, and together with the followers of other religions, unconditionally support the Volunteer Army [志願軍] and the People's Army [人民軍]. The best thing to do is to join the army directly and to learn the spirit in which Śākyamuni, the embodiment of compassion, killed robbers in order to save people and endured suffering on behalf of all living creatures. To wipe out the American imperialist demons, who are destroying world peace, is in accordance with Buddhist doctrines; it is not only blameless but actually will give rise to merit as well.[33]

The Buddhist campaign of patriotism conducted by leading Buddhists certainly affected ordinary monks and nuns, who then demonstrated their patriotic enthusiasm by doing whatever the government asked of them. The Committees of Buddhists for Resisting America and Assisting Korea already existed in different regions and were then gradually established nationwide. Some Buddhists signed their patriotic pledges and undertook political studies while others organized public parades. According to an incomplete record pieced together from *Xiandai Foxue*, monks and nuns in more than twenty cities organized public parades, and more than 10,000 signed patriotic pledges from June 1950 to August 1953.

Marxist education and the socialist transformation of institutional Buddhism inside temples had begun immediately after the founding of the People's Republic of China in 1949. In some places before the war, monks and nuns had already been transformed through the reeducation program into ordinary socialist workers and peasants. Their Buddhist identities gradually disappeared, their activities lost any Buddhist flavor, and monks and nuns became common workers and farmers in new China. Unfortunately, it is difficult to know the activities of these "ex-Buddhists." In some places where Buddhist participation in the war was specifically reported (and even highlighted to demonstrate Buddhist enthusiasm and patriotism), two of the most significant and widespread activities were the donations for the Chinese Buddhist airplane and the recruitment of young monks and nuns into the Chinese Volunteer Army.

Donation of the Buddhist Airplane and Military Recruitment

The Buddhist campaign to donate an airplane and other military equipment was not the first time this had happened in modern Chinese history. Earlier, in the Republic Period, monks and nuns responding to the Nationalist appeal organized such campaigns during the Anti-Japanese War. Yet, at this time, the campaign was more widespread and was permeated with stronger patriotic passion. In the middle of 1951, U.S. troops intensified their counterattacks, causing enormous casualties among Chinese solders and massive destruction of their military equipment. On June 1, the General Committee of Chinese People for Resisting America and Assisting Korea issued an urgent appeal to all Chinese people to participate in the campaign of patriotic pledges, to donate money for airplanes and cannons, and to provide desired services to the families of the Volunteer Army.[34] Quickly, effectively, and with enthusiasm, the Chinese people responded to the appeal, so did the Buddhists.

The Committee of Buddhist Circles in Beijing for Resisting America and Assisting Korea sent an open letter to all Buddhists in China, stating, "All fellow Buddhists, let us actively make contributions! We must donate a Chinese Buddhist airplane [中國佛教號飛機]. We must work hard to increase production."[35] On June 20, 1951, Buddhists in Jiuquan in Guansu province sent another letter to *Xiandai Foxue*, challenging all other Buddhists in China to make contributions to the Buddhist airplane.[36] The letter stated that even children were saving their pocket money to purchase a "children's airplane" for the Volunteer Army. Buddhists, who were family members of the Chinese nation, should not hesitate to do the same. The letter further declared:

> [We Buddhists] should dispel all misgivings in observing precepts that we would perhaps violate the precept of non-killing if we donate the airplane or cannons, which are the instruments of killing. [We] dare to assure that one who practices the bodhisattva's path will take up a knife and kill evil ones so that the good people may live in peace and happiness. The crazy criminals of American imperialists

> have threatened the peace of the whole world. [They] attempt to rule the world and take charge over Asia, so their bombardments and killing have become intensified. It is crystal clear now that peace and invasion cannot live simultaneously together. Safeguarding the nation is definitely the important task of every citizen. We are determined to eliminate all evil enemies through "killing for stopping killing." Removing all sense of worries, we shall further unite all peoples of different nationalities, and take actions to accomplish the donation task.[37]

The letter specified two sorts of donations, one general and one special. The general donation was to fulfill the duty of Buddhists as family members of the Chinese nation; the special donation was for Buddhists to make specific contributions for the purchase of the Buddhist airplane. Finally, the letter challenged all Buddhists to fulfill their patriotic duty in accordance with the Buddhist practices of compassion, loving-kindness, appreciative joy, and equanimity. Within a short period, the call had received overwhelming responses from Buddhists throughout China. Especially in big cities, such as Beijing, Shanghai, Suzhou, and Tianjin, Buddhists established special committees to conduct the campaigns.

Buddhists in Shanghai promised to contribute 750 million yuan which, according to the current value, was half of the cost of an airplane. The Committee of Buddhist Circles in Beijing for Resisting America and Assisting Korea pledged on behalf of all Buddhists in the area that it would collect about 60–100 million yuan within the next half year. Meanwhile, it was proposed that the task of providing the rest of the money needed for the airplane should be shared by Buddhists in other cities.[38] In order to quicken the process of collecting the donations, the committee passionately appealed:

> Fellow Buddhists all over China, everyone is duty-bound to love one's country. How could we Buddhists lag behind . . . ? Please work harder, we must endeavor to accomplish our patriotic task in time as scheduled.[39]

The donation campaign quickly spread among Buddhist communities in different parts of China. It seemed that each province or city, having received a quota from Beijing, in turn shared it among the temples and individual Buddhists in the area. Some individual Buddhists pledged to work longer every day and donate the extra income, while others promised to save a certain amount of money each day. The *sangha* in Shanghai urged individual monks to save 200 yuan or 500 yuan per day; nuns were asked to contribute 200 yuan per day as well. Collectively, temples were sorted into four classes depending on their size and wealth, with the first class donating 20,000 yuan per day, the second donating 10,000 yuan, the third 5,000 yuan, and the fourth 2,500 yuan per day. The Buddhist Youth Society in Shanghai requested its 600 members to donate 6,000, 30,000, 60,000, or 120,000 yuan respectively.[40] It was anticipated that the donation campaign for the Buddhist airplane in Shanghai would be completed within six months.

The donation campaign for the Buddhist airplane was well received in many parts of China due to the prevailing patriotic sentiments at the time and the involvement of well-known Buddhists. The money was gradually remitted to Beijing through the People's Bank, with a specific indication for the Chinese Buddhist airplane. On November 3, 1951, the Panchen Lama[41] in Xining (西寧) issued a statement:

> [I] pledge to do my best to appeal to Tibetan people and Buddhists that they actively participate in the campaign of Resisting America and Assisting Korea, to donate military equipment with enthusiasm. We should make efforts to fulfill the plan of purchasing a Buddhist fighter plane earlier than scheduled.[42]

The available information indicates that, unlike what happened during the Anti-Japanese War—when some Buddhists had questioned the authenticity and legitimacy of a Buddhist airplane (which would cause the massive destruction of human lives)—no such voice was recorded this time. Buddhists in general seem to have supported the campaign; some regretted the difficulty in fulfilling their assigned quotas due to different reasons, such as lack of income. While expressing their difficulty and sorrow, however, these Buddhists never criticized the campaign itself. They did not complain about being rather forcibly assigned donation quotas, nor did they articulate any unwillingness to make such contributions. Quite the contrary, despite bemoaning their poor economic situations, they promised to do their best to donate their assigned share of the money.[43] Meanwhile, some of them who were unable to pay their share donated their products—such as raw rice and wheat—as substitute compensation. Buddhists in Guangzhou City had been asked to donate 100 million yuan, but by the end of November 1951, only 20 million yuan had been collected. The Study Society of Buddhists in Guangzhou then decided to organize a sale of vegetables, with all income to be donated to their quota. For three days, May 29–31, 1952, a vegetable sale was held in Liu Rong Temple (六榕寺), and 12,183,700 yuan were collected.[44] By January 1952, Buddhists in Beijing proudly announced that they had already contributed 58,711,600 yuan and thus almost completed the assigned donation task earlier than scheduled.[45]

At the same time as the campaign for the donation of the Chinese Buddhist airplane, another campaign was under way throughout China to encourage young monks and nuns to join the Volunteer Army. The phenomenon of Buddhist clergy joining the army to defend the nation against a foreign invasion had already been seen during the Anti-Japanese War. This time, however, more *sangha* members were recruited, demonstrating how Buddhists, endowed with patriotism, had supported the Communist government. Shortly after China's involvement in the war, a nationwide campaign for military recruitment among young Chinese people took place and attracted the attention of the Buddhist *sangha*, especially the young monks.

Having gone through a number of sociopolitical campaigns and regular Marxist studies, young monks and nuns gradually transformed themselves, both physically and mentally, into new citizens of the Chinese nation, ready to sacrifice their religion and even their lives for their country. Their religious commitment became secularized and the sacredness of monkhood disappeared from their daily lives, which became no different than that of ordinary secular Chinese. The only exception was that they continued to wear Buddhist robes; in some places, they even wore the same clothing as ordinary secular Chinese. These young monks and nuns were then considered by themselves and by others as common family members of the Chinese nation.

Meanwhile, Buddhist leaders, advised by the government, constantly encouraged the socialist transformation of the *sangha*. They insisted that Buddhists accept the leadership of the Communist Party by following the instructions of the government and by taking part in political campaigns sponsored by the regime. Under these circumstances, the question of whether monks and nuns would violate Buddhist discipline if they followed the government's order became unimportant in comparison to fulfilling their national duty. Some were convinced that their activities (even bearing arms and killing enemies in the war) were actually sanctioned by Buddhist doctrines and justified by the contemporary situation. The question they often asked was not why but how Buddhists should make contributions to the nation by participating in the war. Thus, the phenomenon was often seen where elder monks sent their young monk-disciples to report for military duties; the young monks were happy and proud to become members of the Volunteer Army.

At the beginning of the Korean War, it was often seen that monks and nuns went, alone or together, with other Chinese people and participate in a street demonstration. They would join in shouting anti-American slogans and pledging in public that they were prepared to go to the front and fight against the invaders. Later, when the campaign for military recruitment occurred in China, it was often reported that young monks changed from their robes into military uniforms at the military recruitment stations. Their decision to join the army was considered to be the glory of the entire Buddhist community and thus welcomed by the government and supported by the *sangha*.

In January 1951, a young monk named Shangchun from Qingliang Temple in Changzhou (常州) submitted an application for military enlistment, which was quickly accepted. A farewell celebration party was organized one afternoon inside Qingliang Temple, which was attended by more than forty leading monks and nuns from major temples in the area. All of them extended their blessings and appreciation in support of Shangchun's decision and action.[46] After the party, there was a public parade in which Shangchun rode on a horse while wearing a huge red flower pinned on the front of his clothes. More than twenty Buddhists, including monks and nuns, marched at the front of the parade, carrying red flags, beating drums, and striking gongs. Fireworks announced the event. The parade passed through major streets of the city and attracted large crowds of people who highly praised the patriotic act of the young monk.

After a recruitment meeting held on June 10, 1951, on Jiuhua Mountain (九華山), a number of monks pledged to join the Volunteer Army. One of them, Wu Yunhen, expressed his happiness and willingness:

> Joining the army is a glorious task and we must fulfill [it]. After all, we monks are to save people and the world without any misgiving. I hope we young Buddhists do not cling to such a small place as Jiuhua Mountain, nor should we forget the great cause of serving the nation. Only then could we Buddhists be called Good Men [好男兒].[47]

It is difficult to hear the voices of the *sangha* resisting such recruitment, either because the monks and nuns dared not articulate their resistance, or because such articulation was intentionally kept away from the public. The *sangha* was portrayed as united in voice and action in following the direction of the government. The only negative responses could be seen in the concerned expressions of some older monks and nuns, who were quoted as saying that the temples would be left with only old and weak monks and nuns if young ones went to the front.[48] It is difficult to calculate how many young monks joined the army during this period,[49] yet according to the available information, Buddhist communities in general seem to have encouraged military enlistment, and many young monks showed their readiness for it. For instance, in Jiuhua Mountain, the five monks who joined the army represented one-third of the total number of applicants from the entire village.[50] In Emei Mountain, several dozens (數十人) of young monks joining the army gave it the highest representation among all of the communities in that county.[51]

Several explanations were suggested for the enthusiasm for military enlistment among young Buddhist clergy. One was that it was an expression of patriotism. Another suggestion was that it demonstrated their appreciation of the government's policy on Buddhism. It was also suggested that this was an actual demonstration of true bodhisattva spirit in serving the world. Yet the phenomenon may also indicate that, after various political campaigns, young monks were forced to acknowledge reality: the existence of Buddhism was at risk of disappearing in China, and their future as members of the *sangha* was full of uncertainty. As Holmes Welch said, "The monastery no longer offered a refuge from the dust of the world. And what sort of future lay ahead for those who stayed in it?"[52] Joining the army, which could be the triple blessings for the Buddhist community, the nation, and young monks themselves, perhaps would be one of the wiser choices.

Conclusion

In the early 1950s, China underwent a dramatic transition from neo-democracy to socialism (1949–1956); great changes took place throughout the nation. A new China was founded on the ruins of colonialism and feudalism.[53] Numerous patriotic and political campaigns sponsored by the Communist government were conducted nationwide to cleanse the old thoughts and to transform the Chinese people into new socialist citizens. These campaigns were aimed at stabilizing social, political, and economic developments. The Chinese people participated in such campaigns with complete or, rather, innocent trust and enthusiasm, full of hope for the better future promised by the Communist regime.

The government conducted these campaigns anticipating that all Chinese people would be united under Communist leadership. Monks and nuns were told that they could either act as patriotic citizens or be left behind (and even eliminated) in the new social and political environment. In general, they responded to such campaigns with enthusiasm; they extended their full support to the government with patriotic passion. Indeed, some were fascinated with the idea of being new citizens and family members of the Chinese nation. They eagerly limited or hid their religious differences, mental and physical, from the rest of the Chinese people. Gradually, the gap between the temples and society disappeared as monks and nuns followed the orders and instructions of the government along with other ordinary Chinese people.

At an early period of the People's Republic of China, patriotism reigned supreme in most part of China; it reached its zenith during the Korean War. Patriotism served almost as a new religion, which endeavored to unify the nation by demanding the complete faith and surrender of ordinary citizens to the state. Through the use of the state machinery, the government exercised all of its power in conducting patriotic education and disseminating propaganda among the masses. The Chinese people were requested to love their nation by working hard to strengthen the people's democracy, to defend the nation from invasion, and to make the utmost contributions to the reconstruction of the motherland. Such ideological education and propaganda penetrated deeply into the *sangha*. As a result, Buddhists became obliged to discontinue Buddhist traditions and practices that had endured for thousands of years. Voluntarily or by force, they were prepared for participation in the activities of resisting America and assisting Korea. By these activities, they were identified as true patriotic citizens of the Chinese nation, with high and noble aspirations.

The successful self-transformation and active participation of Chinese Buddhists in the war were made possible largely because of the commitment of some leading Buddhists, both clergy and lay, such as Juzan and Zhao Puchu. It is still unclear whether they were fully convinced that Buddhism could be revived only through self-reform under the Communist leadership, or whether they simply realized the futility of resisting the socialist transformation of the *sangha*. It is clear, however, that they grasped the opportunity presented by the Korean War to push Buddhists into society to work for the nation and to make their contributions to China's efforts in the war.

Buddhists in China at the time seem to have sincerely believed that only the Communist Party could save China and protect Buddhism. Therefore, only by following the path provided, or dictated, by the Communist government could Buddhism survive and revive. On behalf of their Buddhist communities, Buddhist leaders urged ordinary monks and nuns to make self-sacrifices, self-concessions, and self-submissions to the interests of the nation, party, and government. What was said and done during this period may reveal the reality that some Buddhists were even more eager and active to reform Buddhism than were their Communist comrades. Their activities and advocacy can only be understood within the contemporary social and political contexts and might be considered a skillful means of attempting to save Buddhism. The impact of their activities should also be considered in discussing their contributions to both modern Buddhism and the subsequent development of Buddhism in China. On one hand, they helped the government to impose strict policies on Buddhism; on the other hand, they encouraged Buddhists to accept such policies without resistance. As a result, Buddhism almost disappeared from mainland China in the following two decades. Buddhists and especially their leaders probably did not anticipate that they might contribute to its disappearance.

NOTES

1. Holmes Welch, *Buddhism under Mao* (Cambridge, Mass.: Harvard University Press, 1972), 1.

2. Guangwu Lo, *The Outline of Great Events of Religious Works in New China* (Beijing: Huawen Publication Society, 2001), 2 (羅廣武，《新中國宗教工作大事概覽》，北京：華文出版社，二００一年，第二頁。).

3. Lo, *Outline of Great Events of Religious Works in New China*, 3 (羅廣武，《新中國宗教工作大事概覽》，華文出版社，二００一年，第三頁。). Holmes Welch gave a different interpretation, in which he quoted from Juzan's report after he had listened to the brief on Zhou's speech: "The government in its cooperation with religion is after political, not ideological conformity. Every religion should stay within its proper confines" (Welch, *Buddhism under Mao*, 3). This is the second-hand translation from the later report of Juzan. See Juzan, *Collections of Juzan* (Nanjing: Jiansu Guji Publication Society, 2000), 2:713 (巨贊，《巨贊集》，江蘇古藉出版社，二０００年，第二卷，第七一三頁。).

4. The meaning of patriotism has varied in different social, political, and geographic contexts throughout its long history of use. An interesting discussion about its changes is in Mary Dietz's "Patriotism: A Brief History of the Term," in *Patriotism*, ed. Igor Primoratz (New York: Humanity, 2002), 201–215.

5. There are similarities between Chinese nationalism and patriotism in modern Chinese history; see Yongnian Zheng, *Discovering Chinese Nationalism in China* (Cambridge: Cambridge University Press, 1999), 87–95.

6. Peichao Li, *Historic Development of Patriotism of Chinese Nation* (Wuhan: Hubei Jiaoyu Publication Society, 2001), 22–24 (李培超，《中華民族愛國主義發展史》，湖北教育出版社，二００一年，第二二～二四頁。).

7. Such fears and worries already existed before 1949. In some areas, Communists had already carried out land reform to reduce rents, and monks and nuns who used to possess large amounts of temple lands had to either give up their possessions or reduce their rents; otherwise, they would be persecuted and punished as counterrevolutionaries.

8. Richard Bush Jr., *Religion in Communist China* (Nashville, Tenn.: Abingdon, 1970), 15. All public areas outside of any religious premises are available for atheistic and antireligious activities.

9. Chang Chih-i, "A Correct Understanding and Implementation of the Party Policy Concerning Freedom of Religious Belief," *Minzu tuanjie* (Unity of Nationalities) (Bejing: Minzu Publication Society, Apr. 1962), 2–5. Translated in *Union Research Service* 28 (Aug. 31, 1962): 295, here cited by Bush, *Religion in Communist China*, 18.

10. Welch, *Buddhism under Mao*, 1.

11. Burton Kaufman, *The Korean War: Challenges in Crisis, Credibility, and Command* (Philadelphia: Temple University Press, 1986), 31.

12. Jialu Xu, ed, *Daily History of the People's Republic of China* (Chengdu: Siquan Renmin Publication Society, 2003) (許嘉璐主編《中華人民共和國日史》，成都：四川人民出版社，二００三年，卷一，第四七六～四七七頁。); Yongnian Zheng, *Discovering Chinese Nationalism in China* (Cambridge: Cambridge University Press, 1999), 476–477.

13. Xue Yu, *Buddhism, War, and Nationalism: Chinese Monks in the Struggle against Japanese Aggressions, 1931–1945* (London: Routledge, 2005), 143–148.

14. Juzan, *Collections of Juzan,* (Nanjing: Jiansu guji chuban she, 2000), 2:706–708 (巨贊，《巨贊文集》，南京：江蘇古藉出版社，二０００年，第二卷，第七０六～七０八。). An English translation of the summary of the letter can also be found in Welch, *Buddhism under Mao,* 94–96.

15. *Xiandai Foxue* (*Modern Buddhist Studies*) 1.6 (1951): 30 (《現代佛學》，第一卷，第六期，一九五一年，第三十頁。). This news was quoted from *People's Daily,* January 8, 1951. Holmes Welch translated *Xiandai Foxue* (現代佛學) as *Modern Buddhism.* It seems that he understood *foxue* (佛學), Buddhist studies, as equivalent to *fojiao* (佛教), Buddhism. It was rather sensitive at the time to use the term Buddhism in the title of a Buddhist journal. See Welch, *Buddhism under Mao,* 11–17.

16. 北京市佛教界保衛世界和平反對美國侵略委員會. The committee was later renamed as the Committee of Buddhist Circles in Beijing for Resisting America and Assisting Korea ((北京佛教界抗美緩朝委員會)).

17. It was reported by the Xinhua News Agency that about 80 percent of the total number of monks and nuns from about 400 temples in Beijing participated in the parade. As one of the leading monks, Xiuquan, said, "For hundreds of years, we monks did not have the right of parading. Now, we are liberated. Chairman Mao treats us as members of the people's family so that we can participate in the parade." *Xiandai Foxue* (*Modern Buddhist Studies*) 1.6 (1951): 30 (《現代佛學》，第一卷，第六期，一九五一年，第三十頁。).

18. *Xiandai Foxue* (*Modern Buddhist Studies*) 1.6 (1951): 30 (《現代佛學》，第一卷，第六期，一九五一年，第三十頁。).

19. Part of the telegram to Chairman Mao goes like this:

> Since the liberation of Beijing, we Buddhists of four groups [四**衆**弟子] have studied new revolutionary theories. Combining the Buddhist ideas of national protection and patriotism in connection with internationalism, we all have taken part in the campaign of Resisting America and Assisting Korea. . . . We Buddhists of four groups solemnly pledge a vow to you: Under your leadership, we shall intensify our studies, enhance our political consciousness, and work harder in productive activities. We shall follow [Buddhist?] doctrines, endeavor for lasting peace and resist the invasion war. Endowed with the spirit of great courage, we shall fight to the death against American imperialists who are the deadly enemies of the people.

Xiandai Foxue (*Modern Buddhist Studies*) 1.6 (1951): 30 (現代佛學》，第一卷，第六期，一九五一年，第三十頁。).

20. *Xiandai Foxue* (*Modern Buddhist Studies*) 1.6 (1951): 31 (《現代佛學》，第一卷，第六期，一九五一年，第三十一頁。).

21. Buddhist activities in this area can be found in a number of works, such as Walpola Rahula, *The Heritage of the Bhikkhu: A Short History of the Bhikkhu in Educational, Cultural, Social, and Political Life* (New York: Grove, 1974); Stanley Jeyaraja Tambiah, *Buddhism Betrayed? Religion, Politics, and Violence in Sri Lanka* (Chicago: University of Chicago Press, 1992); Yu, *Buddhism, War, and Nationalism;*

and 學愚，『太虛大師的民族主義與世界主義』方立天，學愚編，《佛教傳統與當代文化》，北京：中華書局，二０ ０六，第六一～七九頁。.

22. Juzan, "On Buddhist Patriotism," *Xiandai foxue* (*Modern Buddhist Studies*)1.11 (1951): 4 (巨贊，『論佛教的愛國主義』，《現代佛學》第一卷，第十一期，一九五一年．第四頁。).

23. The original record of this event can be found in Taisho 2 (152):653.

24. The original source can be found in Taisho 50 (2059):340b, although, according to its context, it was originally supposed to show the supernatural power of Gunabhadra that he could predict the future.

25. Juzan, "On Buddhist Patriotism," 4 (巨贊，『論佛教的愛國主義』，《現代佛學》第一卷，第十一期，一九五一年．第四頁。).

26. Their activities in Hunan and Guilin were full of military spirit. See Yu, *Buddhism, War, and Nationalism*. 143–149.

27. *Xiandai Foxue* (*Modern Buddhist Studies*)1.3 (1950): 27 (《現代佛學》，第一卷，第三期，一九五０年（十一月），第二十七頁。).

28. Juzan, "On Buddhist Patriotism," 4–5 (巨贊，『論佛教的愛國主義』，《現代佛學》第一卷，第十一期，一九五一年（７）．第四～五頁。).

29. *Xiandai Foxue* (*Modern Buddhist Studies*) 2.1 (1951): 23 and 24 (《現代佛學》，第二卷，第一期，一九五一年（九月），第二十三～二十四頁。).

30. *Xiandai Foxue* (*Modern Buddhist Studies*) 1.7 (1951): 7 (《現代佛學》，一九五一年（七月），第七頁。).

31. *Xiandai Foxue* (*Modern Buddhist Studies*) 4 (1954): 16 (《現代佛學》第四期，一九五三年（四），第十六頁。). The English translation is quoted from Welch, *Buddhism under Mao*, 278–279.

32. Yiliang, "Patriotic Issues of Four Groups of Buddhists," *Xiandai Foxue* (*Modern Buddhist Studies*) 1.11 (1951): 6–7 (一量，『四衆弟子的愛國主義問題』，《現代佛學》第一卷，第十一期，一九五一年（７）第六～七頁。).

33. *Xiandai Foxue* (*Modern Buddhist Studies*) 1.8 (1951): 35 (《現代佛學》第一卷，第八期，一九五一年，第三十五頁。). The translation is from Welch, *Buddhism under Mao*, 277.

34. Jialu Xu, *Daily History of the People's Republic of China*, 2:190–192 (許嘉璐主編《中華人民共和國日史》，四川人民出版社，二０ ０三年，卷二，第一九０～九二頁。). Meanwhile, on June 2, 1951, an editorial in the *People's Daily* called for a campaign to have all Chinese people take patriotic oaths.

35. *Xiandai Foxue* (*Modern Buddhist Studies*) 6.10 (1951): 1 (《現代佛學》第一卷，第十期，一九五一年（六），第一頁。).

36. It is interesting to notice that Buddhists in Jiuquan had appealed to other Buddhists to donate an airplane for Chinese soldiers during the Anti-Japanese War.

37. *Xiandai Foxue* (*Modern Buddhist Studies*) 1.11 (1951): 33 (《現代佛學》第一卷，第十一期，一九五一年（七），第三十三頁。).

38. *Xiandai Foxue* (*Modern Buddhist Studies*) 1.12 (1951): 28 (《現代佛學》第一卷，第十二期，一九五一年（八），第二十八頁。). On March 1, 1955, 10,000 Chinese yuan was equivalent to about 45 U.S. cents (100,000:4.5).

39. *Xiandai Foxue* (*Modern Buddhist Studies*) 1.12 (1951): 28 (《現代佛學》第一卷，第十二期，一九五一年（八），第二十八頁。).

40. *Xiandai Foxue* (*Modern Buddhist Studies*) 1.12 (1951): 29 (《現代佛學》第一卷，第十二期，一九五一年（八），第二十九頁。).

41. In May 1951, both the Panchen Lama and the Dalai Lama had come to Beijing on the occasion of signing the "Treaty on the Peaceful Liberation of Tibet."

42. *Xiandai Foxue* (*Modern Buddhist Studies*) 2.4 (1951): 16 (《現代佛學》第二卷，第四期，一九五一年（十二），第十六頁。).

43. *Xiandai Foxue* (*Modern Buddhist Studies*) 2.2 (1951): 23 (《現代佛學》第二卷，第二期，一九五一年（十），第二十三頁。).

44. *Xiandai Foxue* (*Modern Buddhist Studies*) 2.8 (1952): 25–26 (《現代佛學》第二卷，第八期，一九五二年（四），第二十六～二十七頁。).

45. In "A Letter to All Buddhists in China," *Xiandai Foxue* (*Modern Buddhist Studies*) 1.12 (1951): 28 (《現代佛學》第一卷，第十二期，一九五一年（八），第二十八頁), The Committee of Buddhist Circles in Beijing for Resisting America and Assisting Korea, promised to contribute 100–600 million yuan. The shortage may be explained by some difficulties in the actual campaign. *Xiandai Foxue* (*Modern Buddhist Studies*) 2.5 (1952): 23 (《現代佛學》第二卷，第五期，一九五二年（一），第二十三頁。).

46. *Xiandai Foxue* (*Modern Buddhist Studies*) 1.6 (1951): 35 (《現代佛學》第一卷，第六期，一九五一年（二），第三十五頁。).

47. *Xiandai Foxue* (*Modern Buddhist Studies*) 1.11 (1951): 34 (《現代佛學》第一卷，第十一期，一九五一年（七），第三十四頁。).

48. In a temple of more than 300 resident monks, both the temple and the old monks were left without care after dozens of young monks joined the army. *Xiandai Foxue* (*Modern Buddhist Studies*) 1.12 (1951): 23 (《現代佛學》第一卷，第十二期，一九五一年（八），第二十三頁 。). They were told by the editor of *Xiandai Foxue* that the reduction in the number of monks would not do any damage to Buddhist institutions in China, but rather be a blessing for the future.

49. According to *Xiandai Foxue*, only one case was reported in which a nun joined the army and went to military college for training. The practice of leaving the *sangha* and joining the army occurred during this period even before the outbreak of the Korean War. By February 1950, twenty-four out of forty monks at the Jing'an Si Seminary in Shanghai had joined the army or entered into military training. See Welch, *Buddhism under Mao*, ch. 1, n. 90.

50. *Xiandai Foxue* (*Modern Buddhist Studies*) 2.2 (1951): 21 (《現代佛學》第二卷，第二期，一九五一年（十），第二十一頁。).

51. *Xiandai Foxue* (*Modern Buddhist Studies*) 1.12 (1951): 30 (《現代佛學》第一卷，第十二期，一九五一年（八），第三十頁。).

52. Welch, *Buddhism under Mao*, 68.

53. Zedong Mao, *Selected Collections of Mao Zedong* (Beijing: Renmin Publication Society, 1967), 2:665 (毛澤東，《毛澤東選集》，第二卷，北京：人民出版社，一九六七年，第六六五頁。).

7

Onward Buddhist Soldiers: Preaching to the Sri Lankan Army

Daniel W. Kent

It is almost nine o'clock in Mihintale, the dusty Sri Lankan city said to have hosted the arrival of Buddhism to the island.[1] The sky is dark, but light and sound pour from the small temple of Bogahayāya. Silver dollar–sized red clay oil lamps cast flickering light on uniformed soldiers sitting cross-legged on the ground, listening to the local monk, Ānandavaṃsa, preaching a sermon on the topic of *sīla*, discipline and morality. Most soldiers in the audience bear physical and mental scars from their times on the battlefield, such as a fidgeting young captain wearing special shoes to reduce the limp caused by a 50-caliber bullet that tore through his upper thigh five years ago. The stocky color sergeant can barely grasp the tray of flowers he offers to the Bodhi tree, having lost movement in three of the fingers on his right hand due to infection after surviving for three days in a swamp after his regiment left him for dead.

For each solider who survives to show scars, others never get the chance for a special shoe or a weak grip. The war dead, physically absent from the sermon at the temple, call to mind the *Yodhājīvasutta*, a story in the Pāli canon of a warrior who asked the Buddha whether it is true that soldiers who die on the battlefield are reborn in heaven. The Buddha remained silent in response. Undaunted, the warrior asked again, but the Buddha again remained silent. After being asked a third time, the Buddha responded, telling the warrior that those who die on the battlefield will not be reborn in heaven. He explained that those who die on the battlefield are

FIGURE 7.1 Ven. Ānandavaṃsa preaches to soldiers of the Sixth Sri Lankan Light Infantry Regiment following a Bodhipūjā ceremony on the evening of March 9, 2007. Photo taken by Daniel Kent.

inevitably overcome with hatred and pain and are born, according to those feelings, in a hell realm (*Saṃyutta Nikāya* XLII.3). Given this bleak outlook, what does Buddhist belief, doctrine, and practice have to offer to the soldiers gathered in Mihintale, listening to Ānandavaṃsa's sermon and considering the fate of their fallen comrades and perhaps their own futures?[2] In an economy ravaged by a quarter century of civil war, there are few employment opportunities; most soldiers come from poor families to fight and kill for the *raṭa*, *jātiya*, and *āgama*: the country, nation, and religion. Are they doomed to hell for their choice of occupation?

Although there are no uniformed chaplains in the Sri Lankan military, monks living at temples near the army camps serve the religious needs of the soldiers both informally and through Buddhist sermons, or *baṇa*. Individual regiments often invite famous preachers to their camps to sponsor ceremonies commemorating Regiment Day, which marks the day they were established, and memorializing the missing, dead, and injured of the particular unit. Other ceremonies may be commissioned by high-ranking officers seeking to increase morale or prepare for specific offensives, while the army as a whole sponsors two major sermons every year. The largest ceremony occurs on October 11, the anniversary of the founding of the Sri Lankan army. This sermon is performed at Panāgoḍa army temple before an audience composed primarily of the families of dead soldiers. Endeavoring to ease the suffering of the families, the monks receive alms and transfer merit to the dead. The second major sermon occurs around the first Sunday of October at the Śrī Mahābodhi Tree in Anurādhapura. This sermon takes place following a ceremony during which all of the flags from all of the regiments in the Sri Lankan army are blessed at the Bodhi tree and then taken back to their respective units.

The guiding question behind the vast majority of studies of Buddhism and war is, how does Buddhism justify, legitimate, or otherwise allow war? Scholars have asked this question, attempting to resolve the perceived conflict between the first precept against killing and the contemporary reality of active Buddhist participation in warfare. Scholarship guided by this question has been, for the most part, quite fruitful, challenging essentialized presentations of Buddhism as a religion of absolute pacifism with more nuanced explorations of Buddhists making the decision to engage in warfare.[3] Justification, however, is not the concern of the warrior in the *Yodhājīvasutta*, nor is it the primary concern of contemporary Sri Lankan Buddhists participating in the war.

In this chapter, I will explore an alternative line of questioning employed by Buddhists engaged in war. Rather than beginning and ending my work with the search for Buddhist justifications of war, I endeavor to discover some of the questions asked and answers provided by the Buddhist soldiers and monks dealing most directly with the conflict. Rather than examining the speeches and writings of the monks and politicians represented frequently in the national media, I have chosen informants whose voices are normally not heard. These voices come from soldiers with experience on the battlefields and from monks residing at temples near military bases. Although they may employ some of the same Sinhalese Buddhist nationalist rhetoric as do politicians, they do so not to build a national consensus on the war, but to address the individual problems facing soldiers.[4]

When asked of their concerns about war, soldiers and monks spoke in terms of karma and intentionality rather than in terms of justice. Soldiers do not ask monks to justify the civil war, but about the karmic consequences of their actions. Indeed, the vast majority of monks deny that Buddhism can ever condone war. "Will I receive negative karma if I kill the enemy on the battlefield?" many soldiers ask. During sermons to soldiers, monks respond to this explicit and implicit question, easing soldiers' concerns and attempting to instill in them a positive state of mind that they hope will protect them and reduce the amount of negative karma that the soldiers create on the battlefield.

Buddhism Does Not Condone War, but...

The wave of anti-Tamil violence that swept through the island of Sri Lanka in July 1983 shook the foundations of Sri Lankan society. Known as Black July, this event challenged scholars to explain how such a thing could possibly happen in Sri Lanka. Immediately after independence in 1948, Sri Lanka had been viewed as an example for other former colonies to follow. The violence of 1983 caused a reevaluation across all fields of study as scholars began to ask why, how, and when Sri Lanka was transformed from a model society to a fractured one.

While scholars from all disciplines rushed into the discursive space ripped open by Black July, anthropologists and scholars of religion turned their collective gaze on religion in general and Buddhism in particular. Less than a year after the riots, Gananath Obeyesekere wrote:

> What then is the background to this violence, unprecedented in the history of a country designated by the people themselves as *dhamma dīpa*, "the land of the Buddha's dharma," a doctrine of non-violence and compassion? I am a Sinhalese and a Buddhist and this is the troubling question that I ask myself.[5]

Stanley Tambiah echoed Obeyesekere, asking: "If Buddhism preaches non-violence, why is there so much political violence in Sri Lanka today[?]"[6] Finally, Ananda Wikremeratne expressed his own remorse, writing, "Isn't it a shame...that all this violence should take place in Sri Lanka? After all, Sri Lanka is a Buddhist country. How can Buddhists resort to violence[?]"[7]

As Buddhist soldiers rushed off to fight and die on behalf of their *raṭa, jātiya,* and *āgama* (country, race, and religion), scholars were forced to reexamine their assumptions about Buddhism as a religion of nonviolence. The first step toward reconciliation was the separation of Buddhism-the-religion from Buddhists who adopt violent means. In 1993, Gananath Obeyesekere questioned the Buddhist identity of those who advocated violence: "To say that the killing of one's enemy is justified is a perversion of Buddhism, and those who condone such acts have rejected their Buddhist heritage."[8] By condemning those who made the decision to go to war, Obeyesekere shifted the focus away from Buddhism to the Buddhists themselves—preserving Buddhism as a tradition of absolute nonviolence, while questioning the legitimacy of contemporary Sri Lankan Buddhists.

Whether they are legitimate in the eyes of scholars or not, however, Buddhist monks, like Ānandavaṃsa, are often invited to deliver sermons and perform

FIGURE 7.2 High-ranking monks bless soldiers within the Śrīṃahābodhi shrine in Anuradhapura on October 1, 2005. In the front row are Sri Lanka's highest-ranking officers, including former army commander Shanta Kottegoda, current army commander Sarath Fonseka, and the late Lt. Gen. Parami Kulatunga, who was killed in a suicide bombing six months later. Photo taken by Daniel Kent.

rituals for the army. As he preached before a mixed audience of uniformed soldiers and white-clad civilians one evening in March 2007, Ānandavaṃsa did not justify the war. Indeed, like most monks, he stated expressly that Buddhism can never condone war or killing. In a conversation two years before this sermon, Ānandavaṃsa stressed to me that monks should never tell soldiers to kill:

> We wouldn't say, "May you have strength. May you defeat the enemy!" We can't pray for that! If monks were to pray for that there, they would face problems with the rules of monastic discipline. A monk can never tell someone to kill. In the same way, they can't say that killing is good.... That is why monks don't have any blessing for killing. We say: "May soldiers be protected! May they be free from sickness and suffering! May they live lives without accidental harm!"[9]

Two weeks before preaching to an audience of over 10,000 white-clad laypeople gathered at Panāgoḍa army temple on a warm evening in October 2006, Ven. Itāpanna Dhammalankāra explained during an interview: "Our dharma does not condone the harming of any type of being. We show *maitrī* for all people and animals. When a war starts, we must only try to stop it."[10] Two years later, on the other side of the island, Ven. Neluwakande Gñānānanda echoed Dhammalankāra's words at a ceremony sponsored by the soldiers at a small infantry camp in Mihintale:

> What we need is to live in peace. Everyone values life. *Buddhadharma* does not condone the murder of humans or even animals. Problems in society arise because of the bad actions of people. The result is that many people suffer. That is why we think that this country must be full of peace. The final result must be peace. That is our goal.[11]

Like Dhammalankāra, Gñānānanda is careful to separate Buddhist teachings from the act of killing.

How is it possible for monks to support soldiers by preaching to them without justifying or condoning the war in Buddhist terms? Is there a way to understand Buddhists who decide to go to war without condemning them for violating their Buddhist heritage? Tessa Bartholomeusz attempted just such a solution in her book *In Defense of Dharma: Just-War Ideology in Buddhist Sri Lanka*. Rather than dismissing Buddhist warfare as an aberration or a rejection of Buddhist heritage, Bartholomeusz argued that Sinhalese Buddhists have employed a prima facie just-war theory. Prima facie obligations refer to ethical obligations, which can be overridden when they come in conflict with each other. For example, the obligation to speak the truth may be overridden if doing so would result in the death or injury of another. Additionally, the obligation to refrain from killing or causing injury could be overridden by the obligation to preserve the life of an innocent. In the case of Sri Lankan Buddhists, Bartholomeusz argued that the obligation to refrain from killing can be overruled by the obligation to protect the Buddhist religion.[12]

Bartholomeusz's work provides a useful framework for understanding how a Sinhalese Buddhist can go to war without violating his or her Buddhist heritage. Bartholomeusz solves this problem by viewing the Buddhist precept against killing as a prima facie ethical obligation that is overridden by the obligation to protect the dharma. The language of "obligation" and "rules," however, is not entirely compatible with Buddhist doctrinal understandings of action. In his article "Can Killing a Living Being Ever Be an Act of Compassion? The Analysis of the Act of Killing in the Abhidhamma and Pali Commentaries," Gethin warns of the dangers of applying etic, or external, concepts to Buddhist beliefs and doctrines:

> Abhidhamma—and hence I think mainstream Buddhist ethics—is not ultimately concerned to lay down ethical rules, or even ethical principles. It seeks instead to articulate a spiritual psychology

> focusing on the root causes that motivate us to act: greed, hatred, and delusion, or nonattachment, friendliness, and wisdom. Thus that intentionally killing a living being is wrong is not in fact presented in Buddhist thought as an ethical principle at all; it is a claim about how the mind works, about the nature of certain mental states and the kinds of action they give rise to.[13]

While Gethin does not reject the possibility of comparison, he argues that scholars in the field of Buddhist ethics often obscure the nature of Buddhist karma theory. Theories of just war are composed of rules and principles unfamiliar to the traditional Sri Lankan frame of reference; they are incompatible with the reasoning behind the decisions made by Sri Lankan Buddhists participating in war.

Although Gethin can be fairly accused of privileging Buddhist doctrine over other sources, such as literature and ritual practice, he makes an important point. Buddhist doctrine does not contain conditions for laying down ethical rules and principles through which war could be justified. On the contrary, he argues, Buddhist doctrine is concerned with psychology, focusing on the root causes and effects of individual actions.[14] The decision to take up arms leading to a just or unjust conflict has little relevance to contemporary Sri Lankan Buddhists. After war begins, however, Buddhist doctrine, literature, and practice all have a great deal to say about actions and particularly the effects of those actions on the battlefield.

If the question of justification is no longer a useful lens for viewing Buddhist warfare, what question could we pose to replace it? In order to discover an alternative, I conducted several group interviews with Buddhist soldiers at Panāgoḍa army base, asking my subjects to explain the kinds of questions that they have asked or would like to ask monks about war. Many answered quickly that they have asked whether negative karma occurs when they fire their weapons at the enemy.[15] Several monks confirmed that this was a question that they commonly received from soldiers. Having heard this question repeated again and again by my informants, I adopted it as my main question for the monks and soldiers whom I interviewed. Rather than asking monks and soldiers how Buddhism justifies war, I asked about the karmic consequences of individual actions on the battlefield.

The Karma of War

"*Hamduruwo,*[16] does negative karma occur when a soldier fires his weapon at the enemy on the battlefield?" I asked Ānandavaṃsa in an interview several weeks before his sermon. Ānandavaṃsa answered definitively: "It couldn't not occur. A negative karma occurs." Ven. Sudarsana, a forest monk and former corporal in the infantry before his ordination seven years before our interview, took a firm position, arguing: "*Cetanā 'ham bhikkhave kammaṃ vadāmi.* Intention becomes karma."[17] He continued, asking: "Can a soldier shoot another person while practicing loving-kindness [*maitrī*] meditation? If he were doing that, how could he kill?"

Monks are not the only ones to argue that killing on the battlefield produces negative karma. A disabled thirty-year-old infantry corporal explained the consequences of actions in war:

> According to the teaching of Buddhism, negative karma occurs. It is impossible to prevent it. According to my knowledge of the *dhamma*, the unwholesome act of killing occurs there. I think that many of our soldiers know this. However, this is our duty. There are many duties like this in the world. Many people give different reasons to justify unwholesome actions, but they are still unwholesome.[18]

The term chosen by Sudarsana to evaluate the actions of soldiers, *cetanā*, or intention, is familiar to all Buddhists. In the most commonly cited formulation of the act of intentional killing, which is found in the Pāli commentarial literature, five conditions must be fulfilled for negative karma to be created: (1) there must be a living creature; (2) one must know that the creature is living; (3) one must intend to kill the creature; (4) one must perform the necessary action; (5) the creature must die.[19] For Ānandavaṃsa and Sudarsana, the act of killing on the battlefield clearly fulfills all of these conditions.

Not all monks or soldiers, however, agree that soldiers produce negative karma when they fire at the enemy. Upon hearing my question, Ven. Ampiṭiyē Sīlavaṃsatissa became flustered and answered: "*Cetanā* is the thing at the root. Soldiers don't take guns with the intention of killing. More than killing, they take them with the principal intention [*cetanā*] of saving the country, the race, and the religion [*raṭa*, *jātiya*, *āgama*]."[20] Before our interview, Sīlavaṃsatissa had lifted his robe to show me the scars left from the shrapnel of a mortar round and from a gunshot wound. The monk had received these injuries during an attack on his temple, which is located next to an army base, by the LTTE (Liberation Tigers of Tamil Eelam) in 2002.

One light infantry soldier explained:

> Soldiers don't shoot the enemy out of personal anger. If they shoot they do so for the common good. This war is on behalf of the country, people, religion, region, and motherland. It would be

> negative karma to shoot one's neighbor over a land conflict, but the intention here is a good one.[21]

This soldier separates the act of killing on the battlefield from intention, transforming the act into a neutral one. This soldier is not alone in his reasoning. Major Chakkrawarthi, the commander of the army temple at Panāgoḍa, also emphasized the lack of personal anger behind the actions of soldiers:

> In Buddhism, one needs to fulfill five conditions for a sin to occur. Those five are not fulfilled by us. Our goal is just to face the enemy with the goal of protecting our own lives and the lives of others. Our soldiers don't kill with anger.[22]

Chakkrawarthi reasons that soldiers fire their weapons at the enemy not with anger, but out of their duty to protect others.

The key to this puzzle is how each individual understands *cetanā*. Some, like Sudarsana, argue that the intention to kill can never be wholesome. Others, like Ampiṭiyē Sīlavaṃsatissa, argue that the soldier's intention to kill is not personal, not rooted in delusion, hatred, or desire. Although these monks and soldiers disagreed in their answers to my question, they harnessed similar terminology and concepts to provide their answers. All of my informants based their arguments not upon justice, but upon whether the actions of a soldier do or do not produce negative karma, and upon the possibility of killing with a positive intention. Everyone with whom I spoke, regardless of their answer to my question, identified intention, or *cetanā*, as the factor which determines the positive or negative effects of an action; none used language applicable to the formation of a just-war theory, prima facie or otherwise. None of my subjects made reference to the idea of ethical obligations coming in conflict with one another.

Soldiers and monks may be united in their use of *cetanā* and karma to evaluate the actions of a soldier on the battlefield, but disagreements are also very common among monks and soldiers regarding *cetanā* and the karmic consequences of acts of killing.[23] Of the twenty monks interviewed over the course of my research, eleven believed that firing a weapon on the battlefield produced negative karma; nine believed that it did not.[24] Soldiers were also split in their assessments. Of fifty-eight soldiers interviewed at the Sixth Sri Lankan Light Infantry (SLLI) camp in Mihintale, thirty-three believed that negative karma did not occur when they fired their weapons at the enemy, while twenty-five believed that it did occur. While each of these soldiers agreed that intention determines the karmic effects of particular actions, they disagreed on whether it was possible to fire their weapons with a positive intention. Even though all of my informants employed the same terminology in their evaluation of actions on the battlefield, they still differed in their understandings of those actions and employed different lines of reasoning to support their claims.

Once we begin viewing war through individual intentions and actions, rather than in terms of justification or legitimation, the sermons that monks deliver to soldiers take on new meaning. If soldiers and monks view individual karma as the primary problem on a battlefield, it follows that preachers will concentrate their sermons on influencing karma, rather than justifying war in objective terms.

Performing Intention

As Ānandavaṃsa preached before his audience of uniformed soldiers, he did not justify the war. One night, Ānandavaṃsa did not even preach about war. Instead, he preached a commentary on the famous Pāli verse *Yo dhammaṃ passati, so maṃ passat* (he who sees the *dhamma* sees me). When I asked Ānandavaṃsa about his goals when preaching to soldiers, he explained that his primary goals were to comfort their hearts, instruct them in morality, and wish for their protection.

The themes of nirvana, meditation, and the fruits of the homeless life, however, were conspicuously absent from Ānandavaṃsa's sermon. Indeed, almost all of the preachers with whom I spoke avoided these topics, explaining that such topics would not help to effect positive change in the soldiers' hearts. Instead, the monks explained, they selected topics that were "timely" and "appropriate" to their audience of soldiers.[25] Ven. Vimaladhajja, a monk who lives two kilometers from Panāgoḍa army base, described the kinds of topics that are appropriate to soldiers:

> When I go to preach to a group of soldiers, I preach in the necessary way to them. I preach about the greatness of King Duṭugämuṇu. Each occasion calls for a timely sermon. Each occasion has an appropriate sermon.[26]

Vimaladhajja explained that stories of Duṭugämuṇu (Pāli: Dutt ạgāmaṇī), the second-century BCE Sinhalese king who conquered the ancient capital of Anurādhapura from the South Indian king Eḷāra, are the most appropriate for soldiers. Duṭugämuṇu, whose name literally means "Gämuṇu the Fierce," is said to have led his armies carrying a spear festooned with a relic of the Buddha.[27] According to the *Mahāvaṃsa* account, after his victory over King Eḷāra, Duṭugämuṇu, like the Mauryan king Aśoka before him, was plagued with guilt

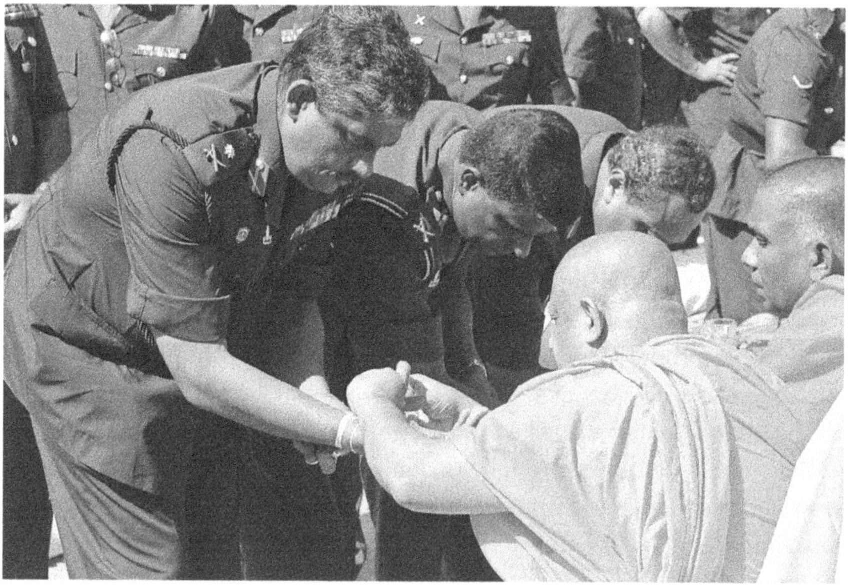

FIGURE 7.3 Monks tie protective threads around the wrist of army commander Sarath Fonseka at the Śrīmahābodhi shrine on October 1, 2005. Photo taken by Daniel Kent.

because he had killed so many people. Eight *arahants*[28] soothed him, explaining that he was only guilty of killing one and a half human beings: one who had taken the five precepts and another who had taken refuge in the triple gem.[29] The *Mahāvaṃsa* records that, after his death, Duṭugämuṇu was reborn in heaven to await rebirth as the chief disciple of the future Buddha Metteya (Maitreya). Duṭugämuṇu is said to have explained his motives, declaring, "Not for the joy of sovereignty is this toil of mine, my striving [has been] ever to establish the doctrine of the Sambuddha."[30]

Vimaladhajja, whose enthusiastic support of the army has earned him the nickname "Brigadier Monk," explained that stories of Duṭugämuṇu can buttress a soldier's courage. There is a fine line, however, between encouraging soldiers and encouraging them to kill. Ānandavaṃsa explained:

> First let's imagine the reason why someone joins the army today. We can think of two reasons. The first is for a job. The guys in our army today joined because they didn't have a job. As for a national army . . . soldiers act according to the orders that they receive from above. If he goes to war, he must first protect himself. When we preach to soldiers, we have to decide whether we should preach in a way that would decrease their belief, self-confidence, and pride in themselves or in a way that would increase their self-confidence.[31]

On the one hand, Ānandavaṃsa does not want to encourage killing; on the other hand, he does not want to put soldiers into danger by reducing their confidence in themselves.

Ven. Mangala shares Ānandavaṃsa's concerns for the immediate well-being of the soldiers. He asserted: "If I were to go to an army camp and tell them to love their enemies, saying, 'Love your enemies. May your enemies be healthy.' What would the enemies do? They would come and destroy the camp!" He continued later: "If a soldier thought, 'I can't shoot this person; it is a sin,' he would not be suitable for that job. If he were to do that, another soldier would come along and shoot him."[32] A soldier who fears the sinful consequences of his actions, Mangala argued, may be more physically vulnerable than a soldier who is confident in the correctness of his actions. If a soldier were to join the army and suddenly decide to not perform his duties, he would be endangering himself, his unit, and ultimately his country; thus, preaching to soldiers of sin would upset their minds and potentially endanger them.

One might argue that monks should not speak to soldiers at all, but should leave soldiers to their wrong livelihood. This, however, is not an option for Ānandavaṃsa or Mangala. They have both known many of the soldiers that visit their temples from the time the soldiers were children attending Buddhist school. Like many other monks, therefore, they cannot remain silent when soldiers come to them, but neither can they discuss the very real possibility that the karma produced by the soldiers in battle will lead to dire consequences in the future. Despite their disapproval of acts of intentional killing from a Buddhist perspective, both Ānandavaṃsa and Mangala remain silent on the consequences of killing on the battlefield,

How does a monk encourage a group of soldiers without encouraging them to kill? Different preachers succeed in this task to varying degrees. While there are monks who in their sermons urge soldiers to go forth and kill, such monks are in the minority.[33] The majority of monks attempt to assist soldiers without specifically encouraging killing. As with Ānandavaṃsa's sermon on one the days I was there, sometimes monks will not even mention war during their sermons to soldiers; instead, they focus upon the importance of *sīla* (morality) or on the importance of the *dhamma*. Ven. Vipuladhamma, the head of the meditation center outside of Mihintale, explained the dilemma that arises when he preaches to soldiers whose job it is to kill:

> Now the soldiers' goal is to create an environment where peaceful and harmonious people can live freely. So it is not good to have

> the intention [*cetanā*] of destroying people. It is not good to have the intention [*cetanā*] to take revenge. That is because everyone living here in Mihintale has the right to live. There are people who are trying to grab away that right. Those people must be stopped in order to give [the rest of the] people the opportunity to live together harmoniously. If they go to battle with that goal, their goal is very good. We give them encouragement for that.[34]

As discussed above, all of the monks and soldiers with whom I spoke drew a clear connection between intention and the karma created by an action. Many argued that a soldier fighting with selfless intentions to save the innocent or protect the country would not create negative karma when he fired his weapon at the enemy. Taking this for granted, monks like Vipuladhamma attempt to instill particular intentions in the minds of soldiers going off to battle.

This strategy is apparent in Ven. Vimaladhajja's sermons praising Duṭugämuṇu. In this short composition of his own, he sang:

Niridun Duṭugämuṇu Maha yuda keruvēya
Bērāganna āgama dana näsuvēya
Pirisidu sirilakama eksatkeruvēya
Avasana sandahāmin suvayak läbuvēya

Duṭugämuṇu, the lord of men, fought a great war.
He killed people in order to save the religion.
He united the pure Sri Lanka
and received comfort from that in the end [of *saṃsāra*].[35]

This poem could be taken as a blanket justification of war. When viewed in terms of individual karma, however, it does not justify war in objective terms at all. On the contrary, it describes the ideal intention that an individual soldier should take into battle.[36] Because Duṭugämuṇu went to battle with the intention of saving religion, he was reborn in heaven. Vimaladhajja suggests that the soldiers in his audience should adopt similar intentions as they go to the battlefield.

Military personnel agree that a good sermon can help soldiers to establish a wholesome *cetanā*. Intention, however, should not be understood merely as a cognitive decision underlying particular actions. On the contrary, the monks and soldiers with whom I spoke used the term *cetanā* interchangeably with the term *hita*, or heart.[37] The state of one's *hita* is directly related to the amount of *piṅ*, or merit (Pāli: puñña), produced by particular activities.

Writing about intention and merit production during acts of ritual alms giving, Jeffrey Samuels explained:

> For the laymen and laywomen with whom I spoke about meritorious giving, conversations rarely, if ever, touched upon the need for giving to be accompanied by a donor's conscious reasoning. Instead, making merit was largely discussed in conversations focusing on the emotional state of the donor.[38]

As one of Samuels' informants put it: "Merit means happiness [*piṅ kiyannē satuṭa*]. Happiness is the heart/mind [*hitē santōṣaya*]. Demerit means unhappiness [*pava kiyannē asatuṭa*]. Merit is based on these two."[39]

Major Chakkrawarthi, the commander of the army temple at Panāgoḍa, stressed the importance of a healthy heart:

> The battleground is uncertain. It is uncertain whether you will die today or tomorrow. Bombs and mortars fall everywhere. Friends die. Then your heart gets upset. That is why we always need to keep our hearts healthy. It is times like that that you need the help of a monk. Not every monk can accomplish that in a sermon.[40]

Chakkrawarthi explained that a beautiful sermon or well-told story can help to keep the hearts of soldiers healthy. Another officer referred to the sermons of monks as "medicine for the heart":

> The monks preach in order to calm [the soldiers'] hearts. They fix their hearts by saying things like "You all are doing a good job." There is a saying that if you break your arm there is medicine, but if you break your heart there is no medicine. So the monks preach in such a way as to calm people's hearts so that they don't break.[41]

These officers testify to the potential transformative healing capacity of a skillfully delivered sermon and a well-told story.

What are the benefits of taking a calm heart into battle? First, soldiers explained that a calm heart is the only real protection that a soldier can receive from religion. Second, monks explain that a calm heart can reduce the negative karma that soldiers create on the battlefield. Finally, not only does a calm heart intrinsically produce less negative karma than an upset one, but soldiers who go to battle with a calm heart will be less likely to engage in activities that produce negative karma.

Many soldiers reported to me that a calm heart is the only sure way of being protected on the battlefield. "A protective medallion cannot stop a bullet," claimed one officer at Panāgoḍa camp. "The only way to get any kind of protection on the battlefield is to have a calm heart."[42] The soldier was not implying that a tranquil heart can magically protect one from enemy artillery, but it allows one to act with equanimity and without obstructive negative emotions.

It should be remembered here that *hita* as an equivalent to *cetanā* does not refer to one's emotional state alone; *hita* is also intimately connected with the creation of karma. Soldiers and monks both explained that actions performed with a calm *hita* do not result in negative karma. As such, shaping the *hita* of soldiers does not just protect soldiers through the evocation of a meritorious state of mind; shaping the *hita* of soldiers also shapes their intentions, thus reducing the negative karma created when they fire their weapons.

Ven. Assaji, an official advisor to the Sri Lankan army's Buddhist association, explained the importance of a composed heart in soldiers: "A soldier's mind must be calm because he has a sharp weapon in his hand. A person with a sharp weapon in his hand must work with wisdom. They have to work with intelligence and efficiency. A soldier must be wise and have a calm heart."[43] Assaji's comments have a dual meaning: not only can a soldier easily harm the enemy, he can also harm himself and those around him. In order to keep himself and his regiment safe, the soldier must have the presence of mind to use his weapon effectively.

Monks hope that their sermons will also limit negative behavior in very concrete terms. Ven. Ratanavaṃsa stressed the potential danger of a soldier with an upset heart:

> Normally when people are fighting with weapons in an extraordinary mental state, they need to have mercy and compassion.... If not, they may go out and use their strength for wrong things.... A soldier can be very skilled at theft. As for murder, a soldier can do that too. That is why he needs to have love, compassion, and mercy to direct his mind towards good things.[44]

Given the dangers of a battlefield, it is very easy for a soldier to fall into negative behavior. Ratanavaṃsa explained that a soldier on the battlefield is often "consumed with hatred for the enemy, thinking, 'Where are they coming from, who shall I kill, who shall I shoot, who is coming forward?'"

As the Buddha points out in the *Yodhājīvasutta*, if a soldier dies seized by anger in the midst of battle, he will be reborn in a hell realm. While it is impossible to control completely the contents of a soldier's heart, many preachers stress that they do their best to shape soldiers in other directions. Ven. Dhammalankāra explained his role in reducing unnecessary violence on the battlefield:

> They could go to war and kill innocent Tamil people. We don't want this at all. On the battlefield there is a war between two groups and people from both sides die. However, we can't condone the killing of innocent Tamils, Muslims, or Sinhala. We tell them to never do such things. We tell them not to harm a single animal whether it is a goat or a cow. There is no need to harm animals like that. They are innocent animals.[45]

By preaching in this way, Dhammalankāra seeks to reduce collateral damage. Soldiers who go to war with calm minds, Dhammalankāra explained, are less likely to harm innocent civilians or animals.

When I asked Vimaladhajja, whose sermons contained the most martial themes of any of the monks with whom I spoke, if he saw anything wrong with his sermons to soldiers, he exclaimed:

> My gods! If we go to the battlefield and recite protective verses, tell them stories of the kings, and preach some sermons about the Buddha, the morale of the boys will increase, won't it? Won't such things increase their spiritual comfort [*adyatmika suvaya*]? It is not an offense or a disgrace for a monk to go to the battlefield. It gives comfort to the boys. Our boys are happy when they hear that our monks are going to the battlefield. How great would it be to turn a battleground into a place of worship? [He was making a play on the Sinhalese words *yuda bīma* and *puda bīma*, "battleground" and "place of worship."][46]

While Vimaladhajja's statements may be troubling to scholars of Buddhism, it should be noted that he never justified nor authorized the war. On the contrary, Vimaladhajja's goal is transformation. By preaching to soldiers and shaping their hearts, he seeks to increase their morale and spiritual comfort. By transforming the hearts of soldiers, he seeks to protect them and limit the violence in which they engage on the battlefield. Through the transformation of individuals, Vimaladhajja hopes to ultimately transform the world itself, making *yuda bīma* into *puda bīma*.

Conclusion

At the end of Ānandavaṃsa's sermon, the gathered soldiers begin distributing orange fruit drink to the civilians in the audience. This ceremony, like the six that had preceded it every night of that week, had been commissioned by the army to correspond with a large-scale military operation that was about to begin in the north of the island. The commander of every army base in the country had been ordered to commission sermons during the week leading up to the operation. This entire ceremony had been sponsored by the army in an attempt to bless its soldiers, protect them, and grant them success in battle.

When a monk preaches before a group of soldiers, he walks a fine line between serving the needs of the soldiers as individuals suffering in *saṃsāra* and serving the Sri Lankan government, which needs soldiers willing to fight and die for its cause. On the one hand, a preacher does not want to encourage soldiers to kill; on the other hand, he does not want soldiers to have any doubts that might put them into danger. At the same time, these monks hope that the soldiers to whom they preach will go into battle with selfless intentions. Rather than fighting for money or out of personal hatred, the monks urge the soldiers to adopt selfless intentions, such as the intention to protect the innocent and defenseless. Whether or not each individual monk believes that it is, in fact, possible to kill without *akusala*, or unwholesome, intention, when they preach, they attempt to instill this intention in the hearts of the soldiers, thus granting them the protection of a calm mind and discouraging theft and unnecessary killing on the battlefield.

In this chapter, I have suggested an alternative approach to Buddhist warfare. Scholarship on the topic of Buddhist warfare has focused primarily on Buddhist justification of war, but there are many other questions that must be asked about Buddhists participating in war or in any type of state-sanctioned violence. Rather than asking how Buddhists can justify war, I have asked, how does an individual Buddhist understand his actions on the battlefield and the consequences of those actions? How do monks balance their desire to assist the young men who go off to war with Buddhist teachings on the negative consequences of killing? How do Buddhists understand death on the battlefield, and how do they remember the dead? By investigating the questions asked by Buddhist soldiers and the responses given by the monks ministering to them, we can get beyond perceived conflicts between Buddhism and war and begin to understand the complicated world of Buddhists engaged in war.

NOTES

1. This chapter is based on interviews and transcripts of sermons collected between October 2004 and March 2007, during research funded by the University of Virginia's Department of Religious Studies and a Fulbright-Hayes doctoral dissertation research fellowship. This research was performed with the cooperation of the Sri Lankan Army Media Corps and the written permission of the former commander of the army Lt. Gen. (ret.) Shantha Kottegoda. All interviews were

performed in Sinhala, recorded on a digital voice recorder and then translated with the assistance of Mr. T. M. Jayatillake.

2. A note on diacritics: all Sinhala and Pāli words, with the exception of proper names, are spelled according to standard Sanskrit conventions. Sinhala proper names appear according to the individual spellings, if known, that are adopted by the informants, e.g., Obeyesekere rather than Obeyasekara.

3. See, for example, Ananda Abeysekara, "The Saffron Army, Violence, Terror(ism): Buddhism, Identity and Difference in Sri Lanka," *Numen* 48.1 (2001); and Tessa J. Bartholomeusz, *In Defense of Dharma: Just-War Ideology in Buddhist Sri Lanka* (London: Routledge Curzon, 2002).

4. When I say "Sinhalese Buddhist nationalist rhetoric," I am using it as shorthand for clusters of discourses used in the national media and personal interactions that have acquired power in reference to a particular vision of Sri Lanka as a unified Buddhist nation ruled by the Sinhala people. Examples of this rhetoric include calls for selfless devotion to *raṭa, jāti,* and *āgama,* as well as references to the Sinhalese cultural hero Duṭugämuṇu, who is said to have reunited the country under the standard of Sinhalese Buddhism.

5. Gananath Obeyesekere, "The Origins and Institutionalization of Political Violence," in *Sri Lanka in Change and Crisis,* ed. J. Manor (London: Croom Helm, 1984), 154.

6. Stanley Jeyaraja Tambiah, *Sri Lanka: Ethnic Fratricide and the Dismantling of Democracy* (Chicago: University of Chicago Press, 1986), 1.

7. Ananda Wickremeratne, *Buddhism and Ethnicity in Sri Lanka: A Historical Analysis* (New Delhi: International Centre for Ethnic Studies, Kandy, in association with Vikas, 1995), xx.

8. Gananath Obeyesekere, "Duttagamini and the Buddhist Conscience," in *Religion and Political Conflict in South Asia,* ed. D. Allen (Delhi: Oxford University Press, 1993), 158.

9. Interview with Ven. Ānandavaṃsa in Bogahayāya, December 5, 2005.

10. Interview with Ven. Dr. Dhammalankāra in Rukmale, September 28, 2006.

11. Sermon delivered on March 9, 2007, at Mihintale by Ven. Neluwakande Gñānānanda.

12. Bartholomeusz's use of prima facie obligations to construct a Buddhist just-war theory is the culmination of several streams of thought. James Childress adopted the concept of prima facie ethical obligations from the early twentieth-century philosopher W. D. Smith to articulate just-war criteria in a way that is useful to just-war theorists and pacifists alike. Childress, "Just-War Criteria," in *War in the Twentieth Century: Sources in Theological Ethics,* ed. Richard B. Miller, 351–372. Louisville, Ky.: Westminster/John Knox, 1992), 369. Charles Hallisey later adopted prima facie ethical obligations as a possible way of describing Theravāda Buddhist ethics as presented in the *Mangalasutta.* Hallisey, "Ethical Particularism in Theravāda Buddhism," *Journal of Buddhist Ethics* 3 (1996): 32–43.

13. Rupert Gethin, "Can Killing a Living Being Ever Be an Act of Compassion? The Analysis of the Act of Killing in the Abhidhamma and Pali Commentaries,"

Journal of Buddhist Ethics (2004): 190. Although I would not go as far as Gethin in identifying the Abhidhamma with "mainstream Buddhist ethics," much less the ethical calculations of contemporary Sri Lankan Buddhists, he makes an important point about the dangers of comparative studies. It is important that comparison does not overwhelm the categories and terms used by Sri Lankan Buddhists themselves.

14. P. D. Premasiri agrees with Gethin's argument in Premasiri, "The Place for a Righteous War in Buddhism," *Journal of Buddhist Ethics* 10 (2003), accessed at http://www.buddhistethics.org/10/premasiri-sri-lanka-conf.html on September 17, 2008. Premasiri writes:

> All wars, according to the Buddhist view, originate in the minds of people. The behaviour of the large majority of living beings is determined by the mental processes referred to in Buddhism as unskilled or unwholesome (*akusala*). Conflict in society is therefore, considered in Buddhism to be endemic.

15. Throughout this chapter, I have chosen to translate the Sinhalese term *pav* (Pāli: *pāpa kamma*) as "negative karma."

16. The term *hamduruwo* is a Sinhalese honorific used when addressing monks.

17. Interview with Ven. Sudarsana, March 9, 2006, at Labunoruwa Araññā. The citation *cetanā 'ham bhikkhave kammaṃ vadāmi* comes from AN III, 416. The full citation is *cetanā'haṃ bhikkhave kammaṃ vadāmi, cetayitvā kammaṃ karoti kāyena vācāya manasā* (O Monks, intention is what I call karma. Having intended, one does karma with body, speech, and mind).

18. Interview with anonymous corporal, September 26, 2005, at Panāgoḍa.

19. Dhs. A. 129; Sdhp. V, 58; Kkvt. 50; Uj. 62.

20. Interview with Ven. Ampiṭiyē Sīlavaṃsatissa, July 24, 2005, at Welgam Vehera near Trincomallee.

21. Interview with anonymous soldier in Panāgoḍa, September 25, 2005.

22. Interview with Major Chakkrawarthi, November 30, 2005, at Panāgoḍa army temple.

23. It should be noted that, with the exception of two of my informants, who are long-time friends, the monks in this sample were chosen specifically because of their relationship with the army. The monks in this sample either live very near to an army camp, participate frequently in ceremonies sponsored by the army, or were members of the army prior to ordination.

24. Ven. Ratanavaṃsa changed his answer over the course of the time that I knew him. In 2005, he answered that firing at the enemy produced *pav*. In 2007, however, he reversed his answer, arguing that a soldier firing at the enemy need not produce negative karma.

25. The terms "timely" and "appropriate" translate the Sinhalese terms *kālena* and *uccita*, respectively.

26. Interview with Ven. Pilassi Vimaladhajja in Panāgoḍa, October 9, 2006.

27. Gethin points out that the Pāli word translated as "spear," *kunta*, probably referred to a banner and not to a weapon at all. See Rupert Gethin, "Buddhist Monks,

Buddhist Kings, Buddhist Violence: On the Early Buddhist Attitudes to Violence," in *Religion and Violence in South Asia: Theory and Practice*, ed. J. R. Hinnells and Richard King (London: Routledge, 2007), 76.

28. Sanskrit for "worthy ones," *arhats* are people who have realized the goal of nirvāṇa in Theravādin traditions.

29. Mhv, xxv, 109–111.

30. Rajjasukhāya vāyāmo nā'yaṃ mama kadācipi: Sambuddhasāsanasseva ṭhapanāya ayaṃ mama, in Majjhima Nikāya, xxv, 17.

31. Interview with Ven. Ānandavaṃsa in Bogahayāya, November 1, 2006.

32. Interview with Ven. Sarasivapatuve Mangala in Kandy, October 4, 2006.

33. Of all of the sermons that I attended, only one preacher told the soldiers directly that they should kill the enemy.

34. Interview with Ven. Vipuladhamma in Mihintale, January 18, 2007.

35. Interview with Ven. Pilassi Vimaladhajja in Panāgoḍa, November 29, 2005.

36. Indeed, one of Richard Gombrich's interview subjects uses the story of Duṭugämuṇu specifically as an explanation of the concept of *ahosi* karma, karma that does not come to fruition. Gombrich's informant explains:

> For example, Duṭugämuṇu killed many Tamils in war, which is *pav*, but he did it to save Buddhism, and then he did so much for Buddhism (founding monasteries at Anurādhapura, etc.) that his *pin* so far outweighed his *pav* that he will stay in heaven [*divyalōkē*] till the time of Maitrī, the next Buddha, when he will be reborn as his right-hand disciple... and attain nirvana. His *pav* will therefore never mature, there being no results [*vipākē*] of bad karma in heaven. (Gombrich, *Buddhist Precept and Practice: Traditional Buddhism in the Rural Highlands of Ceylon* 2nd. [Delhi: Motilal Banarsidass Publishers, 1991], 253)

While one may question this particular informant's interpretation of Buddhist doctrine, his words reveal the terms that are important to him in debates about Buddhist involvement in warfare: karma and *vipāka* (Sinhala: *vipāke*, Pāli: *vipāka*).

37. I follow the work of Jeffrey Samuels here and use the word "heart" to translate the Sinhalese term *hita. Hita* is often used interchangeably with *cetanā* in colloquial Sinhalese and is roughly equivalent to the Pāli term *citta*, which is often translated as "mind." Discussing his translation of *hita*, Samuels writes: "The term *hita* (or *sita*), which I translate as heart in this and subsequent chapters, however, is slightly more problematic as the term, like *shin* in Chinese and *kokoro* in Japanese, refers to both one's cognitive and [one's] emotional center." Jeffrey Samuels, "Attracting the Heart: Buddhism and Emotion in Contemporary Sri Lanka" (forthcoming, University of Hawaii Press), 5, 6.

38. Jeffrey Samuels, "Is Merit in the Milk Powder? Pursuing Puñña in Contemporary Sri Lanka," *Contemporary Buddhism* 9.1 (2008): 123–147, 133.

39. Ibid., 16.

40. Interview with Major Chakkrawarthi in Panāgoḍa, November 21, 2005.

41. Interview with Anonymous Captain in Panāgoḍa, October 11, 2005.

42. Personal communication with anonymous officer in Panāgoḍa, September 22, 2005.

43. Interview with Ven. Dodangoda Assaji in Colombo, November 23, 2005.

44. Interview with Ven. Ratanavaṃsa near Mihintale, December 4, 2005.

45. Interview with Ven. Dr. Itäpanna Dhammalankāra, September 28, 2006.

46. Interview with Ven. Pilassi Vimaladhajja in Panāgoḍa, November 29, 2005.

8

Militarizing Buddhism: Violence in Southern Thailand

Michael Jerryson

In a school within a Thai Buddhist monastery in southern Thailand, a monk in saffron robes sat beside me in a corner of the room; twenty feet away from us, another monk gave a Pāli lesson to seven novices.[1] We spoke in hushed voices; our bodies were relaxed, our countenances devoid of emotion. Our conversation was different from most conversations between a layperson and a monk. I was there to learn more about the issue of military monks. I asked him: "Why did you decide to become a soldier?"

He explained that this decision was quite typical for a twenty-one-year-old Thai man. We talked about the training exercises he went through, the places he stayed, and then I paused. Clearing my throat, I turned to him and asked: "When you became a military monk, did you have to train more?"

"No," he replied. "I finished training when I was twenty-two. Then I ordained as a monk. For this position, we have to start as a noncommissioned corporal and work our way up from there."[2] Our conversation continued, but I could not stop thinking about how publicly, yet covertly, we were discussing the militarization of monks inside this Pāli classroom. With this conversation, I realized that a new space for violence had emerged in the Thai *sangha*.

In this region, once an Islamic kingdom, the predominant local identity is Malay Muslim. Conflicts emerged throughout the twentieth century revolving around the ethnoreligious clashes between the Malay Muslims and the Thai Buddhist state. Since

January 2004, Thailand's three southernmost provinces—Pattani, Yala, and Narathiwat—have been under martial law due to numerous bombings, murders, and arson attacks by unidentified groups. In this most recent surge of violence in southern Thailand, Buddhist monks have been targets and victims of the violence. In the most dangerous districts of southern Thailand, abbots own and sometimes use firearms. These abbots claim that they never plan to use firearms to hurt people; rather, they fire their guns to scare off potential attackers. However, according to Thai Buddhist ecclesiastical codes, the use of firearms by an ordained monk is a misdemeanor. In this respect, by even handling a weapon, one would be performing a military action. A military monk, however, is quite different from a gun-wielding abbot. The role of the abbots remains strictly religious. Military monks, however, maintain both monastic and state values and responsibilities, though this dual political identity is forbidden according to monastic guidelines. Drawing upon my fieldwork during frequent trips to southern Thailand between July 2004 and November 2008, this chapter focuses on the state's militarization of Buddhist roles and the militarization of Buddhist spaces.

Brief Background

The issue of militarization is absent from most introductory books on "Buddhisms" in the United States.[3] The perception, by inference, is that militarization is in direct contrast to Buddhist principles. This perception is well merited, since militarization is grounded in violence and suffering (Pāli: *dukkha*) and reflects a seemingly counterintuitive approach to one of the core tenets of Buddhisms, namely, to overcome suffering. The root word "military" can refer to the positions of uniformed personnel in the armed forces, or to the Weberian category of the state, wherein organized violence is accepted as a legitimate means of realizing social objectives. Following the Weberian view, military organizations, such as the army, are structures for the coordination of activities meant to ensure victory on the battlefield.[4] For the purposes of this chapter, "militarization" will refer to the process that invests social, economic, and political responsibilities in military institutions and values.[5] As such, the Thai state's militarization of Thai Buddhism refers to the process by which the state invests military responsibilities in the Thai Buddhist *sangha*.

Although Buddhist studies has paid little attention to the relationship between Buddhisms and militarization, the military has been involved with Buddhist affairs throughout the history of Buddhisms.[6] Although written over fifty years ago, Paul Demiéville's seminal work "Le bouddhisme et la guerre" has not until now been incorporated into U.S. Buddhist studies; its first English translation is provided in this volume. Even more surprising is that Demiéville's article did not spark broader conversations about the nature of Buddhist traditions in relation to militarization. The one exception to this trend is the isolated, albeit voluminous, discussions on Buddhist militarism in Sri Lanka.

States throughout South and Southeast Asia have long enjoyed a healthy relationship with Buddhist monasticism. This extended tradition led scholars such as anthropologist Stanley Tambiah to argue that Buddhisms were centered not merely on enlightenment, but also on kingship and the polity.[7] The role of the early Indian Buddhist Mauryan emperor Aśoka was an actualization of the religion's political design, not an aberration or evolution of the religion. The design and infrastructure of Buddhist principles and rules were, and continue to be, amenable to militarization.[8]

However, over time as the structure of polities changed, so did state applications of Buddhisms. One important and significant change occurred in Thailand in the early 1900s. At the same time that nation-states were developing in western Eurasia (otherwise referred to in its continental sense, Europe), a new form of religiopolitical Buddhism was surfacing in Siam: State Buddhism.[9] Historian Kamala Tiyavanich applies the term "State Buddhism" to refer to acts of Siamese nation building under King Chulalongkorn (r. 1868–1910).[10] These acts created and perpetuated a new form of Buddhism, one specifically designed to centralize and unify Siam. While further accentuating the Siamese nation-state's application and integration of Buddhist nationalism, King Chulalongkorn's son King Vajiravudh (r. 1910–1925) also instituted his personal politics. Influenced partly by his education at the Royal Military Academy, Sandhurt, and in Christ Church at Oxford, King Vajiravudh publicly identified three ideological canons (*lak thai*) of Siam: nation (*chāt*), religion (*sāsanā*), and monarchy (*phramahākasat*), which bear a striking similarity to England's "God, King, and Country." In a speech to the Wild Tigers Corps, his nationalist party, on May 26, 1911, Vajiravudh first referred to these three ideological canons.[11] In the same speech, Vajiravudh used "religion" as a synonym for Thai Buddhism.[12]

Siam, through bureaucratic reforms, continued to sustain systemic ideological interconnections between the state and Siamese Buddhism.[13] In each instance, the state was an active force in both shaping and utilizing the power of the Thai *sangha*. Peter Jackson, after examining the role of Thai Buddhism in Bangkok, declared that, throughout the twentieth century, using Thai Buddhism to legitimize a bureaucracy was virtually endemic with Thai administrations:

> [E]ach new political regime in the past century has attempted to restructure the organization of the order of Buddhist monks in its political image in order to maintain a legitimatory [*sic*] parallelism between the symbolic religious domain and the secular power structure.[14]

According to Jackson, twentieth-century Thai political regimes continued to garner symbolic capital from state Buddhism to further buttress their own capital and ensure legitimacy.

This closely intertwined relationship between the Thai state and the Thai Buddhist *sangha* continues in the twenty-first century; it is particularly visible in the three southernmost provinces, where the state has situated its forces *within* local Buddhist monasteries. This military presence within the monasteries symbolizes the collapse of any distinction between Thai Buddhism and the state. This intimate relationship is in stark contrast to the distinctive Malay Muslim culture and religion in the area, which is relatively dislocated from the national government and politics. It has also contributed to violence in the area and the targeting of Buddhist monks. Simultaneously with the collapse of any visible distinction between Thai Buddhism and the Thai state has come the advent of the military monk (*thahānphra*).

Military Monks

Military monks are fully ordained monks who simultaneously serve as armed soldiers, marines, or navy or air force personnel. This amalgam of Thai Buddhism and the military reflects the inherent violence. For many, the idea of a militarized monk conflicts sharply with a monk's most fundamental duties. A Buddhist monk's purpose is to avoid life's vulgarities, to aspire toward enlightenment. A soldier's life is virtually the opposite; that job *requires* confrontation with life's worst vulgarities.

In addition to these ideological complications, there is also an ecclesiastical interdiction that prohibits soldiers from becoming monks. However, as anthropologist Hayashi Yukio explains in his study of the Thai-Lao of northeastern Thailand, a people's religious practice is rooted in experience. Buddhism "does not consist merely of cultivated knowledge sealed in texts, or of its interpretation. Rather it consists of practices that live in the 'here and now.' "[15] While the Buddhist textual tradition clearly disallows the existence of a military monk, lived Buddhist traditions demonstrate a different attitude. Throughout the development of Buddhisms in such countries as China, Korea, and Japan, we find traditions that do not follow the idealized notions of Buddhisms. Similar to Thai Buddhists, Chinese, Korean, and Japanese Buddhist monasticisms also have had military monks.

The Thai Theravāda Buddhist tradition is unique among these monasticisms in allowing men to temporarily join the *sangha*. It is common for Thai Buddhist men to ordain as monks for a short time at least once in their lives. Other Theravāda, Mahāyāna, and Vajrayāna traditions treat ordination as a permanent life decision. Anthropologist Charles Keyes notes that Thai men gain considerable esteem by their temporary ordinations, which generally occur during Buddhist Lent (Thai: *khaophansā*). By entering the Thai *sangha*, all men, regardless of class, have access to education and a means of increasing their social status.[16] Moreover, in addition to these social benefits, it is also popularly believed that, by becoming a monk, a son grants his mother merit to enter heaven.

According to the *Vinaya*, certain interdictions surround ordainment. Many such interdictions revolve around physical or social characteristics that would preclude ordination, such as if a person has a disease, is a criminal, or is disabled. Most of these guidelines resulted from the historical Buddha trying to cope with specific sociopolitical and economic dilemmas. For example, a prohibition evolved that specifically relates to the ordaining of soldiers:

> During the time of the Buddha there was a war on the border of the northern Indian kingdom of Magadha, one of the primary supporters of Buddhist monasticism. Several generals who did not want to join the battle entered the Buddhist Sangha. At the request of the king, the Buddha declared that henceforth soldiers were not allowed into the Sangha. (Vin. I, 73–74)

Since this historic incident, the official doctrinal stance has been to prohibit active soldiers from entering the *sangha*, though we have already noted that this interdiction is subject to regional and historical exceptions. Richard Gombrich, a well-respected scholar of Theravāda Buddhism, has offered a slightly different context for this doctrinal prohibition:

> A minister advised the king that anyone who thus deprived him of his soldiers deserved to be executed. As the king was on good terms with the Buddha, he advised him that other kings might not take such as a thing lying down. Reading between the lines, we can deduce that he warned the Buddha that for their own good the Sangha had better not ordain soldiers.[17]

The Thai state has formally acknowledged and supported the ecclesiastical interdiction on ordaining soldiers. In 1905, to avoid the overlapping of duties to the state and *sangha*, the Chulalongkorn administration created a legal provision called the Thai Military Service Act, exempting monks from military service. The act also eliminated the tensions concerning the possibility of monks enlisting in the army. Thus, in accordance with ecclesiastical restrictions, the Thai Military Service Act was designed to prevent the monk-to-soldier process. However, later in contemporary Thai society, it became clear that the tension was not the result of the monk-to-soldier process, but the reverse: the soldier-to-monk process.

By means of its temporary ordinations, the Thai Buddhist tradition allows maneuverability around these obstacles to the existence of Buddhist soldiers. According to stipulations articulated by the Office of National Buddhism, soldiers are allotted one four-month paid leave of absence during their service in order to ordain at a local monastery (*wat*). Soldiers generally take this leave during the annual Buddhist Lent (which generally lasts from June until October). They return to duty after the rainy season retreat has ended. This leniency surrounding ordination is extended even further by another and more covert exercise regarding the status of military monks.

As early as 2002, a covert military unit (authorized by a confidential department) began directing Buddhist soldiers to ordain while remaining on active duty. Every year since, military monks have been assigned to specific posts. According to some of the military monks I interviewed, this secret military unit operates semi-independently. Its operations are unknown to most of the military in Bangkok, although there have been numerous reports implicating the Thai monarchy, especially Queen Sirikit. For example, there have been reports of groups of military monks becoming ordained in honor of the queen's birthday.

It is difficult to determine how many Thais in the military truly do not know about military monks as opposed to those who know but who refuse to disclose what they know. As the state-appointed guardian of Thai monastic lifestyles and activities, the Office of National Buddhism does not acknowledge the presence of military monks. When asked about their presence, the director dismissed the issue:

> Why would soldiers have to dress like a monk? In dangerous monasteries, we have soldiers there to take care of them. And this point is a really serious point in Thai Buddhism. We can't let something like this exist. The monk can't fight and can't have weapons. People may think this is possible, but it's not.[18]

The official position of the Office of National Buddhism mirrors that of the Thai Buddhist *Vinaya*. As historian Craig Reynolds notes, the *Vinaya* goes so far as to forbid monks from even observing an army in battle dress.[19] Although the director of the Office of National Buddhism argues emphatically that military monks do not exist, they are a very real and active part of many monasteries in southern Thailand.

Accounts of military monks in southern Thailand are cloaked in rumors and secrecy.[20] In numerous interviews with abbots, journalists, and local Buddhists, there were allusions to military monks; they were short references but direct confirmations nonetheless. Such brief references to military monks were always followed by bouts of hesitation and reluctance. If not for the fact that I personally and directly interviewed military monks, I might have dismissed these informants' depictions as a communal fabrication.

To dismiss this atmosphere of secrecy as insignificant would be to dismiss the very real ideological efficacy of the military monk. Thai Buddhism is perceived as a peaceful, meditative, and supportive tradition, devoid of any violence. Monks, as embodied agents of this tradition, are considered diametrically opposed to violence and agents of war, i.e., the military. Hence, there is a reluctance to talk about military monks. Anthropologist Michael Taussig postulates that truth comes in the form of a public secret. The importance of this public secret is *knowing what not to know*.[21] One clear indication of this tacit social understanding is the many interviews with abbots in the southernmost provinces who claim to know nothing about military monks. Contrary to their assertions, however, a high-ranking monk in the southernmost provinces confided that abbots throughout the region met in 2004 and discussed the issue of military monks receiving military stipends.[22] Living in an environment that normalizes bombings and armed attacks, southern monks and some privileged members of the Buddhist laity are aware of military monks, but they also know that they should not openly speak of them. Such a discussion would combine elements that socially and religiously are considered opposites: Buddhism and violence.

The very concept of military monks does represent a powerful clash between Thai Buddhist doctrine and the Thai lived Buddhist tradition. This conflict between doctrine and praxis, when made public, creates a palpable discomfort in most Thai Buddhists. One example of this occurred during an afternoon interview with Phra Nirut, a high-ranking monk in southern Thailand. The interview was lighthearted and relaxed until I asked him about military monks. Phra Nirut paused for a few seconds and sighed. Seemingly reluctantly, he nodded, confirming that he knew a little about them. Pressing the issue a bit more, I asked his opinion of military monks: were gun-wielding

FIGURE 8.1 Thai boy mimicking an armed soldier at a Buddhist monastery during a celebration of the annual Kathin ceremony. Photo taken by Michael Jerryson.

monks legitimate? After the question, Phra Nirut squirmed a bit in his chair, smiled faintly, and let out a series of filler words. Finally he replied, "I cannot say. It depends on many things." He paused again and I let the silence linger. Frowning slightly, Phra Nirut spoke again, this time in a soft voice, "For me, it is not okay. For me, it is not okay."[23]

Phra Nirut's inability to condone military monks could very well be a reaction to their changing role in southern monasteries. Beginning in 2002 with limited guidance by the Thai *sangha*, military monks went to areas that lacked monks. Their presence at assigned posts was indefinite and depended upon the circumstances surrounding their assignment. If a military monk decided to quit his post, another would come to replace him.

Thai Buddhist monasteries need a minimum of five monks in order to perform crucial ceremonies, such as the annual Kathin ceremony, in which the Buddhist laity bestows new robes and gifts upon the monks at the end of Buddhist Lent. Populating these understaffed monasteries with military monks enables monasteries to perform important rituals, granting local Buddhists a chance to make merit. At the same time, through its interrelationship with the Thai *sangha*, the presence of these military monks also augments the state's presence.

The situation changed in 2004, however, when Prime Minister Thaksin Shinawatra declared martial law. The Thai state found a new use for military monks. Instead of assigning them to specific monasteries to fill voids in the monastic infrastructure, under martial law the stationing of military monks was to bolster the defense of particular monasteries. In 2006 and the early half of 2007, there were not many military monks in the southernmost provinces, and the ones with whom I conferred stated that there was no networking among them.

Late one evening in 2007, a monk sat with me at a table outside his quarters, relaying what he had heard about military monks:

> A monastery in Narathiwat had a few monks. When insurgents attacked, the monks moved to stay in the city. The monastery became abandoned. Muslims went to the monastery to destroy the Buddha images, buildings, pavilions, and the monks' quarters. The queen ordered soldiers to become monks and go stay in the abandoned monastery, to guard the monastery and its religious objects. In this respect, I agree that there has to be military monks.[24]

One clear indication of this strategy is the commissioning of military monks throughout the three southernmost provinces. The majority is sent to Narathiwat, the second largest group of military monks is assigned to Yala, and the fewest go to Pattani. These proportions correspond to the level of violence and instability in the three provinces since 2004. Typically, a soldier training in southern Thailand is contacted before his graduation that he has been selected to become a military monk. To proceed through full ordination as a military monk, he attends a local monastery, one in his home neighborhood or one in a more clandestine location in southern Thailand. From that point in time, the military monk serves as an active and vigilant protector of his monastery and its monks.

Early one evening, while smoking his hand-rolled cigarette within the monastery, a military monk to whom I refer as Phra Eks, proudly opened his saffron robes to show me the Smith and Wesson handgun tucked beneath the folds around his waist. He keeps his M-16 hidden in his sleeping quarters and generally carries the handgun in case of trouble. For Phra Eks, a military monk's primary duty is to protect monks from terrorists (*phūkokānrai*):

> We need to disguise ourselves as monks to protect [the monks]. If we don't do this, in the future, there will be no monks in the three provinces. We need to give them moral support, to serve our nation, religion, and army, to foster harmony, to prevent social disruptions, and to prevent people from abusing others.[25]

Phra Eks is thirty years old and comes from a poor Thai Chinese family in one of the border provinces. His father, who died when Phra Eks was very young, also served as a soldier in southern Thailand. Being one of seven children, Phra Eks helps his mother take care of his siblings by contributing part of his salary each month to the family. In this way, he is able to provide his mother with both merit and money.

Phra Eks's disguise is more than a superficial undercover persona or a means of preserving a public secret. Seemingly contradicting himself, he also asserts that he is not pretending to be a monk; he is a *real* monk (*phra čhing*). Because he considers himself to be both a soldier and a monk, I pressed Phra Eks as to his ultimate allegiance. He replied that his duties as a soldier simultaneously fulfill his duties as a monk. For Phra Eks, these two separate sets of duties do not conflict with one another. In the event the monastery is attacked and he kills an attacker, he is confident that he would remain a monk. Although killing a human being would transgress the most important of the *pārājikas* (severe offenses that result from violating Buddhist law), Phra Eks explained the apparent contradiction. He stated that there were certain people at the monastery who would "clean up" the situation—in order to allow him to remain at his post.

Although Phra Eks recognizes the gravity of murdering a terrorist, the defense of the monastery and its occupants overshadows it. I asked Phra Eks on several occasions why the existence of military monks is necessary. He explained:

> If the nation does not have Buddhism, it is a country of thievery [*mūang čhon*]. Buddhism as a religion helps to clean the heart and shape the mind. Buddhism teaches people to abandon their greed, anger, and obsessions, to live moderately. If there is no Buddhism to teach and guide people, it would be a nation of chaos filled with selfish people. . . . I will use a gun whenever I see someone who tries to attack monks at the monastery, such as setting fire [to the monastery], or coming to hurt or shoot the monks. I will shoot.[26]

To Phra Eks, a Muslim terrorist attack on Buddhist monks is symbolically an attack on the moral integrity of the nation. Without military monks, Thailand would revert to chaos; its people would become selfish. His rationalization is that this ideological threat of moral turpitude justifies the use of violence. Phra Eks's stance on terrorists is reminiscent of the rhetoric used by ultraconservative monks in describing Communists in the 1970s. At that time, for the staunch Thai nationalist supporter Phra Kittiwuttho, Communism was ideologically antination and antireligion; a Communist was the living embodiment of Māra, the manifestation of desire. Phra Kittiwuttho perceived that the use of violence against Communists was justified:

> [B]ecause whoever destroys the nation, the religion, or the monarchy, such bestial types [*man*] are not complete persons. Thus we must intend not to kill people but to kill the Devi [Māra]; this is the duty of all Thai.[27]

Kittiwuttho's justification for opposing the Communists in the 1970s rests on two concepts: (1) the antagonist to the state is a manifestation of Māra, an embodiment of moral depravity, and (2) killing such a manifestation is not the same as killing a human being, a "complete person."

While Phra Eks does not go so far as to dehumanize Malay Muslim terrorists, his justification for violence is eerily reminiscent of Phra Kittiwuttho's. Phra Eks will attack those who seek to bring about a chaotic and selfish nation, a nation which Kittiwuttho would consider dominated by Māra. It is this ideological threat to the nation and Buddhist principles that provoked both monks—Phra Eks and Phra Kittiwuttho—to condone the use of violence. Unlike Phra Kittiwuttho's rationale, however, Phra Eks's rationalization enables him to *directly enact* violence. Kittiwuttho became the moral voice of the state during the violent crackdowns in 1973 and 1976.

Military Monks in Buddhist Traditions

This rationale of justifying violence due to an endangered tradition may be endemic throughout different Theravādin traditions. In Sri Lanka, Janatha Vimukthi Peramuna (JVP) Buddhism has blurred the lines between sacred duty and murder. Sri Lankan JVP monks rationalize the violence they commit through Buddhist justifications and a legacy of Buddhist precedents. They trace these precedents back to the Sinhalese mythohistorical chronicle called the *Mahāvamsa*. In this second-century BCE work, the Buddhist king Dutthagamani (Pāli: Duṭṭagāmaṇī, Sinhala: Duṭugämuṇu) wages a sacred war against foreign invaders led by the Tamil king Eḷara. The killing of heathens did not constitute murder, since the Tamil warriors were neither meritorious nor, more important, Buddhist.

Centuries later, during the 1980s, JVP monks reconceptualized Dutthagamani's cause in the ethnoreligious war between the secular separatist movement LTTE (Liberation Tigers of Tamil Eelam) and the Sinhalese Buddhist state. As they demanded President Jayewardene's resignation in 1988, JVP monks launched a rash of violent attacks on police, teachers, and politicians. Their threats, brutal physical assaults, and an attempted assassination all became the means toward realizing an important and justifiable cause: the preservation of the nation and Sri Lankan Buddhism.[28] Interestingly, the rhetoric employed by JVP monks is similar to Kittiwuttho's rhetoric regarding Communists, and not too different from the mentality of the Thai military monk Phra Eks. This commonality suggests a uniform latent tendency in Theravādin Buddhist traditions for justifying violence.[29]

In addition, this tendency to justify Buddhist violence—and the advent of military monks—can be traced beyond the borders of southeast Eurasia and beyond the borders of Theravādin Buddhism to Mahāyāna Buddhism. Historically in eastern Eurasia, under the canopy of Mahāyāna Buddhism, there were situations in which both monasteries and monks were militarized. In China, there have been many instances, such as the messianic Maitreya rebellions during the Sui and Tang dynasties (613–626), when soldier-monks led revolts and rebellions. In 1891, after examining the militant aspects of Chinese Buddhism, J. M. M. de Groot offered the following ideological rationale for the militarism:

> A last reason for the warlike behavior of Buddhist monks we see in an imperative order of the *Fan-mang-king* to all the devotees of the Church, to afford protection to the *Sam-Pao*, or the triad embracing the Buddha, the Law and the Clergy. No one, says the book, can ever hope for the bodhisattva-dignity, unless he conforms in every respect to this most holy duty of all the children of Buddha. Now, defending the *Sam-Pao* is identical with protecting monasteries and sanctuaries against hordes of invaders and rebels, who as is fully proved by China's history of all periods, have never manifested one whit more clemency for religious than for secular buildings.[30]

Throughout Chinese Buddhist monks' scriptures, we find Buddhist militarism repeatedly justified in order to protect sacred spaces. This phenomenon is not limited solely to China. During the course of defending Korea's borders between the twelfth and seventeenth centuries, Korean armies enlisted monks as soldiers to fight the waves of successive invaders: Jurchen, Mongol, Japanese, and Manchu.

Japan also has a long history of militarized monks. As early as the tenth century under the abbotship of Ryōgen, Tendai armies marched into battle. These soldier-monks were well aware of their transgressive behavior and, because of their actions, were dubbed "evil monks." Regardless of this sanction against them, the monks perceived their tasks as absolutely necessary. Christoph Kleine explains that the purpose became cosmic in importance: "armed monks had an important task to fulfill, for the sake of Buddhism and thus the sake of all sentient beings."[31] Centuries later, during the Warring States period of the 1500s, Japanese warrior-monks (*ikko-ikki*) became prevalent, and in the Russo-Japanese War (1904–1905),[32] Japanese Zen monks could be seen marching in the front lines of the military.

The rationale for violence in Theravāda Buddhism may be a latent tendency in its adherents and monks. As such, this tendency toward violence would remain inactive until a Buddhist sovereignty is threatened and triggers a defensive (yet aggressive) reaction. In southern Thailand, the ongoing terrorist actions—like the violence committed by the Khmer Rouge (which, according to Kittiwuttho, awoke in him the need to defend Buddhism) or the ethnic fratricide in Sri Lanka during the 1980s—have activated this latent tendency for a militant Buddhist response.

Ordinations, although uncommon in the southernmost provinces due to the low Buddhist population, have drastically decreased in numbers. In one district I visited, there had been only one ordination in over a year. That individual was a young teacher who decided to ordain for a few weeks before defrocking and returning to lay life. Those individuals who remain monks describe the very existence of Thai Buddhism in the region as endangered. For them, the violence is not merely about worldly existence and its mundane matters but, more important, about the survival of the *dhamma*, the Buddhist doctrine. One monk who is in favor of military monks explained that this militancy is a necessity:

> It is beneficial to have military monks in order to protect the religion. I mean to protect religious rituals, the *dhamma*, artifacts, and people.... Buddhist artifacts have been destroyed. It is good to have a guard to keep an eye on these things. The Buddha's teachings, i.e., the books, are still here. The religious people are still here. If you are asking about the military monk's importance, I would like to ask you back—what if there were no military monks? What would happen? The monasteries might be attacked and destroyed. When the monasteries are destroyed, what would happen then?[33]

It is in this respect that military monks and some nonmilitary monks regard Thai Malay Muslims as their enemies. I asked Phra Eks to define Thai-ness (*kwāmpenthai*):

> Thai-ness means good human relationships [that are] gentle, [in which each] helps the other. But now it's not like that here. Thai Buddhists are still the same; they are gentle like [Thai-ness prescribes] but Thai Muslims have only violence.[34]

Violence against monks and monasteries has activated the latent tendency in Thai Buddhism to demonize the Other and justify violence. It is this mentality that has spurred atypical behavior in Thai monks, behavior such as abbots who go to sleep at night with guns next to their beds.

Caught between the conflicting tides of doctrine and practice, a few high-ranking southern monks do offer doctrinal justification for the military monks. According to them, although the *Vinaya* strictly prohibits monks from using any aggressive force, it does allow them to defend themselves. For these southern monks, the advent of the military monk is an example of this allowance. An examination of different Buddhist traditions reveals varying explanations. Richard Jones provides a slightly different view to justify the creation of military monks by the Thai Buddhist state. According to Jones, the monk's most central social obligation is to teach the *dhamma*. Any action taken to preserve this primary social responsibility is secondary in importance to the repercussions of not teaching the *dhamma*.[35]

Employing this rationale, the obligation of some monks to teach the *dhamma* in southern Thailand requires the presence of military monks. Only they can ensure the existence of monks in this region; otherwise, there would be no monks present at all. Military monks may accept the doctrine and the patriotic justification of their actions; nonetheless, they still must conceal their purpose. I once asked Phra Eks if I could take his picture. He quickly refused, explaining, "It would be too dangerous." Indeed, Phra Eks does need to be concerned about exposure. A photograph of him brandishing a gun would expose the secret of military monks and subsequently result in his expulsion from the *sangha* and possible death.

Anthropologist Stanley Tambiah argues that militancy separates a monk from his sacred identity. Referring to the militant activities of the JVP monks in Sri Lanka, Tambiah explains, "The monk who has finally taken to the gun can no longer be considered a vehicle of the Buddha's religion."[36] In this vein, a picture of Phra Eks with a gun would strip him of sacrality, destroy the perceived pacifism of southern monks, and undermine the clandestine nature of the entire military monk program. Although their existence is a secret, military monks embody the militarization of Buddhist roles.

From Monastic to Military Compound

In addition to the militarization of Buddhist roles, Thai Buddhist spaces are also being militarized. On November 9, 2006, the *Bangkok Post* published a brief article about 100 Thai Buddhist villagers who fled their homes in Yala, one of the southernmost provinces. Women, men, and children abandoned their homes and livelihoods and traveled to the capital district to find refuge in Wat Nirotsangkatham.[37] By the beginning of December, their numbers had grown to over 228 people.[38] The Buddhist refugees did not feel that it would be safe to return to their villages; instead, they made temporary homes at the monastery. The villagers were not the only laity then residing at Wat Nirotsangkatham. Thai soldiers were already living at the monastery, guarding the entrance and fortifying its perimeters.

The military encampment at Wat Nirotsangkatham is one of many instances in which the state has militarized Thai Buddhism. Although soldiers protect the monks and refugees at the monastery, they also use the Buddhist space to strategize and execute military commands, effectively converting the monastic compound into a military headquarters.

The most common place signified in Thai Buddhism is and has always been the monastery, which often has been identified by locals as a communal investment. The significance of the site has changed, however, due to the practices that now take place in the monasteries. From the time when martial law was declared in southern Thailand in 2004 through 2007, Buddhist monks reported that Malay Muslims no longer frequented the Buddhist monasteries. Instead of serving as communal gathering places, monasteries became spaces of contestation. Military units and covert operatives situated there guard monasteries against such dangers as power outages and armed assaults. A consequence of this vigilance by the state and its militarization of Buddhist spaces is that Thai Buddhist identity has also been militarized.

The local investment in a monastery can be measured from different vantage points. Although there are many, in this chapter I will outline only two levels for analysis: the religious and the secular.[39] In religious terms, having a monastery allows the surrounding religious community easy access to annual ceremonies and to rituals, such as funerals, ordinations, and holidays. Buddhist monks who live in the monastery go outside it daily for morning alms (*binthabat*). This routine provides the local laity with affordable, continual opportunities to make merit. From a secular perspective, having a monastery allows the community access to basketball and volleyball courts, schools, meeting areas, medical care, and therapeutic counseling for people of all faiths.[40] These two different communal functions lead scholar Donald Swearer to identify a monastery as the "religious, cultural and social center of the community."[41]

In Thailand's southernmost provinces, a monastery's religious function is dominant as it is used to demarcate Buddhist space within every district. According to the Office of National Buddhism's records, Pattani province has eighty-eight monasteries, Narathiwat has seventy-five, and the smallest number is found in Yala province, which has only forty-five monasteries.[42] Interestingly, Buddhist space is not reflective of the Buddhist populations in these three provinces. According to the National Statistical Office in Thailand, Yala, with the fewest monasteries, has the greatest number of Buddhists: 127,442.[43]

Prior to the state's declaration of martial law in January 2004, a southern monastery signified a place for communal gatherings as well as Buddhist veneration. These shared spaces attracted Thai Buddhists, Thai Chinese Buddhists, and Thai Malay Muslims. From 2004 to the present, southern Thai monks have considered the monastery's space altered due to the contemporary violent context. Specifically, they feel that locals view and use their monasteries in a distinctly different manner. Emblematic of this difference are statements made by the abbot of Wat Kūaanai in Pattani province. In a phone interview, he explained that, before the increase in violence: "Islam was just Islam and Buddhism was just Buddhism. They did not intermingle. But, whenever we had Thai cultural events like Mother's Day or Father's Day, Muslims would come to our monastery."[44] Locals, whether they were Malay Muslim or Thai Buddhist, would also gather together at monasteries for Thai national celebrations such as the Thai New Year (*songkran*) and the Thai king's or queen's birthday.

The state's implementation of martial law and the insurgent violence in Buddhist villages in southern Thailand have resulted in a different function for monasteries in the area. Wat Nirotsangkatham serves as a striking example of this new appropriation. On an early December afternoon in 2006, I spoke with the abbot from Wat Nirotsangkatham. In his office, he explained that some of the current refugees living at his monastery had donated money years ago in order to erect the very buildings in which they were now living: "Now, the villagers want the monastery to help them. It's like what they did in the past comes to help them now.... This building where villagers stay now was built by them."

Thai and Thai Chinese Buddhist refugees from Yala's Bannang Sata and Than To districts currently view the monastery as more than a religious and communal space; they have also made the monastery their home. Although many Thai Buddhists believe that a monastery is a sacred space and is endowed with protective powers, many Yala refugees chose the location for more mundane reasons: it contains useful facilities and is a shelter large enough to accommodate them. In December 2006, under one of Wat Nirotsangkatham's pavilions, a community leader relayed some of the refugees' initial considerations for sanctuary. "Other places were not big enough to fit all of us," he said, and then added, "and it is safer here because of the soldiers."[45] The community leader's comment about it being safer at the monastery addresses an important social association in southern monasteries located within violent environments. In addition to their religious and secular significance, monasteries are now recognized as among the most militarily fortified areas in the three southernmost provinces.

One of the more devastating attacks by militants occurred immediately after the Chinese New Year, on February 18, 2007. A number of bomb attacks targeted restaurants, karaoke bars, shops, and Buddhist homes in Pattani and Yala provinces. The *Bangkok Post*, Thailand's most widely read English newspaper, described this as the "biggest wave of coordinated bombings, terrorism and murders" that had occurred in the southern border provinces.[46] At the time of these attacks, I was living in Pattani province in a monk's quarters (*kuti*) at Wat Chang Hai. The monastery, as well as other buildings in Pattani and Yala provinces, lost electricity when the central power stations were bombed.

Wat Chang Hai, known for its connection to Lūang Phō Tuat, one of Thailand's most venerated monks of the late sixteenth century, is an internationally renowned Buddhist pilgrimage site. The facilities at Wat Chang Hai sprawl over thirteen *rai*[47] of land and include a school system and amulet shops.

Because of this and the restaurants located in its vicinity, Wat Chang Hai represents a significant local investment. The existence of Wat Chang Hai is owed largely to the Hokkien Khananurak family, who financed the renovation of the monastery in 1936. Historian Patrick Jory writes that the Khananurak family supported numerous other Thai monasteries, and they exemplify Chinese families in the southern provinces who have enjoyed good relations with the local Chinese, Thai, and Malay communities.[48]

By 2007, many of these shops had been vacated. They were visible reminders of the economic impact that violence has had in the southernmost provinces. A few restaurants remained open, but all closed their doors at 5:00 p.m., which coincided with the time that the monastery's front gates were locked. Monks and locals explained that, before 2004, stores and restaurants used to stay open late into the evening. One restaurant that did receive enough business to stay open was a small family-owned establishment with a dozen wooden tables and a small television mounted on the ceiling in the back. I went to the restaurant the day after the organized attacks and noted the difference between these customers and their conversations and those from previous days.

There were very few customers and all spoke in hushed tones about the recent bombings. The old man who owned the restaurant appeared to be more concerned about the lack of customers than about a potential attack on his restaurant. Wat Chang Hai is surrounded by the heavily Buddhist-populated district of Khokpo. That was only one of his reasons for feeling secure. "There are quite a lot of [Buddhist] people in this area," he explained. "I always leave the lights on at night. Many people walk past [my restaurant] at night. And the police and soldiers are also around. Terrorists would not dare to come here."[49]

At Wat Nirotsangkaham and Wat Chang Hai and throughout the southernmost provinces, soldiers and national police use monasteries as their primary bases of operations and as their homes. Thai monasteries have excellent strategic positions. They are near the highest population of Buddhists in an area, have access to ample supplies of food and water, and contain facilities large enough to accommodate the police and soldiers. Abbots generally feel receptive to the needs of soldiers and police and make efforts to accommodate them. One abbot in the capital district of Pattani explained that the soldiers at his monastery had no daily stipends. "The soldiers need food and need to use the bathroom, so this is why they stay at my monastery. [T]he soldiers depend on lay donations to my monastery for food."[50] One of the policemen stationed at the monastery noted:

> There are many reasons [to be stationed at a monastery]. One is to protect the monks. Another is to help in the development of the monastery.

FIGURE 8.2 Thai pavilion converted into a barracks within a Buddhist monastery. Photo taken by Michael Jerryson.

And the monastery is a convenient place for us as well. Because of the monastery, we do not have to find somewhere else to stay.[51]

The military occupation of monasteries is more than a pragmatic exercise of protection and sustenance. Pierre Bourdieu states, "Space can have no meaning apart from practice; the system of generative and structuring dispositions, or *habitus*, constitutes and is constituted by actors' movement through space."[52] It is *what people practice* in the monasteries that *shapes the significance* of the monasteries. Practices within southern monasteries have changed dramatically—primarily due to their new military occupants.

It is more than thirty years since southern Thai monasteries began to be used by the Thai military. Thai soldiers have a history of living in monasteries during times of crisis and conflict. During World War II, soldiers occupied monasteries in the northeastern and southern provinces. Later, in the 1970s, in areas considered hot beds for Communist forces in the southernmost provinces, monasteries were simultaneously used to house soldiers and as training grounds for the Border Patrol Police's Village Scouts.[53] Now, the military occupation of monasteries has resurfaced in the three southern provinces.

Since 2002, these Buddhist spaces have become militarized by the very existence of military personnel working and living in them. To protect a southern monastery's occupants from being observed and attacked, the military personnel residing at it usually raise the outer walls and stretch barbed wire around the entrance and the perimeter. They also convert Buddhist pavilions into barracks, transform sleeping quarters into bunkers, and create lookout posts near the entrances.

Some monasteries have over forty police officers or soldiers living within them. Military personnel are armed with handguns and M-16s and wear camouflage uniforms. I had been told that both Muslim and Buddhist police and soldiers had been living in the monasteries, but every monastery I visited was staffed solely by Buddhist personnel.[54] This distinction of strictly Buddhist military personnel encourages locals to merge religious and political identifications and to view the Thai state as a Buddhist state, although its constitution (and its many redactions) does not proclaim a religious allegiance.

State police, soldiers, and government officials (*khārāchakān*) maintain that there is no religious preference or requirement for the police and soldiers working at a monastery. This is an important position for the state to take. Both Buddhist and Muslim residents in the south feel alienated from the state due to reoccurring acts of corruption and illicit activity by local and state government officials. The notorious disappearance of Somchai Neelaphaijit, a popular Muslim human rights attorney, symbolized the state's failure to honor and protect the rights of southern Thai Muslims.[55] Due to this and other examples, there has been increasing pressure for the state to appear impartial. Having both Muslim and Buddhist soldiers and police working at monasteries might lessen the symbolic impact of having state officials residing at a Buddhist monastery. However, the absence of any Muslim soldiers or national police in the southern monasteries underscores the perception of a state Buddhism.

Only a handful of large military camps exists in the southernmost provinces. For instance, in Pattani province, there are only two soldier units that have their own military space—apart from the monasteries—one for combat and one for community support activities. Soldiers are sent to live in one monastery for as long as two years before relocating to another. The superior officers will issue commands to relocate, and the new site will generally be in southern Thailand.[56] The advantage of stationing soldiers in the south is that the extended duration allows soldiers to become familiar with locals and to develop trust and contacts in the surrounding communities, which prior to 2004 maintained strong ties to local Muslims. When asked, monks often say that they prefer to have soldiers, rather than police, living in their monasteries;

ultimately, however, the decision is not theirs. Soldiers living in monasteries are characterized as being hard working and more respectful of Buddhist precepts than the police who live at the monastery.

Many abbots in safer areas stress that they did not ask the state for protection; they say that the military is at the monastery due to governmental concerns. Early one evening just before the Chinese New Year, an abbot and I were sitting in front of his quarters. It had just finished raining, and the abbot was smoking a cigarette while relaxing on his front step. He explained to me:

> This monastery is not in danger; it is not in any dangerous scenario. The monastery didn't ask for soldiers, but the government sent them. The monastery has never called for soldiers to be here. But the government felt worried, afraid that the monastery will be destroyed. I'm afraid if I go outside the monastery. But I think in the monastery there is nothing [to be afraid of].[57]

His monastery had over twenty soldiers patrolling its perimeters, with fortified stations at every entrance. The abbot's position on the violence changed considerably after the Chinese New Year, however, when his monastery lost power for an hour and there was an arson attempt just a few kilometers away. Yet even during this period of heightened fear and tension, this abbot's lack of appreciation for the soldiers differed greatly from that of abbots who live in more isolated areas with higher populations of Muslims and higher rates of murders and bombings.

Some of the soldiers have gone outside of Thailand to work with soldiers from other countries. This international experience has provided them with a seasoned view of the violence in the southernmost provinces. Many of the soldiers I interviewed in the monastery have international work experience in areas such as Aceh during the recent conflict (2003–2005). A few fought in Vietnam during the U.S. war. They typically assist with the general upkeep of the monastery, sweeping the grounds and cleaning latrines. Although they make their homes in the monastery, they keep their personal habits private within their quarters. Because of their respectful and helpful nature, as well as the long-term protection they bring, some abbots and monks have built bunkers and living quarters in their monasteries. While monks generally prefer soldiers to police, they are less enthusiastic about the military commanders, who dispatch the soldiers into the area and yet situate themselves outside the sphere of violence. As I sat at a monastery with an abbot underneath his pavilion, accompanied by four members of the laity, the abbot—with much bitterness in his voice—relayed the following:

> The military sent the soldiers here, but didn't provide them with a place to stay, so they have to sleep under the pavilions with the dogs and ants. Because of this, I built a shelter for them. The military officers are really bad. They call themselves men of honor but they sit in air-conditioned rooms while their privates, who have to follow orders, are sent to sleep with mosquitoes and ants. Military officers sent soldiers down here so these officers should care for their welfare. An officer came to check in on the situation once, but he left even before his driver came back from [the] toilet! Didn't even walk around to see where the soldiers slept, how they were living, or what they eat. He just came and left.[58]

As the violence increases, there is more interaction between soldiers and monks within monasteries. This is especially true in monasteries in more remote locations that have a higher percentage of Muslims living in the village. The shared isolation of monks and soldiers sometimes encourages the sharing of resources, and the two groups exchange information about locals in the surrounding area.

Police are gathered from different provinces throughout Thailand and live at monasteries in southern Thailand from six months to a year. A majority of the national police who are stationed in the southernmost provinces are originally from central and northeastern Thailand; consequently, they have little experience with or knowledge of the Thais living in the southern provinces. And unlike the soldiers, very few possess any international experience. The police rotate on and off duty within the monastery, which allows them days or nights to relax and drink. Within the monastery, the conduct of the police contrasts sharply with the conduct of the soldiers. Soldiers generally keep to themselves and maintain strict vigilance while living in the monastery. One reason for the monks' preference for soldiers became apparent at one monastery where I was staying. Policemen had created an outdoor kitchen in which to prepare and eat their food and consume alcohol. This was just meters behind the novices' quarters. After dinner, the police concluded the evening with a few hours of drinking whiskey and soda beneath the abbot's pavilion. This police behavior has resulted in empty whiskey bottles overflowing trash cans within the monk's quarters.

The transgressive act of drinking intoxicants within a monastery is not the only action worth noting. In December 2006, I asked five policemen on duty in a monastery if the police living there make merit (*tham bun*). A policeman in his mid-thirties gestured around at the barracks and to his fellow policemen, who were armed with M-16s; he responded: "Yes, we do. Actually, what we do right now is merit as well."[59] The very act of protecting the monks and the monastery, a duty inherent in national police and soldiers' responsibilities, also has become a means of making merit. This encapsulation of merit making within military duties is another consequence of the collusion of state and Thai Buddhist elements.

The state's appropriation of Buddhist sites has altered the monastery's spatial significance in southern Thailand. Under the banner of a strident nationalism, monasteries serve as home bases for the military; in exchange for this form of nationalism, the monasteries have lost some of their sacrality. Today, if one were to visit multiple monasteries in an area—a common act for Thai Buddhists on pilgrimage—locals might consider those visits to be indicative of military communication rather than religious devotion. This change in the spatial significance of monasteries has had an impact on their patronage; Buddhist monks report that local Muslim officials in the three southernmost provinces try to avoid contact with the monastery as much as possible. Ačhān Mahāwichī, a former secretary to the Pattani *sangha* leader who has been a monk for over twenty years, explained that currently a trip to a monastery is viewed by many Muslims as a sin:

> Muslims have said many times it is a sin to come to the monastery.... An Islamic village leader, who has to sign a paper when someone dies, complains that when someone dies he has to come to the monastery and get the thing signed, because it is a sin to come to the monastery.[60]

Ačhān Mahāwichī is the second highest-ranking monk at Wat Chang Hai. According to him, the monastery has become a profane space for many Malay Muslims in the southernmost provinces. For the Islamic village leader, entering a monastery meant entering a space of impurity, a distinction of the Durkheimian profane as opposed to sacred space. The association of coming to a monastery with the commission of a sin, while not universally recognized, demonstrates a growing public reconsideration of what coming to a monastery signifies and what such an action signifies for group identifications.

Local Malays' newfound negative attitudes regarding monasteries heighten the significance of visiting a monastery. Entering a monastery may imply more than simply a visit; it could indicate one's adherence to Buddhism. As there is no specific ritual or official declaration for conversion to Thai Buddhism, the very public and regular performance of visiting monasteries (and making merit) becomes an identity-making or identity-reaffirming exercise.[61] This emerging perception contrasts with local views prior to the institution of martial law. Before 2004, visiting a monastery held fewer implications, and

Buddhist identity was largely denoted in two ways: by participating in specific merit-making exercises and, one could argue, eating pork (which is still a very powerful religious signifier, as Muslims do not eat pork).

The new significance of visiting a monastery arises out of the violently charged environment and the Thai state's militarization of the monasteries. While the militarization of Thai Buddhist monasteries is not unique within Buddhist traditions, it is still important to assess its social implications in light of the twenty-first-century context.[62] As a safety precaution, religious practices and ceremonies at southern monasteries have either declined or stopped altogether since martial law was imposed. In areas outside of capital districts, funeral rites—which used to occur in the afternoon or night—are now held during the day. In addition, the regular practice of morning alms has ceased throughout the most dangerous areas. At these monasteries, monks rarely go outside their compounds. One sixty-six-year-old monk, seated at a bench outside his quarters, explained:

> I want to go out and meet people, give them blessings, all that and more. However, they forbid it because it is dangerous.... I listen and obey my abbot and the government, so I don't go out.[63]

The absence of monks going in and out of monasteries further accentuates the presence of the military, which can regularly be seen entering and leaving the monasteries to perform checks around the area. Soldiers and police use the monastery as military headquarters and implement and develop military intelligence while sequestered in monastery buildings. For instance, at several monasteries, abbots showed me detailed reports of the villagers in their communities. The reports described areas that should be heavily watched and included pages of information on local suspects. The reports are a compilation of information shared between the monks and the military and specify which of the local people are (1) arrested (*thūk čhap lǣo*), (2) on the run (*lop nī*), and (3) those whose identities are still undetermined (*yang mai sāmāt phisūt sāp tūa bukhkhon dai*). Military intelligence does not necessarily impact the public's perception of a monastery, but it does illustrate the level at which monks and military collaborate and how the monastery functions as a military headquarters in southern villages.

While these documents are private, military practices in a monastery are not. If locals walk past the entrance of a monastery, instead of seeing monks performing daily chores, they see fully armed, uniformed military standing guard day and night. These habits and practices, according to Pierre Bourdieu, shape the significance of the space and have an important effect on the surrounding Thai community. Monks have become less visible as the military has become more visible. The stationing of soldiers and police at monasteries together with their military habits transform the monastery into a military space. As this happens, the problematic relations between Buddhists and Muslims in the southernmost provinces are exacerbated.

The 228 Buddhist refugees who stay at Wat Nirotsangkatham see the monastery as a safer space than their villages. According to the refugees, their villages are over 95 percent Muslim. They say that murders occur almost daily in their villages. While I was visiting them at the monastery, there was a funeral for a man from a neighboring village. The sister of the deceased told me that in her village everyone is a target—from the elderly to two-year-old children. She is a farmer and, like the refugees, considers her village no longer safe. Part of the refugees' decision to come to Wat Nirotsangkatham is due to the recent conversion of southern monastic compounds into military compounds. Buddhist villagers stay inside the protective perimeters of the monastery and leave as seldom as possible—only to buy food. Unfortunately, perceiving a monastery as a sanctuary from violence does not distinguish it from the violence; rather, it highlights the monastery's role and preferential treatment by the state within a violent climate.

Southern Thai monasteries have assumed defensive functions for the Buddhist laity living in the surrounding areas. Much of this change developed due to physical changes made to the monasteries, i.e., barracks, wire, and blockades positioned at the entrances. Another factor that has converted the public's perception is the change in the occupants they see entering and exiting the monasteries. Instead of the monasteries acting as bases for monks, from which they leave for their morning alms, they are now acting as bases for the military as they leave for their daily rounds.

Since 2005 in the three southernmost provinces, there have been more Muslims murdered than Buddhists. Yet, despite all of the fortifications at the monasteries, not one Muslim uses a monastery as a place of refuge. Living under martial law, monasteries in southern Thailand have clearly become an exclusive military space for Thai and Thai Chinese Buddhists.

Conclusion

As stated earlier, the focus of this chapter has been the militarization of Thai Buddhism in southern Thailand. Buddhist monks and monasteries have been and continue to be targets for violence in the southernmost provinces. This started in 2002, with a bomb threat at Wat Chang Hai in Khokpo, Pattani province. In many ways, this attack represented the nascent policy of targeting monks and monasteries. In a phone interview during the summer of 2004, a high-ranking monk explained the motivation behind the attack on this particular monastery:

> People attacked Wat Chang Hai in order to destroy the morale of the Buddhist people. Because people believe that Wat Chang Hai is sacred and since [it is] sacred, bombing it might decrease the degree of sacredness; people might lose their belief in the monastery.[64]

The militarization of monasteries clearly enhances the protection for some monasteries and their monks. Unfortunately, the state's militarization of monasteries also heightens the association of Thai Buddhism with the state. In light of the martial law initiated in 2004 and the current violence in these southernmost provinces, this militarization raises a monastery's political value and exacerbates local Muslim contestation.

Another state action that has led to the militarization of Thai Buddhism comes in the form of the military monk. While militarizing monasteries has resulted in increasing the political value of monasteries, it has simultaneously led some Muslims to identify monasteries as taboo spaces. Unlike the very visible militarization of monasteries, however, the militarization of monks is a covert exercise; fortunately, it has yet to produce a similar result in how Muslims view monks. Nevertheless, military monks embody the nexus that links the militant state to Thai Buddhist principles. This has the dangerous potential of further politicizing the situation and incurring Muslim derision of southern monks.

While working undercover in monasteries as ordinary monks, military monks fulfill obligations to both the Thai *sangha* and the state. Their roles are not publicized; at times, their roles are not even disclosed to the very monks who ordain them. Violence in southern Thailand is saturated in secrecy: anonymous militant agents, unspoken grievances, and victims from both sides who often go unnamed. From this blend of secrecy and violence, another form of secret arises: a *communal* secret. Some Buddhists living and working alongside military monks are aware of military monks' identities but choose not to publicize them. Their decision to protect the secrecy of military monks may be an indirect result of the religious angst many feel concerning the presence of military monks within the monasteries.

In the current Thai milieu and the current understanding of Buddhist doctrine, there is virtually no public support that advocates military monks. This lack of overt support derives from Buddhist interdictions dating back to the time of the Buddha. One of the earliest canonical sources prohibiting military ordination derives from a time when soldiers could deliberately avoid their military duties by entering the *sangha*. Ironically, the current circumstances are inverted, resulting in the near-opposite reaction. Hand-picked Buddhist soldiers who wish to perform their duties can now receive a salary, weapons, and admittance into the Thai *sangha*. The contradictions embodied in the military monk engender a secret that, if publicly disclosed, would most likely yield intense reactions from Thai Buddhists and the local Malay Muslims.

Before 2004, an attack on a southern monk represented an attack on a victim—a pacifist operating outside of the violence. Unfortunately, this representation is changing in southern Thailand. One clear example of this is Phra Eks's monastery, which is now a fortified and heavily guarded military base. Police living inside his monastery collaborate with the abbot and monks. Another example is Phra Eks himself, a soldier doubling as an ordinary monk. These components are powerful influences on the local community. As Buddhist spaces and monks become closely associated with the military and its functions, they increase the religious divide between Buddhists and Muslims.

Prior to the imposition of martial law, some Buddhist and Muslim locals believed that their local strife was the result of an ethno-economic divide between Thai Chinese and Thai Malays. However, with the government's implementation of martial law, the conflict has been exacerbated and polarized into one of religious division. Anthropologist Amporn Mardent, who works with Muslim women in Pattani province, notes how local Malays discerned an increasing amount of distrust and suspicion between Buddhists and Muslims.[65] The militarization of monasteries affects the way Buddhists and Muslims feel about each other and about themselves. Some southern monks still see their monasteries as fortresses of moral integrity. As if embodying the growing socioreligious divide, one abbot stood on a hill overlooking his monastery and pointed to the wire fence surrounding his territory. To him, the space was divided into religious borders—and it was his monastery's perimeter that demarcated the religious space in the community—where Thai Buddhism ended and "Islam" (*tīislam*) began.

NOTES

An earlier version of this chapter was published as "Appropriating a Space for Violence: State Buddhism in Southern Thailand," *Journal of Southeast Asian Studies* 40.1 (Feb. 2009): 1–25.

1. Pāli is the scriptural and liturgical language of Theravāda Buddhist traditions, such as Thai Buddhism.

2. Personal communication with a monk in the southernmost provinces, 2006.

3. For a brief discussion of Buddhisms, see the introduction to this volume.

4. Kurt Lang, "Military," in *International Encyclopedia of the Social Sciences*, ed. David L. Sills (New York: Macmillan, 1968), 10:305.

5. I draw this definition from peace educator Betty Reardon's *Militarization, Security, and Peace Education: A Guide for Concerned Citizens* (Valley Forge, Pa.: United Ministries in Education, 1982), 3.

6. Perhaps the most well researched work on the subject is Paul Demiéville's essay, first released in 1957 (and translated into English for the first time in this volume), which offers a cornucopia of historical examples linking the military and Buddhist monasticism in countries such as India, Korea, Japan, and China. Paul Demiéville, "Le bouddhisme et la guerre," in *Mélanges publiés par l'Institut des Hautes Etudes Chinoises* (Paris: Presses Universitaires de France, 1957), 1:347–385.

7. Stanley Tambiah, *World Conqueror and World Renouncer: A Study of Buddhism and Polity in Thailand against a Historical Background* (Cambridge: Cambridge University Press, 1976), 515.

8. See ibid.

9. All historical references in this chapter will follow Thongchai Winichakul's practice of using Siam and Siamese for the country and people prior to 1941, and Thailand and Thai for any post-1941 or general context. *Siam Mapped: A History of the Geo-Body of a Nation* (Chiang Mai, Thailand: Silkworm, 1998), 18.

10. Kamala Tiyavanich, *Forest Recollections: Wandering Monks in Twentieth-Century Thailand* (Honolulu: University of Hawai'i Press, 1997), 3–17.

11. A. J. Brown, "Awakening the Wild Tigers (An Annotated Translation with Introduction)," B.A. honour's thesis (Canberra: Australian National University, 1983), 47 and 48. As Scot Barmé has already noted, T. W. S. Wannapho was the first to introduce this notion in 1893. *Luang Wichit Wathakan and the Creation of a Thai Identity* (Singapore: Institute of Southeast Asian Studies, 1993), 17.

12. Scot Barmé, *Luang Wichit Wathakan*, 30.

13. Stanley Tambiah, Somboon Suksramran, and Yoneo Ishii provide detailed accounts of bureaucratic parallels and political applications of the Siamese and Thai *sanghas*. Stanley Tambiah, *World Conqueror and World Renouncer: A Study of Buddhism and Polity in Thailand against a Historical Background* (Cambridge: Cambridge University Press, 1976), 368. Somboon Suksamran, *Political Buddhism in Southeast Asia: The Role of the Sangha in the Modernization of Thailand* (New York: St. Martin's Press, 1977), 44. Yoneo Ishii, *Samgha, State, and Society: Thai Buddhism in History*, trans. Peter Hawkes (Honolulu: University of Hawai'i, 1986), 40–52.

14. Peter Jackson, *Buddhism, Legitimation and Conflict: The Political Functions of Urban Thai Buddhism* (Singapore: Institute of Southeast Asian Studies, 1989), 2.

15. Hayashi Yukio, *Practical Buddhism among the Thai-Lao: Religion in the Making of a Region* (Kyoto: Kyoto University Press, 2003), 1.

16. Charles F. Keyes, *Thailand: Buddhist Kingdom as Modern Nation-State* (Boulder, Colo.: Westview, 1987), 138, 139.

17. Richard Gombrich, *Theravāda Buddhism: A Social History from Ancient Benares to Modern Colombo* (London: Routledge & Kegan Paul, 1988), 116.

18. Personal communication with Nopparat Benjawatthananant, director of the Office of National Buddhism, in Nakhon Pathom, December 25, 2006.

19. Craig Reynolds, *Seditious Histories: Contesting Thai and Southeast Asian Pasts* (Seattle: University of Washington Press, 2006), 237.

20. There are no official reports on military monks; the only substantiation of their existence comes from interviews, personal observations, and local rumors in southern Thailand.

21. Michael Taussig, *Defacement: Public Secrecy and the Labor of the Negative* (Stanford, Calif.: Stanford University Press, 1999), 2.

22. Personal communication with a high-ranking monk in the southernmost provinces, 2004.

23. Personal communication with a Phra Nirut, a high ranking monk in the southernmost provinces, 2007.

24. Personal communication with a monk in the southernmost provinces, 2007.

25. Personal communication with Phra Eks in the southernmost provinces, 2006.

26. Personal communication with Phra Eks in the southernmost provinces, 2006.

27. Excerpt from Charles Keyes, "Political Crisis and Militant Buddhism," in *Religion and Legitimation of Power in Thailand, Laos, and Burma*, ed. Bardwell L. Smith (Chambersburg, Pa.: Anima, 1978), 153.

28. Ananda Abeysekara, "The Saffron Army, Violence, Terror(ism): Buddhism, Identity, and Difference in Sri Lanka," *Numen* 48.1 (2001): 31, 32.29. This latent tendency in Theravāda traditions is socio-historically founded on the strong interrelationship between *sangha* and State in Southeast Asia. The construction of a national religion permits the militancy of that religion if the nation is threatened. By isolating this tendency in Theravāda tradition, I do not mean to infer that other Buddhist traditions are absent of militant traits, nor that Theravāda traditions are more violent than other Buddhist traditions. I would like to thank Betty Nguyen of University Wisconsin, Madison, for reminding me to make these distinctions.

30. J. J. M. de Groot, "Militant Spirit of the Buddhist Clergy in China," *T'oung Pao* 2 (1891): 139.

31. Christoph Kleine, "Evil Monks with Good Intentions? Remarks on Buddhist Monastic Violence and Its Doctrinal Background," in *Buddhism and Violence*, ed. Michael Zimmermann (Kathmandu: Lumbini International Research Institute, 2006), 74.

32. Brian Victoria, *Zen at War*, 2nd Edition (Boulder, Colo.: Rowman & Littlefield, 2006), 137.

33. Personal communication with a monk in the southernmost provinces, 2007.

34. Personal communication with Phra Eks in the southernmost provinces, 2007.

35. Richard H. Jones, "Theravāda Buddhism and Morality," *Journal of the American Academy of Religion* 47.3 (Sept. 1979): 383, 384.

36. Stanley Jeyaraja Tambiah, *Buddhism Betrayed? Religion, Politics, and Violence in Sri Lanka* (Chicago: University of Chicago Press, 1992), 99.

37. "Yala Buddhists Flee to Temple Safety," *Bangkok Post*, November 9, 2006.

38. Personal communication with refugees at Wat Nirotsangkatham. The number of refugees fluctuated during the month of December. According to the *Bangkok Post*, by December 24, 2006, there were only 161 people at the monastery. "Buddhist 'Refugees' Demand New Home," Bangkok Post, December 24, 2006.

39. Here, the term *secular* is used to denote that which is not overtly or publicly recognized as religious.

40. This is comparable to the functions that Islamic mosques, Christian churches, and Jewish temples serve throughout the world.

41. Donald Swearer, *Becoming the Buddha: The Ritual of Image Consecration in Thailand* (Princeton, N.J.: Princeton University Press, 2004), 40.

42. Personal communication with Nopparat Benjawatthananant, director of the Office of National Buddhism, in Nakhon Pathom, December 25, 2006.

43. Information translated from Thai into English from "Population and Households Census 1970, 1980, 1990, 2000: Southern Provinces," *National Statistical Office* (Bangkok: Prime Minister Office, 2003).

44. Personal communication with Wat Kūaanai abbot in Khokpo district, Pattani province, August 13, 2004.

45. Personal communication with a refugee at Wat Nirotsangkatham, December 8, 2006.

46. "Update: Extremists Launch Overnight Wave of Violence," *Bangkok Post*, February 19, 2007.

47. A *rai* is the Thai unit of measure for 1,600 square meters.

48. Patrick Jory, "*Luang Pho Thuat* as a Southern Thai Cultural Hero: Popular Religion in the Integration of Patani," in *Thai South and Malay North: Ethnic Interactions on the Plural Peninsula*, ed. Michael J. Montesano and Patrick Jory (Singapore: National University of Singapore Press, 2008).

49. Personal communication with a Thai Buddhist store owner at Wat Chang Hai, February 19, 2007.

50. Personal communication with the abbot of Wat Kajorn in Pattani province, August 8, 2004.

51. Personal communication with a policeman in Pattani province, December 13, 2006.

52. Pierre Bourdieu, *Outline of a Theory of Practice* (Cambridge: Cambridge University Press, 1977), 214.

53. Information on World War II activities is derived from personal communication with Irving Johnson, National University of Singapore, February 27, 2007. Reports on military occupation during the 1970s come from personal communications with monks in Pattani province, September 2006.

54. This information comes from personal communications with commanding officers at the monastery I visited and from Lt. Col. Surathep Nukaeow of Ingkayut Camp, Pattani, December 28, 2006.

55. Human Rights Watch, "Thailand: Government Covers Up Role in 'Disappearance,'" March 11, 2006.

56. Personal communication with Lt. Col. Surathep Nukaeow of Ingkayut Camp, Pattani, December 28, 2006.

57. Personal communication with an abbot in the southernmost provinces, 2007.

58. Personal communication with an abbot in the southernmost provinces, 2006.

59. Personal communication with police in the southernmost provinces, 2006.

60. Personal communication by telephone with Ačhān Mahāwichī, August 15, 2004.

61. The author would like to thank Irving Johnson for raising this subject.

62. Monasteries were used as military bases during and after World War II in southern Thailand. Personal communication with anthropologist Irving Johnson of the Southeast Asian Programme at the National University of Singapore, February 27, 2007. Kamala Tiyavanich also noted the historical presence of the Thai military in the monasteries during King Vajiravudh's reign (personal communication at Cornell University, April 22, 2006).

63. Personal communication with a monk in the southernmost provinces, 2006.

64. Personal communication by phone with a high-ranking monk in the southernmost provinces, 2004.

65. Amporn Mardent, "From Adek to Mo'ji: Identities and Social Realities of Southern Thai People" in *Kyoto Review of Southeast Asia*, accessed at http://kyotoreviewsea.org/Amporn.htm on September 30, 2006.

Afterthoughts

Bernard Faure

In our time of terrorism and rising fundamentalisms, examining the relationships between Buddhism and violence has acquired a certain urgency. This is only indirectly reflected by the chapters contained in this volume and in the book on a similar topic edited by Michael Zimmermann.[1]

I will simply outline a few themes running through these chapters, starting from the observation that they deal mostly with certain *forms of discourse*—textual or oral, representing canonical dogma or extracanonical *doxa*. In other words, they rarely deal with actual cases of Buddhist violence—Vesna Wallace's description of the "spine method" of killing being a significant exception—but essentially with discursive *representations* and *justifications*. Derek Maher, for instance, analyzes the Fifth Dalai Lama's rhetoric, showing how he tried to justify the use of violence or to explain the relation between Buddhism and violence. In Michael Jerryson's chapter, we hear about the politics of representation. Several chapters deal with canonical sources that seem to allow for a certain use of violence, for instance, the *Satyakaparivarta Sūtra* and the *Suvarṇaprabhāsa Sūtra*.[2] The *Satyakaparivarta Sūtra*, mentioned by Wallace in the Mongolian context, was also important in Japan as a scripture for the protection of the state, beginning in the Nara period.

Most of the chapters found in these two volumes start from what is taken to be the basic interdiction against killing, one of the *pārājika* rules whose transgression leads to exclusion from the *sangha*.[3]

The rule in question is actually limited to the killing of human beings, while the killing of other types of beings only entails a lesser offense. Other normative texts, like the *Sutta Nippāta*, forbid the taking or harming of *any* life.

Most of the authors raise the question of whether killing is compatible or not with Buddhist ethics, in light of the *Vinaya* and also of the spirit of compassion promoted most conspicuously by Mahāyāna. The general opinion is that there is some discrepancy between the normative claims of Buddhism and its more pragmatic approach to war and violence. The assumption that the Buddhist teaching fundamentally condemns killing (and lesser forms of violence) is rarely questioned. According to Daniel Kent, the apparent contradiction or inconsistency between the normative claim and the pragmatic approach can be explained by recognizing that abstaining from killing fellow humans is merely a prima facie obligation. As such, this obligation needs to be reconsidered as a function of the context. On the other hand, Stephen Jenkins argues that the Buddhist position is coherent in this respect, inasmuch as the notion of killing with compassion runs through Mahāyāna literature.

Although reasons for bending the principle of nonviolence are never wanting, they often sound like casuistry. They can take a number of more or less sophisticated forms, particularly in the Mahāyāna and Tantric traditions. But "killing with compassion," like the "compassionate torture" mentioned in Wallace's chapter, remains a dubious oxymoron. The definition of torture as skillful means or as a necessary evil calls to mind the worst casuistry of twentieth- and twenty-first-century history. The real evil here, what Jacques Derrida once called the "evil of abstraction," shows its true face when "compassion" takes the concrete form of techniques such as the "spine method" described by Wallace.

Thus, even granting Jenkins that the only killing compatible with Buddhist ethics is "killing with compassion," a sense of uneasiness remains. We hear, for instance, that the "evil" Tibetan king Lang Darma was "killed with compassion in 842."[4] Some historians have questioned the historicity of that regicide, but that is not the problem here. The point is that this murder has become a paradigm that has been periodically reenacted, and still is today, in widely attended rituals. In these rituals, the officiating monk stabs an effigy that personifies the demonic forces. The ritual murder is designated by a euphemism, "liberation"—since the demon, owing to this compassionate killing, is allegedly released from ignorance and can be reborn under better auspices. Incidentally, the same kind of euphemism was used by the Khmer Rouge to describe the physical elimination of their political opponents.

Another oft-invoked argument to justify killing is the claim that, when the dharma is threatened, it is necessary to ruthlessly fight against the forces of evil. The notion of a cosmic battle between the forces of good and evil (which seems to derive from the Hindu myth of the fight between the *devas* and the *asuras*) gives Buddhism an eschatological dimension that it seems to have lacked initially. This notion, promoting the need for violence in order to preserve a cosmic balance (see Wallace), lends itself to the development of a kind of just-war theory (see Maher). A more metaphysical argument arises from the Mahāyāna notion of emptiness. Indeed, how can one kill another person when, according to good Buddhist orthodoxy, all is emptiness? The man who kills with full knowledge of the facts kills no one because he realizes that all is but illusion, himself as well as the other person. He can kill, because he does not actually kill anyone. One cannot kill emptiness, nor destroy the wind.

In Chan Buddhism, the *Jueguan lun* similarly states that, if a murderous act is as perfectly spontaneous as an act of nature, it entails no responsibility:

> Question: "In certain conditions, isn't one allowed to kill a living being?"—Answer: "The fire in the bush burns the mountain; the hurricane breaks trees; the collapsing cliff crushes wild animals to death; the running mountain stream drowns the insects. If a man can make his mind similar [to these natural forces], then, meeting a man, he may kill him all the same." (94a1–5)[5]

As Brian Victoria has shown, the same kind of sophism can be found in the writings of modern Zen advocates like D. T. Suzuki.[6]

Another common justification relies on the Two Truths theory, a cardinal tenet of Mahāyāna. In the best of all possible worlds, or better, from the standpoint of ultimate reality, of course we are compassionate and therefore we should not kill. But we live in the world of *saṃsāra* where we have to cut some corners.[7] One Sri Lankan monk quoted by Kent vividly expresses the Two Truths theory. He emphasizes that, whatever Buddhists may say about the importance of fighting for one's country (which here is conveniently conflated with the dharma), the dharma itself never condones violence or killing. He argues that you would never find any such justification in the Buddhist canon, just like you wouldn't find a recipe for chicken curry there. Now, anyone who has read extensively in the Buddhist canon knows that you will find everything there, even possibly a recipe for chicken curry. Indeed, the Two Truths theory gives you a sense of how you can eat your chicken and have it too.

The Two Truths theory also has more practical variants: for instance, it allows the distinction between two social spheres—those of the priests and of the warriors. A further distinction (one not always maintained in practice) is that between the world of the clerics and the world of the householders and state officials. The semantic dualism of the Two Truths theory, by establishing an absolute distinction between "good" and "bad" violence, allows for preemptive strikes. However, if history has taught us anything, it is that such a distinction is highly problematic.

A related type of argument that is used by modern Thai and Sri Lankan monks (see Kent and Jerryson) is more psychological and seems to rely on the Abhidhamma. This argument emphasizes *intention* and claims that, if the killing is committed with the right state of mind (detachment or compassion), it entails no karmic consequence and therefore can be considered to be a wholesome act.

Let me finally mention an argument that is not a moral one but rather an ontological one. It is used, for instance, by the Fifth Dalai Lama when he argues that his Mongol protector, Gushri Khan, is a man who is "entitled" to violence, because he acts to protect the dharma; or, rather—a slightly different claim—that violence is justified in Gushri Khan's case because of *who* he is, namely, a bodhisattva in disguise (see Maher). It is no longer the act but the agent that matters; when that agent is no longer acting on selfish motives, he is no longer truly a responsible agent. This type of argument has often been invoked in antinomian traditions such as Tantric Buddhism and Chan/Zen.

Those are some of the main Buddhist justifications for killing, some of which are examined at length in the chapters contained in this volume. By focusing on such justifications, however, one may leave the casual reader with the false impression that one endorses them. Yet such justifications are typical of an ideological discourse, i.e., a discourse that misrepresents relations of power and the causes of violence (historical, sociological, economic, political, ethnic). Indeed, a common feature of many discussions on the issue is that they tend to focus solely on normative texts. Concrete practices of Buddhism are largely ignored or, when they are examined, it is still often only to question whether they fit normative texts.

Buddhist exegetical discourse regarding violence is not always apologetic, however: sometimes, it constitutes a kind of speech act. The sermons of modern Thai and Sri Lankan monks, for instance, have pragmatic and performative goals, namely, to boost the morale of the troops and, if possible, to safeguard the soldiers' moral conduct. The chapters by Kent and Jerryson move away from texts to emphasize *performance*—perhaps under the influence of Mark Juergenmeyer's notion of violence as performance.[8] In Kent's chapter, Buddhist sermons justifying violence are presented as a kind speech act in which—an interesting idea in itself—*delivery* is more important than content. In other words, what the monks say matters less than how they say it. The real point is not the semantic (ethical or philosophical) content of their sermons; the content may even at times seem to contradict fundamental Buddhist ethics. Rather, these sermons have pragmatic goals—and a smooth delivery increases the chance that they will achieve their purposes, namely, pacifying the soldiers' minds (thereby diminishing their bad karma) and protecting their lives.

In Jerryson's chapter, performance appears in the fact that alms begging is perceived as a kind of state ritual. In that sense, it is not as pacific an activity as it may seem—from the Muslim minority's viewpoint at least. This brings to mind the case of Bhutan, a state whose official religion is Tantric Buddhism, where the Muslim minority feels increasingly threatened by the performance of Buddhist rituals.

Emphasizing the performative level, however, does not mean that the semantic level has become insignificant and does not need to be submitted to an ideological critique. When Sri Lankan or Thai monks argue that there is no sin for soldiers in firing at the enemy, are we not confronted with an invidious form of false consciousness—or worse, a blatant deception? And those monks who admit in private that it does constitute a sin, yet refrain from saying so publicly for fear of undermining patriotic morale, fare hardly better. In that context, Western followers of the Fourteenth Dalai Lama rightly might have felt disappointed when he (admittedly caught between a rock and a hard place) abstained from condemning the U.S. invasions of Afghanistan and Iraq.

So far, I have been talking about texts and words in their apologetic or performative functions. Yet, apart from words—oral or written—we have images. Mythological imagery and narrative are perhaps as important as normative sources such as the *Suvarṇaprabhāsa Sūtra*. Paradoxically, this text was instrumental for much of the martial imagery that developed in East Asian Buddhism. The *Suvarṇaprabhāsa Sūtra* emphasizes the figures of Vaiśravaṇa (J. *Bishamonten*), one of the four wrathful *deva* kings, and the eight-armed Sarasvatī (J. *Benzaiten*), whose martial appearance (perhaps influenced by the image of Durga) appealed to medieval Japanese warriors. Another example of martial imagery is the conversion of shamanists by a vegetarian Mahākāla (a Buddhist form of Śiva), as described by Vesna Wallace. This is somewhat ironic when we recall that Mahākāla (J. Daikokuten) was initially described by Buddhists as a flesh-eating deity roaming the forest at night with his horde of blood-thirsty demons.

The motif of coerced conversion can be traced back to the myth of the submission of Maheśvara (another avatar of Śiva) by the dharma protector Vajrapāṇi. The latter, whose name appears in several contributions to this volume, is usually depicted as a powerful, wrathful figure. Initially a servant of the Buddha, he plays an important role in Indian Buddhism. Vajrapāṇi also appears in Chinese Buddhism, where he is the muscular protector and model of the Shaolin monks. These monks have played an important paramilitary role and have come to be seen as the founders of several martial arts traditions.[9]

Vajrapāṇi's subjugation of Maheśvara constitutes the paradigm of the esoteric Buddhist relation with non-Buddhist deities: Vajrapāṇi tramples to death Maheśvara and his consort because they refuse to submit to the new Buddhist order. The Buddha, who has witnessed the whole scene without intervening, now feels vaguely sorry for them and asks Vajrapāṇi to resuscitate them. As a result, the couple comes back to life, now duly metamorphosed into Buddhist followers. This happy ending looks very much like an interpolation, a clerical attempt to paper over Vajrapāṇi's hubris.

Images often speak louder than words, and they do not always say the same thing. All of the dialogue about Buddhist compassion cannot erase the impression produced by the above scene of subjugation and similar ones. Tantric imagery reveals, in a most obvious and at times obscene fashion, a kind of violence that, once noticed, can also be found throughout Mahāyāna Buddhism. Despite all arguments to the contrary, this imagery seems to contradict the claim of compassion made at the level of normative discourse. Imagery is obviously an important dimension that tends to be neglected by textual scholars, and it is just mentioned in passing by some of the authors in this volume. On the iconographic plane, if compassion is well expressed by serene images of meditating buddhas, conversely, the angry gods of Buddhism and Mongolia partake in a puzzling symbolic violence: does this symbolic violence mark a return of the repressed or an outlet for real violence, or is it its mirror image, indeed, its underlying cause? The question must remain open.

A theme such as "Buddhism and violence" entails some more fundamental issues, beginning with the problem of defining these two terms. What one calls *Buddhism* is admittedly an elusive entity. There are many kinds of Buddhist discourses, which do not so much reveal a common essence as what Wittgenstein would call a "family resemblance." It is therefore at best problematic to posit, as we often do, an "authentic" Buddhist teaching, one allegedly based on "what the Buddha taught" (to use the title of Walpola Rahula's influential book).[10]

Brian Victoria's chapter is the only one in this book that definitely denounces Buddhist war ideology. While acknowledging that other Buddhist schools were involved in the Japanese war effort, he restricts his sharp criticism to Zen, the tradition that nurtured him and that he tends to contrast too quickly with some timeless, universalist Buddhist ethics. Although, as a Buddhist, he is justified in underscoring the moral imperative of non-killing, I find it more difficult to follow him when he seems to imply that this moral imperative has been and should remain the horizon of Buddhist ethics and was once historically embodied in a specific ("authentic") form of Buddhism. This view of an authentic early Buddhism (as opposed to "decadent" Zen) flies in the face of reality. As far as we can tell, Buddhism has always been closely associated with rulers, even if the Indian context gave Indian monks more autonomy than their Chinese and Japanese counterparts had. From the start, Buddhism was seen in these countries as an instrument of power. The same is also true in Tibet and Southeast Asia. This conventional view also tends to view later forms of Buddhism—and in particular Tantric or esoteric Buddhism—as degenerations (a few exceptions in the case of "reformers" like Dōgen notwithstanding).

In a word, there is no generic, fundamental (or even mainstream) Buddhism. It may not even be sufficient to say that we are dealing with a multivocal tradition, or multiple traditions that we could call "Buddhisms." Rather, we are dealing with a variety of people—clerics and lay believers, kings and commoners—who call themselves Buddhists. From their respective vantage points, these people hold discourses that are, not surprisingly, often at odds with each other. Among them, some may deplore violence, others condone it, and we find all kinds of intermediate positions between pure affirmation and pure rejection, including various types of denial.

Defining the term *violence* is equally difficult. Most authors so far seem to have restricted its meaning to "war." This is legitimate as a first approach, to the extent that war is the most obvious and massive form of violence. For instance, this approach was taken by Paul Demiéville in his seminal essay "Le bouddhisme et la guerre," originally written as an appendix to Gaston Renondeau's detailed historical survey of the warrior-monks (*sōhei*) of medieval Japan.[11]

Violence is often implicitly defined in contrast to compassion and tolerance. Indeed, compared to other world religions, Buddhism does seem relatively tolerant. The Two Truths theory, for instance, allows Buddhists to integrate various alien doctrines as belonging to the level of conventional truth, which the dharma (the ultimate truth) both complements and transcends. The Buddha himself is said to have preached on the conventional truth in order to adapt his teaching to disciples of shallow understanding while reserving the ultimate truth for an elite. The use of "expedient means" (*upāya*) renders dogmatism difficult, inasmuch as any dogma belongs to the realm of speech, hence, of conventional truth. This approach allows several forms of militant syncretism. Using militant syncretism, rival doctrines were co-opted and integrated at a lower rank in a doctrinal classification (Ch. *panjiao*) that placed one's own doctrine at the top. Needless to say, this kind of syncretism easily led to sectarianism.

As in the case of Maheśvara's "conversion," the mythological realm reflects Buddhism's encounter with local cults. Indeed, it is in this realm that a certain intolerance most clearly manifests itself. Buddhism claims that it "pacified" the new lands to which it spread. A case in point is the myth of Tibet's pacification by Padmasambhava. Padmasambhava, owing to his wondrous powers, subjugated all of the local "demons" of that land (actually, they were the former gods). The metaphor behind the conversion of local deities is often that of sexual submission. In all of these tales, Buddhism is fundamentally male, whereas local cults are often feminized. For instance, prior to Padmasaṃbhava's conquest, we are told that the first Tibetan king, Songtsen Gampo, subdued the telluric powers symbolized by a demoness, Srinmo. The Tibetan king subdued the demoness, whose body covered the Tibetan territory, by "nailing" her down to the ground. He did so by erecting (no pun intended) *stūpas* that served as so many metaphoric nails driven into the twelve points of her body. The Jokhang Temple in Lhasa, the most holy place of Tibetan Buddhism, is said to be the nail driven into the central part of the demoness's body, her genitalia. The rape imagery could hardly be more explicit. An even cruder sexual symbolism is found in a variant of the myth of Maheśvara's submission, in which Rudra (another form of Śiva) is literally sodomized by his Buddhist nemesis, Hayagrīva (a terrible form of the "compassionate" Avalokiteśvara).

The claim that Buddhism is a tolerant religion is based on the fact that Buddhist history does not show the kind of fanatic excesses familiar in the histories of Christianity and Islam. Opponents of the Buddha may have been labeled "heretical masters," but (in part for lack of an ultimate authority) the accusation of heresy rarely led to physical purges. In China, the teaching of the three stages (*sanjie jiao*) was suppressed merely for political reasons. In Japan, the doctrine of the "heretical" Tachikawa branch of the Shingon school was apparently censored because of its sexual elements. It was eventually forbidden in the fifteenth century, and almost all of its texts were destroyed in a kind of Buddhist *autodafé*. Other cases of Buddhist intolerance include the denunciation of the new Pure Land school of Hōnen (1133–1212), his exile in 1207, and the profanation of his grave after his death. We should also mention the sectarian antics of Nichiren (1222–1282), the founder of the Nichiren school, who liked to compare the priests of other schools to dogs wagging their tails in front of their masters and to mice afraid of cats. Nichiren barely escaped execution; he was sent into exile. One of his successors, Nichiō (1565–1630), launched the so-called *fuju fuse* (not giving, not receiving) movement, which required his adherents to forsake all relationships with outsiders. Through their intransigence, Nichiō's disciples were even led to refuse allegiance to the *shōgun* and eventually had to go underground. The Nichiren sect is also well known for its coercive conversion methods (*shakubuku*). Yet, in part because of this, it is one of the most powerful Buddhist sects in Japan today. But these cases are the exception that proves the Buddhist rule, and they underscore the contrast with the practices of the Inquisition in Christianity.

Violence is not always directed at the Other, however. Well-ordered violence begins with oneself. As with all established institutions, the Buddhist *sangha* has remained ambivalent toward the interiorized form of violence known as asceticism. Monastic discipline and practice, whose aim is to form an obedient body and mind, can also be seen as a kind of muted violence against oneself. To show their determination, Chinese monks would sometimes mutilate themselves—including cutting off or burning one or more of their fingers. In extreme cases, self-denial could extend to self-immolation by fire. As James Benn's book has demonstrated, many such cases have been recorded.[12] We still recall the disturbing image of the Vietnamese monk who immolated himself as a sign of protest during what is known in Vietnam as the American war. Paradoxically, one of the main scriptural sources that legitimizes that form of violence is the apocryphal *Fanwangjing* (*Brahma-Net Sūtra*), a disciplinary text that most vehemently condemns any direct or indirect participation in murder.

Another important aspect of violence which has come to light is the Buddhist discrimination against women. Despite the theoretical equality between genders asserted by Mahāyāna, Buddhism has always been and remains a fundamentally patriarchal, and therefore largely sexist, tradition. Even in the twenty-first century, nuns in most Buddhist cultures have a subaltern status that largely derives from the eight "heavy rules" (*gurudharma*) allegedly laid down by the Buddha. The media reported the case of a Thai nun who was physically attacked by some monks for requesting an improvement of that status. But a discussion of this form of violence, as well as various forms of sexual abuse toward children, for instance found in Buddhist monasteries, is beyond the scope of this chapter.[13]

In the name of objectivity, Buddhist scholars often content themselves with presenting their materials without passing judgment. Brian Victoria's chapter is the exception, even though his expression of moral outrage does not quite replace a thorough ideological critique. His chapter—like Vesna Wallace's—provides us with a wealth of information concerning actual acts of violence committed in the name of Buddhism, whereas representations of violence found in the Buddhist forms of discourse analyzed by other authors tend to misrepresent the *causes* of violence. These representations may assist in replicating a form of false consciousness, although the notion of false consciousness may sound paradoxical when applied to Buddhist masters. Regardless, we need to know more about the causes—structural, sociopolitical, psychological—of violence before we can pass judgment on Buddhist representations of violence.

When confronted with the complex relationships between Buddhism and various forms of violence, a more fundamental question arises: is violence contextual, parasitic, or intrinsic to Buddhism? The Buddhist apologies of violence presented in this book are mostly contextual, in other words, they owe as much, or more, to the cultural context as to Buddhism per se. When that context is violent (as is too often the case), Buddhists tend to use their casuistic resources to reinterpret creatively the first *pārājika* rule and to condone the use of certain forms of violence.

Buddhists repeatedly have gone beyond the call of duty, confusing the Buddhist dharma with the reasons of State and with patriotism. For instance, the esoteric Buddhist monks of medieval Japan argued that the law of the Buddha and the kingdom's law were identical (*ōbō soku buppō*). Thus, nationalism or patriotism surreptitiously replaced the alleged monastic detachment toward worldly values. Buddhist doctrine has become at times a quasi-magical device to acquire peace of mind and protection of the body during battle. In the Mongolian case studied by Wallace, for instance, we are dealing with a culture of violence in which Buddhism merely serves as an alibi for repression. Like the Mongol ruler Gushri Khan, whom the Fifth Dalai Lama praised as a *cakravartin* king, the Manchu rulers of Mongolia were glorified as emanations of the wrathful form of the bodhisattva Mañjuśrī. Likewise, the death penalty was generously inflicted in the name of King Yama, the ruler of the underworld. As Wallace points out, the image of the Mongol monarch is closer to that of the Hindu god Indra than to that of the *cakravartin* king. Like the Indian ruler following the injunctions of the *dharmaśāstra*, he punishes in order to preserve cosmic order, a notion that is at first glance alien to early Buddhist or Mahāyāna ideals. However, if the Indian Buddhist discourse on kingship is itself largely indebted to such non-Buddhist texts, can its position on violence be seen as representative?

In Thailand, monks are perceived (and perceive themselves) as symbols of patriotism (Jerryson chapter) and as members of a community that is not only the *sangha*, but the whole nation. As such, they feel obliged to participate in nationalist discourse and to condone acts of violence committed in the name of the nation. Here again, much of the Buddhist discourse on violence is contextual.

Not surprisingly, when it had to adapt to societies such as those of China and Japan, the Buddhist *sangha* had to make hard compromises. But Buddhist monks often went one step, or several steps, further. This can be seen in the case of Japanese warrior-monks embroiled in internecine struggles, or in the cases of modern Thai and Sri Lankan monks yielding to patriotic frenzy. During the Mongol attempts to invade Japan, in the second half of the thirteenth century, Buddhist priests gave their unrestricted support to both sides of the conflict. A more recent example is the Japanese Buddhist support of the war effort during the Second World War. In the process, Buddhist monks came at times to legitimize the worst kind of brutality in the name of "ruthless compassion."

Although the dharma often has had to bow to reasons of State, in some instances it also provided an ideology for counterforces, inspiring peasant revolts in the name of a millenarianism centered on the coming of the future Buddha, Maitreya. In one of these movements, which arose in China at the start of the sixth century CE, the rebels, claiming for themselves the name Great Vehicle (Mahāyāna), undertook to rid the world of its demons—among which they included the established Buddhist clergy.

In Japan, on the other hand, Buddhism paved the way to feudalism, with a new type of religious figure, the warrior-monk. It was only at the end of the sixteenth century, after centuries of feudal struggles, that the power of the great monasteries was crushed by military leaders. The subordinate status of Buddhism during the Tokugawa rule explains in part why, after the Meiji restoration (1868), Buddhists did not express any resistance to the rising militarism; eventually, they fell in line with "spiritual mobilization." The Buddhist theory of selflessness served, for instance, to justify giving one's life for the emperor, while the notion of the Two Truths was used to explain the contradiction between the principle of respect for human life and patriotic duty.

But contextual explanation, while it accounts for a large part of the Buddhist discourse on war and violence, soon reaches its limits. For some reason, however, scholars have been reluctant to consider the idea that violence could be intrinsic to Buddhism, that the nondual dharma could include violence. Yet this question, which raises the specter of Buddhist fundamentalism, must be asked.

If Buddhism is not reducible to its sociopolitical and economic contexts, there may be something more disturbing in it. What if the discourse on compassion turns out to be, in some cases at least, merely a form of lip service or wishful thinking? Could one go so far as to speak of the "sacrificial nature" of Buddhism? As is well known, Buddhism rejected animal sacrifices. Yet exceptions to that rule could still invoke a Buddhist argument. Buddhist vegetarianism, too, suffers many exceptions—beginning perhaps with the Buddha himself, who allegedly died from meat indigestion, and more recently with the Fourteenth Dalai Lama's tongue-in-cheek statement that he is a Buddhist monk, not a vegetarian.

Are there deeper explanatory models to be found below the surface of the texts? Could violence result from specific intrinsic structures, for instance, ritual mechanisms? Despite the importance of ritual in Buddhism—and the fact that a lot of work has been done in this area by anthropologists and historians—it still seems beyond the purview of Buddhist scholars. Among some possible theoretical frameworks for the data discussed here, we could consider

Émile Durkheim's notion of social effervescence; Michel Foucault's discussion of discipline and punishment; René Girard's explanation of the intimate link between violence and the sacred, between mimetic desire and its resolution through sacrifice and scapegoating;[14] Georges Bataille's theory of violence as a form of expenditure belonging to the "general economy."[15]

Another interesting model is Maurice Bloch's analysis of the ritual structure of violence.[16] Like Foucault in his analysis of power, Bloch shifts the focus from psychological forms of aggressiveness to systemic violence. This systemic violence derives from a certain ritual structure that is aimed at obtaining (through initiation) an identification with the transcendental realm (symbolized by apparently permanent social institutions). Bloch argues that the subject's attempt to reach transcendence at the cost of human vitality already implies violence; so does the "rebounding violence" required in order to regain this vitality. Bloch actually discusses Buddhism, and more specifically Japanese Buddhism, although this is an area where his fieldwork is clearly insufficient and his model's application most problematic. Without following him completely in his claim that Buddhist ritual (like all ritual aimed at transcendence) is fundamentally violent, it is clear that much of Tantric Buddhist ritual is centered on exorcisms and black magic. Without forcing an alien theory at all costs on our data, there are many theoretical tools that could prove useful in better grasping that complex problem.

Indeed, the fundamental Tantric narrative is one of subjugation, a forced conversion of the non-Buddhists or a taming of the infidels. Conversely, like the *maṇḍala*, the Buddhist *sangha* looks sometimes like a besieged citadel. Even a cursory look at esoteric ritual manuals gives the feeling that the world is a dangerous place, where humans are constantly threatened by demonic forces. This category of demonic forces conveniently includes social rebels and political opponents. In other words, Buddhists have constantly resorted to the demonization of their rivals, Buddhist or non-Buddhist. A similar term for demonic forces was used by the priest Dōgen (1200–1253) to label some Chinese monks that the Chan/Zen tradition accused of having murdered the first "Chinese" Chan patriarch, the Indian monk Bodhidharma. The tendency to debase outsiders (or sometimes rival insiders, as in this case) and to deny them the status of human is quite common in religious groups. The notion of nonhumans (J. *hinin*) has played an important role, for instance, in Japanese Buddhism and has justified a social discrimination that is still rampant. In the *Kālacakratantra*, a text often used by the Dalai Lama and recently translated by Vesna Wallace, the narrative speaks of a final showdown between Buddhists and heretics—clearly designated as Muslims—who threaten the mythical kingdom of Shambhala. On the other hand, many eschatological movements have inserted themselves into this mythological narrative context of a cosmic fight between the forces of good and evil—as was the case with the millenarian rebellions in China.

Let me return to my question: could the dharma, or ultimate reality, be intrinsically violent? Would that not explain figures such as Vajrapāṇi and the "Bright Kings" (Skt. *vidyārāja*, Ch. *mingwang*, J. *myōō*), emanations of the cosmic Buddha, who are represented as fierce beings bent on destroying the gods or demons they were supposed to convert or tame? To speak of ruthless compassion here is, at best, a euphemism, at worst, an ideological sleight of hand.[17] In Japanese Buddhism, we find a divine/demonic figure called Kōjin (also read in Japanese as *aragami*, or "wild god"). The term designates an individual deity that is both a dharma protector (known as Sanbō Kōjin, "Kōjin of the Three Treasures") and a "god of obstacles" (sometimes identified with the elephant-headed Vināyaka, a Buddhist version of the Hindu god Gaṇeśa). *Aragami* also designates a category of autochthonous spirits not yet individualized and tamed by ritual. The term *ara*, which is contained in their name, is related to the verb *aru*, "being." At the risk of anachronism, one could perhaps heuristically read it as referring to some quasi-Heideggerian "ground of being" (a manifestation of ultimate reality that is really violent) and to the idea that the dharma manifests itself violently. This interpretation seems to reflect the general thrust of Tantric Buddhism.

The fundamental ambivalence of this kind of deity calls to mind a cardinal tenet of Mahāyāna Buddhism, reflected for instance in the Tendai notion of "original awakening" (J. *hongaku*). This notion finds its expression in such mottos as "Passions are no different from awakening" (*bonnō soku bodai*), or "Māra and the Buddha are one and the same" (*mabutsu ichinyo*). Playing with this kind of nondualism leads to the perception that evil is intrinsic to our real nature and that enlightenment is, again, the manifestation of that evil reality within us.

Because Buddhists have made compassion their trademark, their complicated (and at times, disingenuous) relation with violence has raised more questions than in the case of followers of other religions. In a time of fear and terrorism, when the only form of tolerance that seems to increase is, sadly, the tolerance toward banalized violence, Buddhists too have tended to lower their standards, even though such compromise is clearly in opposition to the ethical absolute against killing. This is because, now more than ever, the religious sphere is unable to exist outside of the political sphere. In Asia at least, Buddhism has become ancillary to nationalism. More fundamentally, however, it is time to ask ourselves whether being Buddhist does not *require* a confrontation with the violence that lurks at the heart of reality (and of each individual), rather than eluding the question by taking the high metaphysical or moral ground.

NOTES

1. See Michael Zimmermann, ed., *Buddhism and Violence* (Kathmandu: Lumbini International Research Institute, 2006).

2. On this text, see Emmerick, R. E., trans., *The Sūtra of Golden Light: Being a Translation of the Suvarṇabāsottama Sūtra* (London: Luzac and Company, 1992).

3. See, for instance, Charles S. Prebish, *Buddhist Monastic Discipline: The Sanskrit Prātimokṣa Sūtras of the Mahāsāṃghikas and Mūlasarvāstivādinsa* (Delhi: Motilal Banarsidass, 1996), 51.

4. On this question, see, for instance, Carmen Meinert, "Between the Profane and the Sacred? On the Context of the Rite of 'Liberation' (sgrol pa)," in Zimmermann, *Buddhism and Violence*, 99–130; and Jens Schlieter, "Compassionate Killing or Conflict Resolution," ibid., 131–158.

5. "Jueguan lun," in *Suzuki Daisetsu Zenshū, Vol. 2*, ed. D. T. Suzuki (Tokyo: Iwanami shoten, 1980 [1968]).

6. See Brian Victoria, "D. T. Suzuki and Japanese Militarism: Supporter or Opponent?" in Zimmermann, *Buddhism and Violence*, 106–194.

7. *Saṃsāra* refers to the cycle of rebirths within this world, which is considered a world of suffering.

8. See Mark Juergensmeyer, *Terror in the Mind of God: The Global Rise of Religious Violence* (Berkeley: University of California Press, 2000).

9. See Etienne Lamotte, "Vajrapāṇi en Inde," in *Mélanges de Sinologie offerts à Monsieur Paul Demiéville* (Paris: Presses Universitaires de France, 1966), 113–159; and Meir Shahar, *The Shaolin Monastery: History, Religion, and the Chinese Martial Arts* (Honolulu: University of Hawaii Press, 2007).

10. Walpola Rahula, *What the Buddha Taught: Revised and Expanded Edition with Texts from Suttas and Dhammapada* (New York: Grove Press, 1974).

11. See Paul Demiéville, "Le bouddhisme et la guerre: Post-scriptum à *l'Histoire des moines guerriers du Japon* de G. Renondeau," in *Mélanges publiés par l'Institut des Hautes Études Chinoises* (Paris: Presses Universitaires de France, 1957), 347–385; a translated version appears as the first chapter in this volume. In his introduction, Demiéville examines the canonical sources against killing and devotes some space to the prohibition against suicide. In the first part of the essay, Demiéville examines the participation of Chinese Buddhist monks in war. He gives in particular some interesting information on the history of the Shaolin tradition, traced back to the C patriarch Bodhidharma. (For more on this question, see Shahar, *Shaolin Monastery*.) In the second part, he examines the doctrinal justifications for killing, as found in particular in Mahāyāna casuistics. Unfortunately, he leaves aside the Tantric or esoteric Buddhist tradition.

12. See James A. Benn, *Burning for the Buddha: Self-Immolation in Chinese Buddhism* (Honolulu: University of Hawaii Press, 2007).

13. See Bernard Faure, *The Red Thread: Buddhist Approaches to Sexuality* (Princeton, N.J.: Princeton University Press, 1998); Faure, *The Power of Denial: Buddhism, Purity and Gender* (Princeton, N.J.: Princeton University Press, 2003); Liz Wilson, *Charming Cadavers* (Chicago: University of Chicago Press, 1996); and

Barbara Ruch, ed., *Engendering Faith: Women and Buddhism in Premodern Japan* (Ann Arbor: Center for Japanese Studies of Michigan, 2002).

14. Émile Durkheim, *The Elementary Forms of Religious Life*, trans. Joseph Ward Swain (New York: Oxford University Press, 2008); Michel Foucault, *Discipline and Punish: The Birth of the Prison*, trans. Alan Sheridan (New York: Vintage, 1995); René Girard, *Violence and the Sacred*, trans. Patrick Gregory (Johns Hopkins University Press, 1979).

15. Bataille has argued, for instance, that Buddhism, far from transforming Tibet into a pacific nation, as is too often claimed, actually turned violence inward, in the structures of the "theocratic" state led by the Dalai Lama. See Georges Bataille, *The Accursed Share: An Essay on General Economy*, trans. Robert Hurley (New York: Zone, 1991).

16. Maurice Bloch, *Prey into Hunter: The Politics of Religious Experience* (Cambridge: Cambridge University Press, 1992).

17. See Rob Linrothe, *Ruthless Compassion: Wrathful Deities in Early Indo-Tibetan Esoteric Buddhist Art* (Boston: Shambhala, 1999).

Appendix

Examples of Buddhist Warfare

Date	Country/Government	Event
402–517	Tabgatch empire, China	Six Buddhist-inspired revolts against Māra
613–626	Sui and Tang dynasties, China	Monk rebellions focusing on Maitreyan messianism
815	Tang dynasty, China	Soldier-monk-led revolts; spiritual murder as path of deliverance
841	Tibet	Assassination of Tibetan ruler Lang Darma
1173–1262	Japan	Shinran's Shin sect monks fight over the belief in Amita paradise
1100s–1200s	Northern Wei dynasty, China	Buddhist monk military squadrons versus Mongols and Jurchens
1100s, 1300s, 1500s, 1600s	Korea	Monks enlisted to fight against Jurchen, Mongol, Japanese Hideyoshi, and Manchu invasions
1400s	Japan	Ryōgen calls on Tendai sect to embody principles of Mañjuśrī and carry bows and arrows to battle
1400s–1500s	Ming dynasty, China	Dhyāna Buddhist monks combat Japanese pirates
1500s	Nara Empire, Japan	Japanese warrior-monks (*ikko-ikki*) active during Warring States period
1600s	Tibet	Fifth Dalai Lama offers just-war ideology in support of Mongol armies and their attacks
1699–1959	Northeastern Thailand	Holy Man revolts led by Buddhist monks
1904–1905	Japan, Russia, Korea, China	Zen monk-soldiers in the Russo-Japanese War
1980s	Sri Lanka	JVP monks kill Sinhalese citizens and politicians who oppose their politics
1996	Tokyo, Japan	Asahara Shōkō's Aum Shinrikyō gas bombs Tokyo subway
2002–present	Thailand	Buddhist soldiers work undercover as fully ordained monks

Bibliography

Abeysekara, Ananda. "The Saffron Army, Violence, Terror(ism): Buddhism, Identity, and Difference in Sri Lanka." *Numen* 48.1 (2001): 1–46.

Almond, Philip C. *The British Discovery of Buddhism*. Cambridge: Cambridge University Press, 1988.

Altangerel, T. *XVI–XVII Zuuny Mongol Tsaazyn Bichgüüd*. Ulaanbaatar, Mongolia, 1999.

Altan Khany Tsaaz. In *Mongolyn Tör, Erkh Züin Tüükh*, vol. 1. Translated by B. Bayarsaikhan into modern Mongolian. Ulaanbaatar: University of Mongolia, School of Law, Research Center for Mongolian State and Law History, 2006.

Ārya-Bodhisattva-gocara-upāyaviṣaya-vikurvāṇa-nirdeśa Sūtra. Tarthang Derge, mDo-sde, text 146, bKa'-'gyur, vol. Pa 203, Derge, folio 82a–141b.

Āryadeva and Candrakīrti. *Catuḥśatakam: Candrakīrtipraṇītaṭīkayā Sahitaṃ: Sanskrit and Tibetan Edited with Hindi Translation*. Edited by Gurucharan Singh Negi as Ph.D. diss., Central Institute of Higher Tibetan Studies, Sarnath, India, 2005.

Asaṅga. *Bodhisattvabhūmi*, ed. K. P. Nalinakṣa Dutt (Sanskrit). Patna: Jayasawal Research Institute, 1978.

———. *Asaṅga's Chapter on Ethics with the Commentary of Tsong-kha-pa*, trans. Mark Tatz. New York: Mellen, 1986.

Atwood, P. Christopher, ed. *Encyclopedia of Mongolia and the Mongol Empire*. New York: Facts of Life, 2004.

Austin, J. L. "Performative Utterances." In *Philosophical Papers*, ed. and trans. O. Urmson and G. J. Warnock, 233–252. Oxford: Clarendon, 1979.

Babbitt, Irving, trans. *The Dhammapada*. New York: New Directions, 1965.

Bangkok Post. "Yala Buddhists Flee to Temple Safety." November 9, 2006.

———. "Buddhist 'Refugees' Demand New Home." December 24, 2006.

———. "Update: Extremists Launch Overnight Wave of Violence." February 19, 2007.

Barmé, Scott. *Luang Wichit Wathakan and the Creation of a Thai Identity*. Singapore: Institute of Southeast Asian Studies, 1993.

Bartholomeusz, Tessa J. *In Defense of Dharma: Just-War Ideology in Buddhist Sri Lanka*. London: Routledge Curzon, 2002.

Basham, A. L. *The Wonder That Was India*. New York: Grove, 1959.

Bataille, Georges. *The Accursed Share: An Essay on General Economy*, trans. Robert Hurley. New York: Zone, 1991.

Bawden, Charles. "A Juridical Document from Nineteenth-Century Mongolia." *Zentralasiatische Studien* 3 (1969): 225–256.

———. *The Modern History of Mongolia*. London: Kegan Paul International, 1989.

Bawden, Charles, trans. *Tales of an Old Lama*. Tring, England: Institute of Buddhist Studies, 1997.

Bayarsaikhan, Batsukhiin. "Khalkh Juram, Manjiin Tsaazyn Bichgüüd, Tedgeeriin Khoorondyn Khamaaral." In *Erkh Züi* 2–3 (2001).

———. *Mongol Tsaazyn Bichig*. Ulaanbaatar, 2001.

———. *Mongol Ulsyn Arvan Buyant Nomyn Tsagaan Tüükh*. Ulaanbaatar, 2002.

———. *Khuuly Züin Tailbar Toly: Mongol Ulsyn Tör Erkh Züin Tüükh*. Ulaanbaatar, 2003.

———. *"Mongol Tsaazyn Bichig" Khiisen Erkh Züin Sudalgaa*. Ulaanbaatar: University of Mongolia, School of Law, Research Center for Mongolian State and Law History, 2005.

———. *Mongolyn Tör, Erkh Züin Tüükh*, vol. 1. Ulaanbaatar: University of Mongolia, School of Law, Research Center for Mongolian State and Law History, 2006.

Beal, Samuel. *Si-Yu Ki: Buddhist Records of the Western World*, vol. 2. London, 1884; reprint, Delhi: Motilal Banarsidass, 1981.

Benn, James A. *Burning for the Buddha: Self-Immolation in Chinese Buddhism*. Honolulu: University of Hawaii Press, 2007.

Berger, Peter L. *The Social Reality of Religion*. New York: Penguin, 1973.

Bhagavat, Durga N. *Early Buddhist Jurisprudence*. Poona, India: Oriental Book Agency, 1939.

Bhikkhu Bodhi, trans. *The Connected Discourses of the Buddha: A New Translation of the Saṃyutta Nikāya*. Boston: Wisdom, 2000.

Bhikkhu Ñānamoli and Bhikkhu Bodhi, trans. *The Middle Length Discourses of the Buddha: A Translation of the Majjhima Nikāya*. Boston: Wisdom, 1995.

Bira, Sh. "A Sixteenth-Century Mongol Code." In *Studies in Mongolian History, Culture, and Historiography*, ed. Sh. Bira. Tokyo: Institute for Languages and Cultures of Asia and Africa, 1994.

———. "Khublai Khan and Phags-a Bla-ma." In *Studies in Mongolian History, Culture, and Historiography*, vol. 3, ed. Ts. Ishdorji and Kh. Purevtogtokh. Ulaanbaatar: International Association for Mongol Studies, 2001.

———. "The Worship of Subvarnaprabhāsottama Sūtra in Mongolia." In *Studies in Mongolian History, Culture, and Historiography*, vol. 2, ed. Sh. Bira. Ulaanbaatar, 2001.

Bloch, Maurice. *Prey into Hunter: The Politics of Religious Experience.* Cambridge: Cambridge University Press, 1992.

Blondeau, Anne-Marie, and Yonten Gyatso. "Lhasa: Legend and History." In *Lhasa in the Seventeenth Century: The Capital of the Dalai Lamas,* ed. Francoise Pommaret. Leiden: Brill, 2003.

Borradori, Giovanna. *Philosophy in a Time of Terror: Dialogues with Jüergen Habermas and Jacques Derrida.* Chicago: University of Chicago Press, 2003.

Bourdieu, Pierre. *Outline of a Theory of Practice.* Cambridge: Cambridge University Press, 1977.

Bush, Richard, Jr. *Religion in Communist China.* Nashville, Tenn.: Abingdon, 1970.

Chakravarti, Uma. *The Social Dimensions of Early Buddhism.* Delhi: Munshiram Manoharlal, 1996.

Chang Chih-i. "A Correct Understanding and Implementation of the Party Policy concerning Freedom of Religious Belief." In *Minzu Tuanjie* (Unity of Nationalities), Beijing: Minzu Publication Society, 1962.

Chayet, Anne. "The Potala, Symbol of the Power of the Dalai Lamas." In *Lhasa in the Seventeenth Century: The Capital of the Dalai Lamas,* ed. Francoise Pommaret. Leiden: Brill, 2003.

Chen, Kenneth. *Buddhism in China.* Princeton, N.J.: Princeton University Press, 1964.

Childress, James F. "Just-War Criteria." In *War in the Twentieth Century: Sources in Theological Ethics,* ed. Richard B. Miller, 351–372. Louisville, Ky.: Westminster/ John Knox, 1992.

Cleary, Thomas. *The Japanese Art of War.* Boston: Shambhala, 1991.

Collins, Steven. *Nirvana and Other Buddhist Felicities: Utopias of the Pali Imaginaire.* Cambridge: Cambridge University Press, 1998.

Coomaraswamy, Ananda K. *Buddha and the Gospel of Buddhism.* New York: Harper Torchbooks, 1964.

Davids, T. W. Rhys, trans. *The Questions of King Milinda,* vol. 1. New York: Dover, 1963.

Davidson, Ronald M. *Indian Esoteric Buddhism: A Social History of the Tantric Movement.* New York: Columbia University Press, 2002.

Day, Terence P. *The Conception of Punishment in Early Indian Literature.* Waterloo, Ont., Canada: Wilfrid Laurier University Press, 1982.

Deegalle, Mahinda. "Buddhist Preaching and Sinhala Religious Rhetoric: Medieval Buddhist Methods to Popularize Theravada." *Numen* 44.2 (1997): 180–210.

———. "Is Violence Justified in Theravāda Buddhism?" *Ecumenical Review* 55.2 (2003): 122–140.

De Groot, J. J. M. "Militant Spirit of the Buddhist Clergy in China." *T'oung Pao* 2 (1891): 127–139.

Devahuti, D. *Harṣa: A Political Study,* 3rd rev. ed. Delhi: Oxford University Press, 1998.

Dietz, Mary. "Patriotism: A Brief History of the Term." In *Patriotism,* ed. Igor Primoratz. New York: Humanity, 2002.

Dreifus, Claudia. "The Dalai Lama." *New York Times,* November 28, 1993.

Dreyfus, Georges B. J. "The Shuk-den Affair: History and Nature of a Quarrel." *Journal of the International Association of Buddhist Studies* 21.2 (1998): 227–270.

Durkheim, Emile. *The Elementary Forms of Religious Life*, trans. Joseph Ward Swain. New York: Oxford University Press, 2008.

Eckel, Malcom David. *Bhāviveka and His Buddhist Opponents*. Cambridge: Harvard University, 2008.

Emmerick, R. E., trans. *The Sūtra of Golden Light* (*Suvarnaprabhāsottamasūtra*). Oxford: Pali Text Society, 2004.

Faure, Bernard. *The Rhetoric of Immediacy*. Princeton, N.J.: Princeton University Press, 1991.

———. *The Red Thread*. Princeton, N.J.: Princeton University Press, 1998.

———. *The Power of Denial*. Princeton, N.J.: Princeton University Press, 2003.

Fitzgerald, James L., trans. *The Mahābhārata: Book 11, The Book of Women; Book 12, The Book of Peace*, pt. 1, vol. 7. Chicago: University of Chicago Press, 2004.

Florida, Robert. *Human Rights and the World's Major Religions*: vol. 5, *The Buddhist Tradition*. Westport, Conn.: Praeger, 2005.

Foucault, Michel. *Power/Knowledge: Selected Interviews and Other Writings 1972–1977*. New York: Pantheon, 1980.

———. *Discipline and Punish: The Birth of the Prison*, trans. Alan Sheridan. New York: Vintage, 1995.

Futaki, Hiroshi. "A Study of the Newly Discovered Juridical Documents of Khalkha-Mongolia." *Journal of Asian and African Studies* 21 (1981): 49–73.

Geiger, Wilhelm, trans. *The Mahāvaṃsa: The Great Chronicle of Ceylon*. New Delhi: Asian Educational Services, 1993.

Gethin, Rupert. "Can Killing a Living Being Ever Be an Act of Compassion? The Analysis of the Act of Killing in the Abhidhamma and Pali Commentaries." *Journal of Buddhist Ethics* 11 (2004): 167–202.

———. "Buddhist Monks, Buddhist Kings, Buddhist Violence: On the Early Buddhist Attitudes to Violence." In *Religion and Violence in South Asia: Theory and Practice*, ed. J. R. Hinnells and Richard King. London: Routledge, 2007.

Girard, René. *Violence and the Sacred*, trans. Patrick Gregory. Johns Hopkins University Press, 1979.

Gokhale, Balkrishna. "Dhamma as a Political Concept." *Journal of Indian History* 44 (Aug. 1968): 249–261.

———. "The Early Buddhist View of the State." *Journal of the American Oriental Society* 89.4 (Oct. 1969): 731–738.

Gombrich, Richard. *Theravāda Buddhism: A Social History from Ancient Benares to Modern Colombo*. London: Routledge & Kegan Paul, 1988.

———. *Buddhist Precept and Practice: Traditional Buddhism in the Rural Highlands of Ceylon*. Delhi: Motilal Banarsidass, 1991.

Greenwald, Alice. "The Relic on the Spear: Historiography and the Saga of Duṭṭhagāmaṇī." In *Religion and Legitimation of Power in Sri Lanka*, ed. Bardwell L. Smith. Chambersburg, Pa.: Anima, 1978.

Guangwu Lo. *The Outline of Great Events of Religious Works in New China*. Beijing: Huawej Publication Society, 2001 (羅廣武 ，《新中國宗教工作大事概覽》，北京：華文出版社，二００一年。).

Hakamaya Noriaki. *Hihan Bukkyō*. Tokyo: Daizō Shuppan, 1990.

Hallisey, Charles. "Ethical Particularism in Theravāda Buddhism." *Journal of Buddhist Ethics* 3 (1996): 32–43.

Harris, Elizabeth J. "Violence and Disruption in Society: A Study of the Early Buddhist Texts." *Dialogue* 17.1–3 (Jan.–Dec. 1990): 29–91.

———. "Buddhism and the Justification of War: A Case Study from Sri Lanka." In *Just War in Comparative Perspective*, ed. Paul Robinson. Hampshire, England: Ashgate, 2003.

Heissig, Walter. "A Mongolian Source to the Lamaist Suppression of Shamanism." *Anthropos* 48 (1953): 1–29, 493–536.

Heller, Amy. "The Great Protector Deities of the Dalai Lamas." In *Lhasa in the Seventeenth Century: The Capital of the Dalai Lamas*, ed. Francoise Pommaret. Leiden: Brill, 2003.

Heuschert, Dorothea. "Legal Pluralism in the Qing Empire: Manchu Legislation for the Mongols." *International History Review* 20 (1998): 310–324.

Holt, John Clifford. *Buddha in the Crown: Avalokiteśvara in the Buddhist Traditions of Sri Lanka*. New York: Oxford University Press, 1991.

Horner, I. B., trans. *The Book of the Discipline*: vol. 1, *Suttavibhanga*. Oxford: Pali Text Society, 1992.

Human Rights Watch. "Thailand: Government Covers Up Role in 'Disappearance.'" March 11, 2006.

Ishii, Yoneo. *Samgha, State, and Society: Thai Buddhism in History*, trans. Peter Hawkes. Honolulu: University of Hawai'i, 1986.

Jackson, Peter. *Buddhism, Legitimation and Conflict: The Political Functions of Urban Thai Buddhism*. Singapore: Institute of Southeast Asian Studies, 1989.

Jackson, Roger, and John Makransky, eds. *Buddhist Theology: Critical Reflections by Contemporary Buddhist Scholars*. London: Routledge Curzon, 2003.

Jamspal, Lozang. "The Range of the Bodhisattva: A Study of an Early Mahāyānasūtra, 'Āryasatyakaparivarta,' Discourse of Truth Teller." Ph.D. diss., Columbia University. Ann Arbor, Mich.: University Microfilms International, 1991.

Jamtsarano, Ts. J., and A. N. Tarunov. "Obrozenie pamyatnikov pissannogo prava mongol'skiikh plemen." *Sbornik trudov professorov i prepodavatelei gosudarstvennogo irkutskogo universiteta*, sec. 1, no. 1 (1921): 1–13.

———. "Khalkha Dzhurom (opisanie pamyatnika)." *Sbornik trudov professorov i prepodavatelei gosudarstvennogo irkutskogo universiteta* 6 (1923): 1–18.

Jinkhene Dagaj Yavakh Khuuly Dürem (*Ekh Bichgiin Sudalgaa*), trans. Khereid J. Urangua and Khuntaiji B. Bayarsaikhan. Ulaanbaatar: National University of Mongolia, School of Law, Institute of Historical Studies, 2004.

Jory, Patrick. "Luang Pho Thuat as a Southern Thai Cultural Hero: Popular Religion in the Integration of Patani." In *Thai South and Malay North: Ethnic Interactions on the Plural Peninsula*, ed. Michael J. Montesano and Patrick Jory. Singapore: NUS Press, 2008.

"Jueguan lun." In *Suzuki Daisetsu Zenshū, Vol. 2*, ed. D. T. Suzuki. Tokyo: Iwanami shoten, 1980 [1968].

Juergensmeyer, Mark. *Terror in the Mind of God: The Global Rise of Religious Violence*. Berkeley: University of California Press, 2000.

Juzan. "On Buddhist Patriotism." *Modern Buddhist Studies* 1.11 (1951) (巨贊，『論佛教的愛國主義』，《現代佛學》第一卷，第十一期，1950).

———. "Editor's Letter to Chao Peilin." *Modern Buddhist Studies* 2.1 (1951) (《現代佛學》，第二卷，第一期，一九五一年。).

———. *Collections of Juzan.* Nanjing: Jiansu Guji Publication Society, 2000 (巨贊，《巨贊集》，江蘇古藉出版社，二０００年。).

Karmay, Samten. *Secret Visions of the Fifth Dalai Lama: The Gold Manuscript in the Fournier Collection.* London: Serindia, 1988.

Kaufman, Burton. *The Korean War: Challenges in Crisis, Credibility, and Command.* Philadelphia: Temple University Press, 1986.

Kautilya. *The Arthaśāstra,* trans. L. N. Rangarajan. New York: Penguin, 1992.

Keown, Damien. "Attitudes to Euthanasia in the Vinaya and Commentary." *Journal of Buddhist Ethics* 6 (1999). Accessed at http://www.buddhistethics.org/6/keown993.htm on September 17, 2008.

———. "A Response to 'The Place for a Righteous War in Buddhism' by P. D. Premasiri." *Journal of Buddhist Ethics* 10 (2003). Accessed at http://www.buddhistethics.org/10/keown-sri-lanka-conf.html on September 17, 2008.

Keyes, Charles F. "Political Crisis and Militant Buddhism." In *Religion and Legitimation of Power in Thailand, Laos, and Burma,* ed. Bardwell L. Smith. Chambersburg, Pa.: Anima, 1978.

———. *Thailand: Buddhist Kingdom as Modern Nation-State.* Boulder, Colo.: Westview, 1987.

Kleine, Christoph. "Evil Monks with Good Intentions? Remarks on Buddhist Monastic Violence and Its Doctrinal Background." In *Buddhism and Violence,* ed. Michael Zimmermann. Kathmandu: Lumbini International Research Institute, 2006.

Lama Chimpa, trans. *Tāranātha's History of Buddhism in India.* Delhi: Motilal Banarsidass, 1970.

Lamotte, Etienne. "Vajrapāṇi en Inde." In *Mélanges de Sinologie offerts à Monsieur Paul Demiéville,* 113–159. Paris: Presses Universitaires de France, 1966.

Lang, Karen. "Āryadeva and Candrakīrti on the Dharma of Kings." *Asiatische Studien: Zeitschrift der Schweizerischen Gesellschaft für Asienkunde/Études Asiatiques: Revue de la Société Suisse d'Études Asiatiques* 46.1 (1992): 232–243.

Lang, Kurt. "Military." In *International Encyclopedia of the Social Sciences,* vol. 10, ed. David L. Sills. New York: Macmillan, 1968.

Lawrence, Bruce, and Aisha Karim, eds. *On Violence: A Reader.* Durham, N.C.: Duke University Press, 2007.

Lindtner, Chr. *Nāgārjuniana: Studies in the Writings and Philosophy of Nāgārjuna.* Delhi: Motilal Banarsidass, 1987.

Ling, Trevor. "Introduction." In *Buddhist Trends in Southeast Asia,* ed. Trevor Ling. Singapore: Institute of Southeast Asian Studies, 1993.

Lingat, Robert. *The Classical Law of India,* trans. J. Duncan and M. Derret. Berkeley: University of California Press, 1973.

Linrothe, Rob. *Ruthless Compassion: Wrathful Deities in Early Indo-Tibetan Esoteric Buddhist Art.* Boston: Shambhala, 1999.

Loy, David. "What's Buddhist about Socially Engaged Buddhism?" Accessed at http://www.zen-occidental.net/articles1/loy12-english.html on March 29, 2007.

Maher, Derek F. "The Rhetoric of War in Tibet: Toward a Buddhist Just War Theory." *Journal of Political Theology* 9.2 (2008): 179–191.

Maiskii, Ivan Mikhailovich. *Sovremennaya Mongolia*. Irkutsk, 1921.

———. *Orchin Üeiin Mongol: Avtonomit Mongol XX Zuuny Garaan Deer*. Ulaanbaatar, 2001.

Mardent, Amporn. "From Adek to Mo'ji: Identities and Social Realities of Southern Thai People." In *Kyoto Review of Southeast Asia*. Accessed at http://kyotoreviewsea.org/Amporn.htm on September 30, 2006.

Meinert, Carmen. "Between the Profane and the Sacred? On the Context of the Rite of 'Liberation' (sgrol pa)." In *Buddhism and Violence*, ed. Michael Zimmermann. Kathmandu: Lumbini International Research Institute, 2006.

Mizuno Kōgen. *Basic Buddhist Concepts*, trans. Richard L. Gage. Tokyo: Kōsei, 1980.

Modern Buddhist Studies. 《現代佛學》，天津古籍出版社 ，一九九五年 . (reprinted).

Mongol Ulsyn Arvan Buyant Nomyn Tsagaan Tüükh Nert Sudar Orshivoi. In *Mongolyn Tör, Erkh Züin Tüükh*, vol. 1. Ulaanbaatar: University of Mongolia, School of Law, Research Center for Mongolian State and Law History, 2006.

Nartsupha, Chatthip. "The Ideology of 'Holy Men' Revolts in North East Thailand." In *History and Peasant Consciousness in Southeast Asia*, ed. Andrew Turton and Shigeru Tanabe. Osaka: National Museum of Ethnology, 1984.

Ngag dbang blo bzang rgya mtsho (Fifth Dalai Lama). *rgyal rabs dpyid kyi rgyal mo'i glu dbyangs/Song of the Queen of Spring: A Dynastic History*. Lhasa, 1643; reprint, Gangtok, Sikkim, India: Sikkim Research Institute of Tibetology, 1991.

———. *za hor gyi bande ngag dbang blo bzang rgya mtsho'i 'di snang 'khrul pa'i rol rtsed rtogs brjod kyi tshul du bkod pa du kU la'i gos bzang/The Good Silk Cloth, the Play of Illusion, Setting Forth the Biography of Ngag dbang blo bzang rgya mtsho, the Monk of Za hor*. Lhasa: Tibetan People's Printing Press, 1991.

Obeyesekere, Gananath. "The Origins and Institutionalization of Political Violence." In *Sri Lanka in Change and Crisis*, ed. J. Manor. London: Croom Helm, 1984.

———. "Duttagamini and the Buddhist Conscience." In *Religion and Political Conflict in South Asia*, ed. D. Allen. Delhi: Oxford University Press, 1993.

Olivelle, Patrick, trans. *The Law Code of Manu*. Oxford: Oxford University Press, 2004.

———. *Dharmasūtra Parallels: Containing the Dharmasūtras of Āpastambha, Gautama, Baudhāyana, and Vasiṣṭha*. Delhi: Motilal Banarsidass, 2005.

Peichao Li. *Historic Development of Patriotism of Chinese Nation*. Wuhan: Hubei Jiaoyu Publication Society, 2001 (李培超 ，《中華民族愛國主義發展史》，湖北教育出版社 ，二００一年。).

Pozdneyev, A. M. *Mongolia and the Mongols*, vols. 1–2, ed. J. R. Krueger. Bloomington: Indiana University Press, 1971–1977.

———. *Religion and Ritual in Society: Lamaist Buddhism in Late 19th Century Mongolia*. Bloomington, Ind.: Mongolia Society, 1978.

Prebish, Charles S. *Buddhist Monastic Discipline: The Sanskrit Prātimoksa Sūtras of the Mahāsāṃghikas and Mūlasarvāstivādins*. Delhi: Motilal Banarsidass, 1996.

Premasiri, P. D. "The Place for a Righteous War in Buddhism." *Journal of Buddhist Ethics* 10 (2003). Accessed at http://www.buddhistethics.org/10/premasiri-sri-lanka-conf.html on September 17, 2008.

Purevjav, S. *Mongol Dakhi Sharyn Shashny Khuraangui Tüükh*. Ulaanbaatar, 1978.

Rahula, Walpola. *The Heritage of the Bhikkhu: A Short History of the Bhikkhu in Educational, Cultural, Social, and Political Life*. New York: Grove, 1974.

———. *What the Buddha Taught: Revised and Expanded Edition with Texts from Suttas and Dhammapada*. New York: Grove Press, 1974.

Reardon, Betty. *Militarization, Security, and Peace Education: A Guide for Concerned Citizens*. Valley Forge, Pa.: United Ministries in Education, 1982.

Reynolds, Craig. *Seditious Histories: Contesting Thai and Southeast Asian Pasts*. Seattle: University of Washington Press, 2006.

Rhie, Marylin M., and Robert A. F. Thurman. *Wisdom and Compassion: The Sacred Art of Tibet*. New York: Abrams, 1991.

Riasanovsky, A. Valentin. Fundamental Principles of Mongol Law. Bloomington: Indiana University Press, 1965.

Rotman, Andy. "Marketing Morality: The Economy of Faith in Early Indian Buddhism." *International Association of Buddhist Studies Meeting*, Atlanta, GA, June 23–25, 2008.

Ruch, Barbara, ed. *Engendering Faith: Women and Buddhism in Premodern Japan*. Ann Arbor: Center for Japanese Studies of Michigan, 2002.

Samten, Ācārya Ngawang, ed. *Ratnāvalī of Ācārya Nāgārjuna with the Commentary of Ajitamitra*. Sarnath: Central Institute Higher Tibetan Studies, 1990.

Samuels, Jeffrey. "Is Merit in the Milk Powder? Pursuing *Puñña* in Contemporary Sri Lanka." *Contemporary Buddhism* 9.1 (2008): 123–147.

———. *Attracting the Heart: Buddhism and Emotion in Contemporary Sri Lanka*, forthcoming.

Sans-rGyas rGya-mTSHo: Life of the Fifth Dalai Lama, vol. 4, pt. 1: *The Fourth Volume Continuing the Third Volume of the Ordinary, Outer Life Entitled "The Fine Silken Dress," of My Own Gracious Lama, Ńag-dBan Blo-bZan rGya-mTSHo*, trans. Zahiruddin Ahmad. New Delhi: International Academy of Indian Culture, 1999.

Śāntideva. *Śikṣāsamuccaya: A Compendium of Buddhist Teaching Compiled by Śāntideva Chiefly from Earlier Mahāyāna Sūtras*, ed. Cecil Bendall. The Hague: Moutons, 1957.

Sárközi, Alice. "Mandate of Heaven: Heavenly Support of the Mongol Ruler." In *The Concept of Sovereignty in the Altaic World: Permanent International Altaistic Conference, 34th Meeting, Berlin, 21–26 July 1991*, ed. Barbara Kellner-Heinkele. Wiesbaden, Germany: Harrassowitz, 1993.

Schlieter, Jens. "Compassionate Killing or Conflict Resolution." In *Buddhism and Violence*, ed. Michael Zimmermann. Kathmandu: Lumbini International Research Institute, 2006.

Schmithausen, Lambert. "Aspects of the Buddhist Attitude towards War." In *Violence Denied: Violence, Non-Violence and the Rationalization of Violence in South Asian Cultural History*, ed. E. M. Houben and K. R. Van Kooij. Leiden: Brill, 1999.

Serruys, Henry. "Qaths and Qalqa Jirum." *Oriens Extremus* 19 (1972): 131–141.

Shahar, Meir. *The Shaolin Monastery: History, Religion, and the Chinese Martial Arts.* Honolulu: University of Hawaii Press, 2007.

Shakabpa, Tsepőn W. D. *bod kyi srid don rgyal rabs* (*An Advanced Political History of Tibet*). Kalimpong, India: Shakabpa House, 1976. The latest edition is *One Hundred Thousand Moons: An Advanced Political History of Tibet*, trans. Derek F. Maher. Leiden: Brill, 2009.

Skidmore, Monique. *Karaoke Fascism: Burma and the Politics of Fear*. Philadelphia: University of Pennsylvania Press, 2004.

Southwold, Martin. *Buddhism in Life: The Anthropological Study of Religion and the Sinhalese Practice of Buddhism*. Dover, N.H.: Manchester University Press, 1983.

Strong, John S. *The Legend of King Aśoka: A Study and Translation of the Aśokāvadāna.* Princeton, N.J.: Princeton University Press, 1983.

Sugimoto Gorō. *Taigi*. Tokyo: Heibonsha, 1938.

Suksamran, Somboon. *Political Buddhism in Southeast Asia: the Role of the Sangha in the Modernization of Thailand*. New York: St. Martin's Press, 1977.

Suzuki, D. T. *Zen and Japanese Culture*. Princeton, N.J.: Princeton University Press, 1959.

Swearer, Donald. "Fundamentalist Movements in Theravada Buddhism." In *Fundamentalisms Observed*, ed. Martin E. Marty and R. Scott Appleby, 628–690. Chicago: University of Chicago Press, 1992.

———. *Becoming the Buddha: The Ritual of Image Consecration in Thailand*. Princeton, N.J.: Princeton University Press, 2004.

Syrkin, A. "Notes on the Buddha's Threats in the Dīgha Nikāya." *Journal of the International Association of Buddhist Studies* 7 (1984): 147–158.

Tambiah, Stanley Jeyaraja. *World Conqueror and World Renouncer: A Study of Buddhism and Polity in Thailand against a Historical Background*. Cambridge: Cambridge University Press, 1976.

———. *Sri Lanka: Ethnic Fratricide and the Dismantling of Democracy*. Chicago: University of Chicago Press, 1986.

———. *Buddhism Betrayed? Religion, Politics, and Violence in Sri Lanka*. Chicago: University of Chicago Press, 1992.

Tatz, Mark. *Asaṅga's Chapter on Ethics with the Commentary of Tsong-kha-pa*. New York: Edwin Mellen Press, 1986.

Taussig, Michael. *Defacement: Public Secrecy and the Labor of the Negative*. Stanford, Calif.: Stanford University Press, 1999.

Thapar, Romila. *Early India: From the Origins to AD 1300*. Berkeley: University of California Press, 2002.

Tsong-kha-pa. *The Great Treatise on the Stages of the Path to Enlightenment: Lam Rim Chen Mo*, vol. 1, trans. Lamrim Chenmo Translation Committee. Ithaca, N.Y.: Snow Lion, 2000.

Victoria, Brian (Daizen). *Zen War Stories* London: Routledge Curzon, 2003.

———. "D. T. Suzuki and Japanese Militarism: Supporter or Opponent?" In *Buddhism and Violence*, ed. Michael Zimmermann. Kathmandu: Lumbini International Research Institute, 2006.

———. *Zen at War*, 2nd ed. Boulder, Colo.: Rowman & Littlefield, 2006.

Vostrikov, A. I. *Tibetskaya tibetoyazychnaya istoricheskaya literatura* (XVII–XIX). Ulaanbaatar, 1960.

Walshe, Maurice, trans. *Thus Have I Heard: The Long Discourses of the Buddha*. London: Wisdom, 1987.

———. "*Cakkavatti-Sīhanāda Sutta*: The Lion's Roar on the Turning of the Wheel." In *The Long Discourses of the Buddha: A Translation of the Dīgha Nikāya*, trans. Walshe. Boston: Wisdom, 1995.

Weirong, Shen. "Tibetan Tantric Buddhism at the Court of the Great Mongol Khans: Sa skya paṇḍita and 'Phags pa's works in Chinese during the Yuan Period." In *Questiones Mongolorum Disputatae*, ed. H. Futaki and B. Oyunbilig. Tokyo: Association for International Studies of Mongolian Culture, 2005, pp. 61–89.

Welch, Holmes. *Buddhism under Mao*. Cambridge, Mass.: Harvard University Press, 1972.

Wickremeratne, Ananda. *Buddhism and Ethnicity in Sri Lanka: A Historical Analysis*. New Delhi: International Centre for Ethnic Studies, Kandy, 1995.

Willemen, Charles, trans. *The Storehouse of Sundry Valuables* (*Tsa-pao-tsang-ching/ Kṣudrakāgama*). Berkeley, Calif.: Numata Center for Translation and Research, 2004.

Wilson, Liz. *Charming Cadavers*. Chicago: University of Chicago Press, 1996.

Witzel, Michael. "The Case of the Shattered Head." *Studien zur Indologie und Iranistik* 13–14 (1984): 363–415.

Xu, Jialu ed. *Daily History of the People's Republic of China*. Chengdu: Siquan Renmin Publication Society, 2003 (《中華人民共和國日史》，四川人民出版社 ，二００三年。).

Yilian. "Patriotic Issues of Four Groups of Buddhists." In *Modern Buddhist Studies* 1.11 (1951) (一量，『四眾弟子的愛國主義問題』，《現代佛學》第一卷，第十一期，一九五一年).

Yokoi, Yūhō, and Brian (Daizen) Victoria. *Zen Master Dōgen: An Introduction with Selected Writings*. New York: Weatherhill, 1976.

Yu, Xue. *Buddhism, War, and Nationalism: Chinese Monks in the Struggle against Japanese Aggressions, 1931–1945*. London: Routledge, 2005.

Yukio, Hayashi. *Practical Buddhism among the Thai-Lao: Religion in the Making of Religion*. Kyoto, Japan: Kyoto University Press, 2003.

Yumiko, Ishihama. "On the Dissemination of the Belief in the Dalai Lama as a Manifestation of the Bodhisattva Avalokiteśvara." *Acta Asiatica* 64 (1993): 38–56.

Zahiruddin Ahmad. *Sino-Tibetan Relations in the Seventeenth Century*. Rome: Instituto Italiano per il Medio ed Estremo Oriente, 1970.

Zedong, Mao. *Selected Collections of Mao Zedong*, vol. 2. Beijing: Renmin Publication Society, 1967 (毛澤東，《毛澤東選集》，第二卷，北京：人民出版社，一九六七年，第六六五頁。).

Zheng, Yongnian. *Discovering Chinese Nationalism in China*. Cambridge: Cambridge University Press, 1999.

Zimmermann, Michael. "A Mahāyānist Criticism of *Arthaśāstra*, the Chapter on Royal Ethics in the *Bodhisattva-gocaropāya-viṣaya-vikurvaṇa-nirdeśa-sūtra*." *Annual Report*

of the International Research Institute for Advanced Buddhology at Soka University for the Academic Year 1999 (2000): 177–211.
———. "War." In *Encyclopedia of Buddhism*, vol. 2, ed. Robert Buswell Jr., 893–897. New York: Macmillan, 2003.
———. "Only a Fool Becomes a King: Buddhist Stances on Punishment." In *Buddhism and Violence*, ed. Michael Zimmermann. Kathmandu: Lumbini International Research Institute, 2006.
Zimmermann, Michael, ed. *Buddhism and Violence*. Kathmandu: Lumbini International Research Institute, 2006.

Index

Italicized page numbers refer to illustrations. Bolded page numbers indicate authors of selections.

Lightning Source UK Ltd.
Milton Keynes UK
UKHW022353130921
390516UK00006B/1463

9 780195 394849